"十四五"职业教育国家规划教材

国家示范性高职院校建设成果·职业英语系列

胡扬政 主编

刘玥 胡霞 胡冰冰 苑丽娟 刘梅 副主编

现代酒店服务英语
（第3版）

Service English in Modern Hotel

(The Third Edition)

清华大学出版社
北京

内 容 简 介

本书根据高职高专"工学结合"培养模式编写。作者根据酒店行业的工作环境和岗位要求,营造了仿真的工作情境,使学生在逐项完成服务工作任务的同时,掌握相应的英语词汇、英语表达方法和沟通技巧,具备顶岗工作的能力。书中设计了 Service Position、Skills and Attainments、Position Knowledge 等教学栏目,实现了酒店英语语言运用能力培养和酒店服务能力培养的有机结合。

本书适合高职高专酒店管理专业和旅游相关专业教学使用,也可作为酒店行业的培训教材,或酒店从业人员自学之用。

《现代酒店服务英语》和《酒店英语服务实训》为配套教材,前者供课堂教学使用,后者用于模拟实训和酒店岗位实训。本套教材获评"十二五"和"十三五"职业教育国家规划教材。

本书封面贴有清华大学出版社防伪标签,无标签者不得销售。
版权所有,侵权必究。举报:010-62782989,beiqinquan@tup.tsinghua.edu.cn。

图书在版编目(CIP)数据

现代酒店服务英语/胡扬政主编. —3 版. —北京:清华大学出版社,2017(2024.8重印)
国家示范性高职院校建设成果. 职业英语系列
ISBN 978-7-302-47516-3

Ⅰ.①现… Ⅱ.①胡… Ⅲ.①饭店－商业服务－英语－高等职业教育－教材 Ⅳ.①F719.2

中国版本图书馆 CIP 数据核字(2017)第 142120 号

责任编辑:吴梦佳
封面设计:常雪影
责任校对:李 梅
责任印制:沈 露

出版发行:清华大学出版社
网　　址:https://www.tup.com.cn,https://www.wqxuetang.com
地　　址:北京清华大学学研大厦 A 座　　邮　编:100084
社 总 机:010-83470000　　邮　购:010-62786544
投稿与读者服务:010-62776969,c-service@tup.tsinghua.edu.cn
质量反馈:010-62772015,zhiliang@tup.tsinghua.edu.cn
课件下载:https://www.tup.com.cn,010-83470410
印 装 者:三河市龙大印装有限公司
经　　销:全国新华书店
开　　本:185mm×260mm　　印 张:19.5　　字 数:458 千字
　　　　　(附光盘1张)
版　　次:2009 年 5 月第 1 版　2017 年 7 月第 3 版　印 次:2024 年 8 月第 11 次印刷
定　　价:49.00 元

产品编号:070591-02

丛书编写委员会

专业总策划：
　　王成荣　吕一中　李宇红　平若媛

总　主　编：
　　胡扬政　王莉莉

副　总　编：
　　刘　玥　周欣奕　胡冰冰　苑丽娟　胡　霞
　　王　艳

委　　　员：
　　Glenn L. Hyatt　Udo Schwarzboeck　Mariah J. Xu
　　郭远志　李作聚　苏　讫　王海龙　宋　娜
　　冯茂芳　李维维　田志英　刘　莉　包　博
　　宋光辉　谷书霞　申　巍　杨明军　王金红
　　高亚妹　李　梅　高兰凤　苏玉刚　周其艳
　　徐庆颖

总 序

在经济全球化的今天,既具有专业能力又具有职业英语能力的毕业生已成为各行各业亟须的人才。在越来越多的工作岗位上,具有较强的职业英语能力已成为竞聘的重要条件甚至是首选条件。随着中国经济的迅猛发展,各行各业对新职业人的职业英语能力的需求和要求还会更加强烈。

因此,提升学生的职业英语素养与职业英语能力,实现学生高质量就业,成为北京财贸职业学院示范校建设的一项重要任务。该校坚持英语教学改革三原则,即:为专业建设服务,为特色人才培养服务,为示范校建设服务;以学生职业英语能力发展为中心,通过专业英语课程、普通商务英语课程等职业英语课程模块的建设,通过课堂教学和实践教学体系的建设,构建高职职业英语能力培养体系;以 DCPEA(Development-Centered in Professional English Ability)为高职专业英语课程建设新模式,以"6P"为知识载体,实现英语语言运用能力的培养与实际的英语工作技能养成的有机结合;把课程建设、教材建设和科研相结合,努力建设职业英语精品教材,实现专业英语教学内容、教学方法和训练方式的完全转变;探索高职双语课程的建设及其教材的开发;提高学生用英语"能财会商"的能力,提高学生在未来职业发展中的竞争能力,提升专业的综合实力,满足首都市场经济发展对财贸人才的新需求,满足社会对新职业人多变的需求。

我们的职业英语系列教材建设力求体现以下特色。

(1) 理念与目标:以学生职业英语能力发展为中心,建设财经专业类职业英语精品教材。

(2) 建设任务:以"6P"为知识载体,培养学生的职业英语素养与多种职业英语能力。"6P"知识载体具体如下。

- Profession(职业):以不同的职业英语工作为教材编写主线。
- Position(岗位):以不同岗位的英语工作任务构成教学模块,或以行业内对英语需求高的岗位的不同工作任务为教材编写重点或模块。
- Procedure(工作流程):以具体的英语工作任务为技能,以其工作过程为教学内容。
- Point(要点):以工作流程中的语言要求和工作注意事项为技能要点。
- Performance & Practice(演练与实训):通过模拟演练和(岗位)实训提高学生英语工作中的实际应用能力。

(3) 建设过程:以学生所学专业及其对应的未来职业为切入点开展调研,确定职业英语工作任务和职业英语能力;由行业专家和专业教师指导或策划,由一线专业英语教师任主编，多名英语教师及行业专家共同编写，努力体现教材的职业性、实用性、规范性、现代性和趣味性。

（4）建设策略：英语语言运用能力的培养服务于职业英语的工作要求，并根据不同的职业英语工作需求，决定英语语用能力培养的侧重点；融入职业资格考试内容，教材内容和岗位英语工作任务努力配套，课堂教学教材和实训教材配套。在实训教材中引进案例教学和项目教学。教学栏目、教学情境、教学任务和教学实践的设计体现不同的职业英语能力培养的特色，使教材成为专业英语课程改革、实现职业英语工作能力培养的助推器。

前任院长王茹琴教授不仅为我院的英语教学改革指明了方向，还为职业英语教材的编写提出了宝贵的建议并给予了大力的支持；国际教育学院院长潘勇为职业英语课程的建设和为青年作者队伍成长积极铺路搭桥，出谋划策；清华大学出版社为本套丛书的策划出版付出了不懈努力，在此一并表示谢意。

胡扬政　王莉莉
2022 年 1 月

再版说明

《现代酒店服务英语(第3版)》和《酒店英语服务实训(第3版)》(以下简称《现代酒店服务英语》套书)互为配套的 DCPEA 模式的课堂和实训教材。其中的《酒店英语服务实训》为 2007 年北京市高等教育精品教材立项项目(项目编号 561)。这套书不仅是最早的高职专业英语工作过程导向教材,而且是北京财贸职业学院"国家示范性高职院校建设成果·职业英语系列"的范本,本套教材均被评为"十二五"和"十三五"职业教育国家规划教材。

建设和不断完善《现代酒店服务英语》套书 DCPEA 模式研究型规划教材,旨在构建以"6P"为知识载体的高职酒店英语 DCPEA 新课程模式,实现学生五星级酒店实训和就业"零距离",并为高职高专及应用型本科的专业英语(ESP)教学改革、课程和教材建设提供系统、翔实、可供借鉴的模式、理念、经验和对策,为从根本上改变专业英语课程教材和教学严重滞后于专业人才培养需求的现状,实现专业英语课程职业英语能力培养的完全转变尽绵薄之力。

一、DCPEA 模式的《现代酒店服务英语》套书的建设过程

1. 第 1 版

DCPEA 是 Development-Centered in Professional English Ability 的缩写,意为"以职业英语能力发展为中心"。这个模式是主编带 2003 级和 2004 级学生参加酒店面试而引发的一系列思考和调研并结合酒店英语课程改革和建设提出来的,经过对 2005 级学生全方位的教学改革验证之后,被用在《现代酒店服务英语》套书中。2008 年 8 月出版了全套教材的第 1 版。

2. 第 2 版

(1) 美籍专家对每一篇对话进行仔细的修改并在美国录音;根据专家的意见,我们又认真修改了全书,以确保本书英语语言的质量,确保美国现代口语进课堂。

(2) 根据学生对教材使用的反馈要求,为全套教材配置了光盘和音频文件。

3. 第 3 版

(1) 在实训教材(主教材第 3 版)增加"再版说明",并引入高职专业英语 DCPEA 课程和教材建设模式,为任课教师教学改革、课程建设和科研提供借鉴。

(2) 根据社会发展及酒店自身的发展对酒店服务的新需求,全套教材第 3 版由专业英语教师重新编写商务中心服务等模块。在课堂教材中,作者把自己曾经在知名酒店商务中心服务经历改写成教学内容,以提高学生的酒店英语综合服务能力。在实训教材中删掉了酒店现在实际中已乎存在的服务,还删掉了学生在酒店实训中一直没有接触到的服务。

（3）为更好地提高学生的职业英语实用能力，结合语言学习的规律，在实训教材中增加"实训回望"，并给出"部分参考答案"。

（4）增加教学附件。本书在修订中增加了二维码，手机扫描二维码可直接播放对话录音。

4. 第4版修订初步预期

（1）对课堂教材的部分模块和个别章节进行重写。

（2）酒店业人员流动性较强，进入酒店除了实训能力考核外，还有许多次的酒店英语面试，课堂教材第4版将补充酒店英语面试能力的培养。

二、酒店英语 DCPEA 课程与教材建设模式的构建

一个发展中心：以学生"职业英语能力发展为中心"为理念。

两个教学导向：以服务任务和服务过程为导向，并以服务任务为技能。

两种实践教学体系：建立课堂演练和酒店岗位实训或模拟实训相结合的实践体系。

"6P"知识载体(6P 模式)：将"6P"知识载体渗透到酒店英语服务能力的培养中。

（1）Profession(职业)：以酒店，特别是五星级酒店的英语服务内容为主线。

（2）Position(岗位)：以不同服务岗位的工作组成教学模块；以相同岗位的不同服务为技能构成教学单元。

（3）Procedure(过程)：以具体的服务任务和流程构成教学内容。

（4）Point(要点)：以服务工作中的英语语言要求和实际操作注意事项为技能要点，并作为教学重难点。

（5）Performance & Practice（演练与实训）：通过模拟服务演练和岗位实训来提高"新酒店人"的酒店英语职业素养和职业技能。

多种英语服务能力培养(十种)：用英语与客人有效沟通的能力、酒店英语礼仪服务得体的应用能力、酒店英语服务的实操能力、用英语销售酒店产品的能力、用英语进行销售策划的能力、用英语处理投诉的能力、用英语解决突发事件的应变能力、用英语进行个性化服务的能力、用英语解决问题的能力、用英语进行创新服务和创新工作的能力。此外，还有用英语应对面试的能力(第十一种)。

五法运用：任务或情境教学、实践教学、项目教学、案例教学、讨论式教学等教学方法融入《现代酒店服务英语》全套教材。

两结合、两侧重、两设计的教学策略："两结合"即将英语语言习得与酒店岗位服务功能结合，将英语语用能力的培养与英语服务技能养成结合并服务于职业能力的培养；"两侧重"即侧重听说；"两设计"即将服务要求和案例演练提高设计在酒店英语教学和职业英语技能的养成中，培养高职学生娴熟的英语服务应用能力。

三、DCPEA 模式的现代酒店服务英语配套教材的建设创新与特色

本书以多方位的调查与研究为依据，以全方位的课程改革为实证，首创高职酒店英语 DCPEA 新的课程和教材模式；建设以"6P"为知识载体的高职酒店英语精品教材和国家规划教材；创建以学生"职业英语能力发展为中心"的课堂教学和与岗位实践相结合的教学体系，培养学生英语礼仪的应用能力等十种酒店英语服务能力。课堂情境教学和岗位实训配套，课堂教材与实训教材配套，相辅相成。引进旅游饭店职业英语证书的考试内容，提高酒

店管理专业学生的酒店英语实用技能和职业素养，提高他们在未来职业发展中的创新能力和综合竞争实力。

富有创意的教材构架、新颖独特的教学栏目和融入不同教学方法的教学设计，以及受学生喜爱的由实训实例改写的案例故事，还有根据教师实践经历改写的教学内容，这些颠覆了传统的专业英语教材的编写模式和体例，实现了英语语用能力培养与酒店岗位英语服务能力培养的有机结合，不仅有助于教师进行课堂教学改革，还将对学生职业发展产生深远的影响。本书体现了职业性、实用性、时代性及语言的规范性。教材建设与课程建设和科学研究相结合，尽显DCPEA职业英语培养的研究色彩。

好的专业英语(ESP)教材不能只是教学内容简单的输出器，更不能是公共英语教材的翻版。它需要作者特别是主编对专业、人才培养和课程进行深入研究，并植根于成功的教学改革和课程建设的肥田沃土之中，实现对已有教学体系和教学内容创造性的重构，有企业需要的现代新知识和职业素养与技能，有专业和课程需要的地道规范的英语知识，有独到的适合本课程能力培养的模式和载体，有作者将先进的教学法融入其中的教学内容和实践任务的教学设计，有新颖独特的体现本专业职业能力培养的教学栏目设计，有融进使用教材的师生反馈和时代变化需求对教材的多次修订、重写和不断提高，实现英语应用能力培养和职业英语工作能力养成的有机结合，能真正成为执教教师职业英语能力培养教学改革的推助器，实现专业英语教学内容、教学方法和训练方式的完全转变，还要方便学生自学。我们正是朝着这些方面努力的！

本套教材自出版以来一直受到广大师生和读者的欢迎，得到专家的好评，"代表了目前高职专业英语教材编写的水平，对其他层次专门用途英语教材编写和教学极具启发意义"。这套教材不仅是国内酒店英语精品课程广泛使用的教材，而且为多门酒店英语精品课程的建设助力。编者提出的DCPEA理念和"6P"知识载体，所归纳提炼的十种英语服务能力及所设计的教学栏目等被用在一些教师教学改革、课程建设和科研文献中。编者还在《中国外语》等期刊上发表了DCPEA课程和教材建设研究文献共8篇，教材和文章均受到众多学者的引证和科研运用；DCPEA教材编写模式也被其他专业英语教材建设所引用。这套教材两次荣幸地获评职业教育国家规划教材，其中的实训教材是北京市高等教育精品教材立项项目。借教材再版之机，对广大师生、读者、学者和专家对本套教材及其研究文献的厚爱表示由衷的感谢！

编　者

2022年1月

前　言

中国酒店业的快速发展有目共睹。现在在校的酒店管理专业的学生正处于职业环境的黄金时段——酒店业的快速发展时期,这将为具有较高的酒店英语服务技能和管理技能的酒店人才提供更为广阔的发展空间。

高等职业院校酒店管理专业教育培养的是具有一定职业竞争力的酒店实用型专业人才,要让他们在未来的职业生涯中有能力去施展,有才华去发挥。提高这些学生的酒店英语服务技能,增强他们的职业竞争力,培养受星级酒店欢迎的实用型高技能特色人才,不仅是酒店业快速发展对高水准服务人才和管理人才的迫切要求,更是酒店管理专业课程建设和教学改革的方向与重要任务。而教材则是实现以学生英语服务能力培养为目标的酒店英语课程改革的重要载体和根本保证。

《现代酒店服务英语》是一本工学结合的教材。编者根据酒店行业的工作环境和岗位要求,营造了仿真的工作情境,使学生在逐项完成服务工作任务的同时,掌握相应的英语词汇、表达方法和沟通技巧,训练顶岗工作的能力。

本书按照高职专业英语 DCPEA(Development-Centered in Professional English Ability,以职业英语能力发展为中心)课程模式的宗旨组织内容,将英语语言能力的培养与英语服务技能的养成相结合,以酒店特别是五星级酒店职业(Profession)英语服务内容为编写主线,以不同服务岗位(Position)的工作内容构成教学模块,以相同岗位的不同服务任务为服务技能组成教学单元,以具体服务任务和工作流程(Procedure)构成教学内容,以服务工作中的英语语言要求和实际操作注意事项为技能要点(Point),并作为教学重点和难点。通过这些模块的服务英语教学和模拟服务演练与实训(Performance & Practice),提高"新酒店人"的酒店英语职业素养和职业技能。

本书在编写体例上进行了精心的设计,具有一定的创新性。

(1) 设立 Service Position、Skills and Attainments 和 Position Knowledge 等教学栏目,培养学生的岗位职业素养。

(2) 以"6P"为知识载体,注重对学生酒店英语实用服务技能的提高,包括用英语进行有效沟通的能力,用英语进行优质服务的能力,用英语完成实际操作的能力,用英语处理投诉和解决突发事件的应变能力,用英语进行酒店产品销售的能力,用英语进行个性化服务的能力,用英语解决问题的能力,用英语进行创新服务和创新工作的能力。

(3) 教学栏目、教学情境、教学任务和教学实践的设计体现了英语语用能力培养和酒店岗位英语服务能力培养的有机结合,体现了酒店英语服务能力培养的特色。

(4) 课堂教学教材和岗位实训教材配套，相辅相成。《现代酒店服务英语》和《酒店英语服务实训》是配套教材，其中《酒店英语服务实训》为 2007 年度北京市高等教育精品教材立项项目。

(5) 配套音频涵盖全部 Service Conversation，便于学生自我学习，自我实践。

(6) 本书所有对话均配有二维码，扫描二维码可在线播放音频。

本书由胡扬政担任主编，美国专家 Glenn L. Hyatt 担任主审。本书共有十四个服务模块，胡扬政编写了前台服务、客房预订部服务和客房服务三个模块；李维维，刘莉编写了商务中心两个模块，刘梅编写了康体中心服务三模块；苑丽娟编写了总机服务和商场部服务两个模块；胡冰冰编写了收银台服务和会展中心服务两个模块；刘玥编写了酒吧服务和其他服务两个模块；胡霞编写了礼宾部服务和餐厅服务两个模块。苏立刚、杨明军、李梅参加了修订。美国专家 Glenn L. Hyatt 先生、Mariah J. Xu 女士和 Elena H. Hyatt 女士为本书的 Service Conversation 音频作英文配音。本书读者可登录 www.tup.com.cn 下载本书配套音频文件。

酒店经理郭远志先生为本书的编写和修改提出了宝贵意见，我们还得到了北京财贸职业学院旅游系王琦教授、国际教育学院潘勇副教授、王莉莉副教授的鼎力支持，在此深表感谢。

由于时间仓促，编者水平有限，错漏之处在所难免，恳请使用者多提宝贵意见，以便再版时补充更正。

编　者
2017 年 5 日

Contents 目 录

Chapter One   Front Desk Service
前 台 服 务

▶ **Unit One   Check-in**
单元 1   入住登记 ·· 3
　　Service Conversation 1　You Are Our Guests ································ 5
　　Service Conversation 2　Registering a Group That Has a Reservation ········ 6

▶ **Unit Two   Complaints and on the Guest's Request**
单元 2   处理投诉和回应客人要求 ·· 11
　　Service Conversation 3　Our Housemaid Will Bring Them to Your
　　　　　　　　　　　　　Room Soon ·· 12
　　Service Conversation 4　We Do Apologize for the Inconvenience ·········· 13

Chapter Two   Reservation Desk Service
客房预订部服务

▶ **Unit Three   Room Reservation**
单元 3   客房预订 ·· 19
　　Service Conversation 5　Accepting a Reservation ······················· 21
　　Service Conversation 6　Recommending Other Hotels ··················· 22

▶ **Unit Four   Revising the Reservation**
单元 4   预订变更 ·· 26
　　Service Conversation 7　Changing a Reservation ························ 28
　　Service Conversation 8　Canceling a Reservation for the Guest ········· 29

Chapter Three Concierge Desk Service
礼宾部服务

Unit Five Luggage Service
单元 5 行李服务 ………………………………………………………… 35
- Service Conversation 9   Welcome to the Great Wall Hotel ……………… 37
- Service Conversation 10 Is It Charged or Free ………………………… 38

Unit Six Car Reservation Service
单元 6 车辆预订服务 …………………………………………………… 42
- Service Conversation 11 Calling a Taxi at the Hotel Gate ……………… 43
- Service Conversation 12 Car Reservation at the Concierge Desk ……… 44

Chapter Four Cash Desk Service
收银台服务

Unit Seven Foreign Currency Exchange
单元 7 外币兑换 ………………………………………………………… 51
- Service Conversation 13 Exchange US dollars into Chinese yuan ……… 53
- Service Conversation 14 Changing at the Airport Exchange Office …… 54

Unit Eight Check Out
单元 8 结账退宿 ………………………………………………………… 58
- Service Conversation 15 Checking Out in Cash ………………………… 60
- Service Conversation 16 Checking Out by Credit Card ………………… 61

Unit Nine Solving Problems with the Bill
单元 9 解决账单问题 …………………………………………………… 65
- Service Conversation 17 Explaining the Bill …………………………… 66
- Service Conversation 18 Here Is the Money You've Overpaid ………… 67

Chapter Five Telephone Desk Service
总 机 服 务

Unit Ten Telephone Operator
单元 10 转接电话 ………………………………………………………… 73
- Service Conversation 19 Outgoing Calls ………………………………… 74

Service Conversation 20　Incoming Calls ·················· 75

Unit Eleven　Other Service
单元 11　其他服务 ·················· 79
Service Conversation 21　The Wake-up Call ·················· 80
Service Conversation 22　Leaving the Message ·················· 81

Chapter Six　Housekeeping Service
客房服务

Unit Twelve　Chamber Service
单元 12　客房服务 ·················· 87
Service Conversation 23　May I Do the Room Now ·················· 88
Service Conversation 24　What Time Would You Like Me to Come Back ······ 89

Unit Thirteen　Room Service
单元 13　客房送餐服务 ·················· 93
Service Conversation 25　Your Order Will Arrive in 15 Minutes ·················· 94
Service Conversation 26　Here Is Your Chinese Breakfast ·················· 95

Unit Fourteen　Maintenance Service
单元 14　维修服务 ·················· 99
Service Conversation 27　The Repairman Will Come to Your Room Soon ······ 101
Service Conversation 28　Repairing the Facilities in the Bathroom ·········· 101

Chapter Seven　Restaurant Service
餐厅服务

Unit Fifteen　Table Reservation
单元 15　餐厅预订 ·················· 107
Service Conversation 29　Reserving a Table on Valentine's Day ············ 108
Service Conversation 30　Book a Table by the Window ·················· 109

Unit Sixteen　Greeting the Guests
单元 16　餐厅迎客服务 ·················· 115
Service Conversation 31　Arranging One Table for the Non-reserved Guest ··· 116

Service Conversation 32　Arranging One Table for the Reserved Guest ·········· 117

▶ **Unit Seventeen　Taking Orders**
单元 17　点菜服务 ··· 120
　　Service Conversation 33　Can You Recommend Some Chinese Food ·········· 121
　　Service Conversation 34　The Chinese Cuisine Is Divided into Eight Styles ······· 122

▶ **Unit Eighteen　Service During the Meal**
单元 18　上菜服务与席间服务 ·· 126
　　Service Conversation 35　Serving the Guest During the Meal ·············· 126

▶ **Unit Nineteen　Setting Accounts**
单元 19　结账 ·· 128
　　Service Conversation 36　I Forgot to Bring My Wallet with Me ············ 129
　　Service Conversation 37　Do You Accept Credit Cards ···················· 130

Chapter Eight　Bar Service
酒 吧 服 务

▶ **Unit Twenty　General Service**
单元 20　常规服务 ·· 137
　　Service Conversation 38　Serving Drinks ································· 138

▶ **Unit Twenty-one　Dealing with Complaints and a Drunken Guest**
单元 21　处理投诉和醉酒客人 ·· 144
　　Service Conversation 39　I Am Not Happy with the Steak ················· 145
　　Service Conversation 40　A Drunken Guest ······························ 145

Chapter Nine　Business Center Service（Ⅰ）
商务中心服务（一）

▶ **Unit Twenty-two　Secretarial Service**
单元 22　文秘服务 ·· 151
　　Service Conversation 41　Printing and Photocopying of the Documents ··· 152
　　Service Conversation 42　I Need an Interpreter and a Translator Tomorrow ··· 153

Unit Twenty-three　Computer Renting and Internet Services
单元 23　计算机租赁和网络服务 ·· 158
　　Service Conversation 43　I Wonder If I Can Rent a Computer from You ········ 159
　　Service Conversation 44　We Have Free Wi-Fi Service ···························· 160

Chapter Ten　Business Center Service (Ⅱ)
商务中心服务(二)

Unit Twenty-four　Ticket and Tour Assistance
单元 24　票务预订协办 ·· 164
　　Service Conversation 45　Booking a Bullet Train Ticket ·························· 166
　　Service Conversation 46　Booking a Transfer Air Ticket ·························· 167

Unit Twenty-five　Business Event and Courier Services
单元 25　商务活动承办和快递服务 ··· 172
　　Service Conversation 47　Reserving a Business Event and a Tour Package ······ 174
　　Service Conversation 48　Delivering a Parcel ·· 176

Chapter Eleven　Health & Recreation Center Service
康体中心服务

Unit Twenty-six　Body Care Service
单元 26　康体服务 ·· 184
　　Service Conversation 49　Serving Basketball ·· 186
　　Service Conversation 50　Serving Bowling ·· 187

Unit Twenty-seven　Bathing Service
单元 27　洗浴服务 ·· 192
　　Service Conversation 51　Serving Sauna ··· 194
　　Service Conversation 52　Serving Swimming ······································· 195

Unit Twenty-eight　Entertaining Service
单元 28　娱乐服务 ·· 201
　　Service Conversation 53　Serving Ballroom ··· 202
　　Service Conversation 54　Serving Net Bar ··· 204

Chapter Twelve Convention & Exhibition Center Service
会展中心服务

Unit Twenty-nine Convention Service
单元 29 会议服务 212
Service Conversation 55 Reserving the Conference on the Phone 214
Service Conversation 56 Discussing the Service Details 216

Unit Thirty Exhibition Service
单元 30 展览服务 221
Service Conversation 57 Reserving an Exhibition 223
Service Conversation 58 We're in an Urgent Need for Your Help 224

Chapter Thirteen Shopping Service
商场部服务

Unit Thirty-one Recommending the Article for the Guest
单元 31 为客人推荐商品 231
Service Conversation 59 Shopping at the Jewelry and Crafts Shop 233
Service Conversation 60 Shopping at the Textile and Knitwear Shop 234

Unit Thirty-two Displaying the Articles for the Customer to Choose
单元 32 展示商品供客人挑选 239
Service Conversation 61 Shopping at the Chinese Arts and
                         Stationery Shop 240
Service Conversation 62 Shopping at the Chinese Tea Counter 241

Chapter Fourteen Other Service
其他服务

Unit Thirty-three Lost and Found Service
单元 33 失物招领服务 250
Service Conversation 63 Don't Worry, Sir 251
Service Conversation 64 Claiming My Ring 252

Unit Thirty-four Depositing Service
单元 34 寄存服务 ………………………………………………… 256
   Service Conversation 65 Luggage Depositing ……………………… 257
   Service Conversation 66 Safe-Deposit Box ………………………… 257

Unit Thirty-five Tourism Service
单元 35 旅游信息服务 …………………………………………… 261
   Service Conversation 67 Showing the Way ………………………… 262
   Service Conversation 68 Booking a Tour …………………………… 262

Unit Thirty-six Baby-sitting Service
单元 36 托婴服务 ………………………………………………… 266
   Service Conversation 69 Baby-sitting Service ……………………… 266

Key to the Exercises
练习答案 ……………………………………………………………… 270

参考文献 ……………………………………………………………… 289

Chapter One　Front Desk Service
前台服务

Unit One　Check-in
单元 1　入住登记

Unit Two　Complaints and on the Guest's Request
单元 2　处理投诉和回应客人要求

Service Position 服务岗位

The Front Desk/Reception Desk/Front Office/General Service Counter(前台/总台/总服务台)is not only a very important position of the Front Office Department, but also the hub of activities of the hotel. It is mainly responsible for selling the products and services of the hotel, and dispatching the operation of the hotel. The service effect and the service quality represent the whole level of the management of the hotel. The Front Desk is called as "Nerve Center" or "Open Window" of a hotel.

In most of the hotels, the Front Desk is located near the main entrance.

Skills and Attainments 服务技能与素养

The receptionists of the Front Desk need to complete the following main services in English:

Check-in for the guests or the group with reservations, handling walk-in guests; extending the stay; changing the room; assigning the rooms; leaving a message; meeting the needs of the guests, dealing with the guests' complaints; giving the information that the guests want.

The Front Desk is the answer station for residence halls. If a guest has questions about housing, needs assistance, or does not know the direction to a new location, he will stop by or call and ask the desk clerks. Sometimes, the guests will ask how to get to the hotel. So the staff of the Front Desk ought to know how to get to it by car, by bus or by subway. Besides the courteous and warm-hearted attitude, the receptionists must have the excellent English ability of services. Only in this way, can they answer the guests' inquiries, meet the guests' needs and solve the guests' problems and deal with the guests' complaints.

Key Words and Expressions

the Front Desk	前台
room reservation	客房预订
the FIT reservation	散客预订
dispatch (*n. & vt.*)	调度,处理
entrance (*n.*)	入口,进口,门口
extend/cancel the reservation	延长/取消预订
walk-in guests	没有预订的客人
extending the stay	延宿
check-in (*n.*)	入住登记
room rate	房价

Unit One Check-in

Procedure of Service 服务流程

Check-in for the guest

- Greet the guest.
- Ask the guest whether he has a reservation with the hotel.
- Find out the reservation in the computer for confirmation.
  For a walk-in guest:
  Check the reservation list for the vacancies in the computer, and introduce them to the guest.
- Ask the guest to show his identification.
- Ask the guest to fill in the registration list.
- Ask the guest how to make the payment.
- Form the check-in record.
- Give the key card to the guest.
- Tell the guest that the bellman will show him to the room.
- Extend best wishes to the guest.

Registering the group that has a reservation

- Find the tour leader.
- Self-introduce.
- Confirm the group name and the number of rooms.
- Ask the group leader whether there is any change in the schedule or in the number of the persons.
- Ask the group leader to help his members to complete the registration cards.
- Form the check-in record.

- Give the key cards and breakfast vouchers to the group leader.
- Tell the group leader about the arrangement such as:
  The place and the time of the activities.
  How and where to collect the luggage when they leave.
- Wish them to enjoy their stay.

Points of Service Language 服务语言要点

1. **Polite expressions 礼貌用语**

   Welcome to our hotel. Is there anything I can do for you?
   欢迎您来到我们酒店。需要我为您服务吗？
   Nice to have you here.
   欢迎您来到我们酒店。
   My pleasure. You are our guest.
   很高兴为您服务。您是我们的客人。
   Just a minute, please. A bellman will show you to your room. I hope you enjoy your stay here.
   请稍等。我们的服务员会带您到您的房间。祝您住得开心。
   Hope you have a pleasant stay here.
   祝您入住愉快。
   You're always welcome. We are glad to serve you at any time. Have a pleasant stay here.
   不用谢。我们很高兴随时为您服务。祝您入住愉快。
   I'm afraid that your room is not ready yet, would you mind waiting, please? We are very sorry for the inconvenience.
   恐怕您的房间还没能准备好，请您等会儿好吗？由此带来的不便我们深表歉意。

2. **Asking the guest whether he has a reservation with the hotel 询问客人是否有预订**

   Have you made a reservation with our hotel?
   Do you have a reservation?
   请问你们有预订吗？
   In whose name was the reservation made?
   用谁的名字预订的？
   When was it made?
   什么时间订的？

3. **Registering a guest 为客人登记**

   May I see your passports?
   我可以看看您的护照吗？
   Would you please fill in the registration form?
   您能填写这张登记表吗？
   Please fill in the registration forms—your nationality, age, occupation, passport number, and your signature.

请填写入住登记表——填上您的国籍、年龄、职业、护照号码等,还要签名。

What's your occupation, please?

请问您从事什么职业?

4. **Asking the guest how to make the payment** 询问客人怎样付款

How would you like to make your payment?

How will you be paying?

How would you like to settle your bill?

您用什么方式付款?

How would you like to pay, by credit card, in cash or with a traveler's check?

请问您怎样付款,是用信用卡、现金还是旅行支票?

In cash/With US dollars traveler's check, I think.

我想用现金/美元旅行支票。

Here is the receipt. Please keep it.

这是您的收据。请您妥善保存。

Service Conversation 1

You Are Our Guests

01-01　You Are Our Guests. mp3

Ⓡ: Receptionist

Ⓖ: Guest

R: Good morning. Welcome to China World Hotel. Is there anything I can do for you?

G: We'd like to check in, please.

R: Do you have a reservation?

G: I'm afraid not.

R: Please wait a moment, sir. Let me check the registration list.
Thanks for waiting so long. We only have a suite available.

G: What's the room rate per night?

R: 175 US dollars.

G: We'll take it.

R: How long do you intend to stay?

G: Two nights.

R: May I see your passports?

G: Certainly. Here you are.

R: Thank you. Please fill in the registration forms, your nationality, age, occupation, passport number, and your signature.

G: OK. Is that all right?

R: Yes. Thanks. How would you like to make your payment?

G: In cash.

R: Would you please pay 150 US dollars as a deposit?

G: OK. Here you are.

R: Here is the receipt. Please keep it.

G: Thank you.

R: Here are your key cards and your breakfast coupons. Your rooms are on the sixteenth floor.

G: Thank you.

R: My pleasure. You are our guests. Just a minute, please. The bellman will show you to your room. I hope you enjoy your stay here.

Practice   Answer the questions according to the service conversation.

1. The guest has a reservation with the hotel, doesn't he?
2. How does the receptionist deal with the walk-in guest?
3. What does the guest pay 150 US dollars as?

Service Conversation 2 — Registering a Group That Has a Reservation

R: Receptionist

G: Guest

R: Good afternoon, ladies and gentlemen. Welcome to our hotel. Who is your group leader?

G: Good afternoon. I'm the group leader. My name is Li Fen. We have made a reservation in your hotel. I'd like to check in for our group.

01-02 Registering a Group That Has a Reservation. mp3

R: Nice to have you here. I'm Zhou Jun at the Front Desk. I'd like to confirm the schedule for your stay here first.

G: I see.

R: Is there any change in the number of your group?

G: No.

Chapter One　Front Desk Service
前台服务

R: You will have an evening party at 8 this evening, won't you?

G: Yes. Where can we have the evening party?

R: The hall on the second floor. You will have breakfast at 5:40 tomorrow morning, and leave our hotel at 6:20, is that right?

G: Yes.

R: We will arrange a wake-up call at 5:20. Will that be all right?

G: That's fine.

R: Could you please place your luggage in front of the desk on the left of the lobby at 6:10? The bellman will pick them up.

G: OK.

R: Could you help your members to fill in the registration cards?

G: Certainly. Here are the registration cards.

R: Thank you. Your key cards and breakfast vouchers are all in the envelopes with your names on them. Your rooms are on the sixth to ninth floors and there are five rooms on each floor. Would you please sign your name here?

G: OK.

R: Thank you. If you have any changes, please contact the Front Desk. Hope you have a pleasant stay here.

Practice　Answer the questions according to the service conversation.

1. Is there any change in the schedule of the group?
2. What does the hotel arrange for the group to do?
3. How many rooms are there on each floor?
4. What do you think of Zhou Jun's service in the service conversation?

Key Words and Expressions

check-in (n.)	入住登记
vacancy (n.)	空房
registration card /form	登记卡/表
make the payment	付款
identification (n.)	身份证
schedule (n.)	计划表,时间表
luggage (n.)	行李
receptionist (n.)	接待员
signature (n.)	签名,署名,盖章
receipt (n.)	收据
breakfast voucher	早餐券
contact (n.& vt.)	联系,交涉

Points of Service Performance 服务演练要点

- When checking in, first ask the guest whether he has a reservation with the hotel. If he is a guest with a reservation, you need to find out his information record for confirmation. If there is no reservation for this particular guest, you should check the reservation list for the vacancies and then introduce them to the guest.
  客人要办理入住手续,先要询问是否有预订。如果是有预订的客人,须找出相关的信息记录予以确认;如果是没有预订的客人,须查一下预订记录单看是否有空房,然后给客人介绍。

- Be sure to politely ask the guest to present his valid certificates, such as ID card and passport.
  要礼貌地请客人出示身份证、护照等有效的身份证明。

- When you ask the guest to fill in the registration form and fill out the registration record in the computer, make sure to get the following information from the guest: nationality, age, occupation, passport number; the dates of arrival and departure; the room type, the room number and the room rate; and the signature of the guest.
  要求客人填写登记表和在计算机上形成登记记录时,都要注意留下下列信息:国籍、年龄、职业、护照号码等,到达日期和离店日期、房型、房间数和房价,还有客人签名。

- When you handle a group check-in, confirm the group name and the number of rooms, and then ask whether there are any changes in the schedule or the number of persons.
  在做团队入住登记时,不仅要确认团队名称和房间数,还要询问客人的时间安排和人数有无变化。

Performance for Service 模拟演练

Task A

Practice making a registration in pairs according to the following two cards.

Guest Card		
	Guest name:	Tom Smith, a tour leader
	Reservation:	20 standard rooms for 20 persons; 2 nights
	Change:	22 standard rooms for 23 persons; 2 nights
	Special request:	special rate

Receptionist Card	
	Greet the guest
	Introduce
	Confirm the reservation
	Deal with the change
	Discount: 15% off

Chapter One Front Desk Service
前台服务

Task B

Mr. Jenny Brown is standing at the Front Desk. He says that he booked a single room a month ago. But unfortunately the receptionist Liu Ying can't find it, he can't check in. Liu Ying checks in the computer and she finds out that a guest just checked out 15 minutes ago. It will take 20 minutes for the room to be cleaned.

Position Knowledge 岗位知识

- Another name for hotel keeping is the "courtesy industry". We advocate conventional and good manners and politeness. Practice these till they become second nature—till you are courteous automatically.
  宾馆行业,又称"礼貌行业"。我们提倡传统的良好仪态和彬彬有礼,要在实践中使这些成为你的第二天性——使这些习惯成自然。
- If the guest pays in cash, he has to hand in some deposit in advance. If the guest pays by credit card, you should ask him to give his credit card to be pre-authorized.
  如果客人用现金付款,须先交押金。如果客人用信用卡付款,须预授权。
- When seeing the passport, pay more attention to the following information of the guest: nationality, age, occupation, passport number and the date of expiry.
  检查客人护照时要注意客人的下列信息:国籍、年龄、职业、护照号码以及护照的有效日期。

Exercises

Ⅰ. Topics for discussion.

1. How to register a walk-in guest?
2. What will you pay more attention to when seeing the passport?
3. How to express your wishes to the guest when finishing registration?

Ⅱ. Answer the following questions.

1. How would you like to settle your bill?

   _____

2. How to say to the guest if you want to know his occupation?

   _____

3. What will you say to the guest if the room is not ready?

   _____

4. What will you tell the guest to do when he hands in the deposit?

   _____

Ⅲ. **Translate the following sentences into English.**

1. 不用谢,我们很高兴随时为您服务。祝您入住愉快。
2. 请稍等。我们的服务员会带您到您的房间。祝您住得开心。
3. 请填写入住登记表——填上您的国籍、年龄、职业、护照号码等,还要签名。
4. 请您在这儿签个字,好吗?
5. 你们的房卡和早餐券都放在写有你们名字的信封里了。
6. White 小姐,请稍等,我查一下预订表。谢谢您,让您久等了。您预订了 4 个晚上的 11 个标准间和 1 个套间,对吗?

Ⅳ. **Translate the following sentences into Chinese.**

1. You need to show the key card when you sign for your meals and drinks in the restaurant and the bar.
2. We have the room available you need. How many nights would you like?
3. If you don't understand what the guest says, be sure not to guess nor pretend to know at all. Certainly you aren't afraid of this. Ask the guest to say again with "I beg your pardon". "Pardon me?", or "Sorry, I don't understand. Could you please repeat that?"
4. Unfortunately the suite you stayed last time was booked this morning. But we have a suite available facing the lake. The room rate is just the same with the one you stayed in last time.
5. We advocate old-fashioned and good manners and politeness. Practice these till they become second nature—till you are courteous automatically.

Unit Two Complaints and on the Guest's Request

单元 2 处理投诉和回应客人要求

Procedure of Service 服务流程

- Greet the guest.
- Be patient to listen to what the guest says and take notes.
- Say "sorry" or make an apology to the guest.
- Repeat what the guest says for confirmation.
- Tell the guest the measures to be adopted at once.
- Tell the guest when the problem will be solved.
- Ask the guest to tell his name and room number.
- Say "thank you" to the guest.
- Tell the related clerk what to do at once.
- Exam the result and make a record.

Points of Service Language 服务语言要点

1. **Asking what has happened 询问发生了什么**

    May I know what's wrong?
    Could you tell me what has happened?
    请问有什么问题吗?

2. **Saying "sorry" or making an apology 道歉或表示遗憾**

    I do apologize.
    我向您道歉。
    I'm sorry to hear that.
    听到这样的事,我很抱歉。
    We make an apology for...
    我们为……向您道歉。
    We do apologize for the inconvenience.

我们为给您带来的不便深表歉意。
There could have been some mistakes. I do apologize.
可能是出了什么问题,实在是对不起。

3. **Making an apology and taking measures 道歉和采取措施**

We do apologize for the inconvenience firstly. My name is Wang Li. Our repairman will come to your room within five minutes.
首先,我们为给您带来的不便深表歉意。我叫王莉。我们的维修人员五分钟内到达您的房间。
I'm sorry to hear that, but I will send someone to fix it at once.
听到这样的事,我很抱歉,我马上派人来修。
Wait a minute, please. I'll send a housemaid immediately.
请稍等,我马上派一个服务员过去。
The housemaid will bring the pillow and slippers to you.
服务员会把枕头和拖鞋一起给您送去。

4. **Showing sincerity to the guest 表示诚恳**

I assure you that it won't happen again.
您尽管放心,不会再发生这种事情了。
You're welcome. If there is anything else I can do for you, please don't hesitate to call me.
不用谢,如果有什么我能做的,请打电话给我。
We might have overlooked some details. Thank you for bringing the matter to our attention.
我们可能忽略了一些细小的地方。感谢您提醒我们注意。
You're welcome. We sent you complimentary flowers to express our regrets for all the trouble.
不用谢,我们给您带来了那么多麻烦,为了表示歉意,我们送您一个免费的花篮。

Service Conversation 3

Our Housemaid Will Bring Them to Your Room Soon

02-03 Our Housemaid Will Bring Them to Your Room Soon. mp3

R: Receptionist
W: Tom White

R: Good evening. Front Desk. Can I help you?

Chapter One　Front Desk Service

前台服务

W: Good evening. This is Tom White. I want to have a bath, but I find there is neither shampoo nor toothpaste in the bathroom.

R: I'm very sorry to hear that, Mr White. We might have overlooked some details. Thank you for bringing the matter to our attention. Wait a minute, please. I'll send a housemaid immediately. May I know your room number?

W: Room 2567.

R: Thank you. Is there anything I can do for you?

W: I have a cold these days. Can I have an extra blanket?

R: Certainly. You need a blanket, shampoo and toothpaste. Our housemaid will bring them to your room soon.

W: Thank you very much.

Practice　Answer the questions according to the service conversation.

1. Why does Tom White call the receptionist?
2. What does the receptionist say to Tom White?
3. What will the housemaid send to the guest's room soon?

Service Conversation 4

We Do Apologize for the Inconvenience

02-04　We Do Apologize for the Inconvenience. mp3

R: Receptionist

S: John Smith

R: Good evening. Front Office. What can I do for you?

S: This is Mr. Smith in Room 2256. I've just checked in. I'm not satisfied with my room.

R: May I know what's wrong?

S: The air-conditioner doesn't work, and the room is terribly hot. I want to wash my hands, but there is neither water nor soap. The light is so dim that I can't read.

R: We do apologize for the inconvenience. My name is Wang Li. Our repairman will come to your room within four minutes. Our housemaid will bring soap to your room.

S: That's fine.

13

(*Fifteen minutes later*)

R: This is Wang Li speaking. Is everything all right?

S: Everything is OK. Thanks very much.

R: You're welcome. Mr. Smith, if there is anything else I can do for you, please don't hesitate to call me.

Practice　Answer the questions according to the service conversation.

1. The guest is not very satisfied with the room. Why?
2. How does Wang Li deal with the complaint?
3. What does Wang Li do fifteen minutes later?

Key Words and Expressions

complaint (*n.*)	投诉,申诉,牢骚
make an apology	道歉
adopt measures	采取措施
toothpaste (*n.*)	牙膏
housemaid (*n.*)	女服务员
air-conditioner (*n.*)	空调
repairman (*n.*)	维修人员
satisfy (*vt.*)	使满足,使满意

Points of Service Performance 服务演练要点

- When a guest makes a complaint against something to you, be sure not to argue with the guest. Certainly, don't make excuses and blame others. Listen carefully and take notes. Then say "sorry" to him and tell him what will be done. You'd better tell him in what time the problem will be solved.
  当客人因某事向你投诉时,记住千万别同客人争论。当然,也不要找借口,责怪他人。仔细听,做记录。向客人道歉,告诉他你要采取的措施。你最好还要告诉他问题何时能解决。

- Avoid being defensive, irritated, or angry, even though these reactions are natural.
  避免出现辩解、烦躁或恼怒,即使这些反应是正常的。

- Show your sympathy and empathy. Don't only look at things from your view points. Try to put yourself into the place of the guest.
  要有同情心,要理解对方的心情。不要仅从自己的角度看问题,要设身处地地为客人想一想。

Chapter One Front Desk Service
前台服务

Performance for Service 模拟演练

Task A

Performance in meeting the guest's need in pairs according to the following two cards.

| Guest Card | Rose Smith in Room 5678
Need an extra pillow
There is something wrong with the hair-dryer in the room. |

| Receptionist Card | Wang Ping receives the call.
A housemaid will be sent to meet her needs. |

Task B

Mr. Jenny Brown in Room 1156 calls the receptionist Wang Li at the Front Desk because the water closet(抽水马桶)can't be used, and there is something wrong with the air-conditioner as well. He shows his dissatisfaction.

Wang Li tells Mr. Jenny Brown that the repairman will go to his room within five minutes to repair the water closet and the air-conditioner.

Position Knowledge 岗位知识

- Getting into an argument with the guest is the most undesirable thing to a staff member and a hotel. When a guest makes a complaint against something to you, be sure not to argue with the guest, but you can try your best to make clear what it is. Certainly you can ask the guest some questions, so that the guest can have the chance to explain.
对于酒店员工和酒店来说,最不可取的就是和客人争吵。当客人因某事向你投诉时,千万要记住别同客人争论,不过,你可以尽自己的努力去弄清事实的真相。当然,你还可以向客人提问题,这样,客人也有机会解释。
- A dissatisfied guest means a loss of potential future business for the hotel, whereas a pleased guest leaves the hotel with a warm memory of the hospitality he has enjoyed and will have an inclination to repeat his visit to our hotel.
一位扫兴离去的客人,意味着酒店将会失去可能得到的一笔生意;而一位满意的客人将带着自己在酒店所享受到的热情周到的服务的美好记忆离开,他会愿意再次光顾我们的酒店。

Ⅰ. Topics for discussion.

1. Simply introduce the procedure of meeting the needs of the guest.
2. Speak out some sentences about how to express apology to the guest.

Ⅱ. Read the following passage and answer the questions.

In handling complaints, the hotel staff should always be polite and helpful. He should be always ready to lend an attentive ear to what the guest has to say and always hear the guest out. He must not interrupt guest unless necessary, it is also advisable for him to jot down what the guest has said. He should then make a short apology and express his understanding of the guest's situation or sympathy with the guest. Only when he puts himself in the guest's shoe, can he look at the problem from the other person's perspective(观点,看法). And only when the staff member looks at the guest's problem in the guest's way, can he be ready to sympathy with the guest. After that the staff member should take actions quickly to remove the complaint, either by making polite, patient and detailed explanations, or making swift, effective correction and remedies, or reporting the complaint to a superior. But whatever he intends to do, he must keep the guest informed of the measures or actions he plans to take and when he will carry them out.

Questions:

1. How should the hotel staff be when dealing with the guest's complaint?
2. What does "jot down" mean?
3. What does the hotel staff do when the guest finishes the complaint?
4. How can the hotel staff look at the problem from the other person's perspective?

Ⅲ. Translate the following sentences into English.

1. 我们为给您带来的不便深表歉意。
2. 我担保,不会再发生这种事情了。
3. 非常抱歉,我们可能忽略了一些细小的地方。感谢您提醒我们注意。请稍等,我马上派一个服务员过去。
4. Smith 先生问王平能否多要一个枕头和一个吹风机。
5. 一位满意的客人将带着自己在饭店所享受到的热情周到的服务的美好回忆离开,他会愿意再次光顾我们的酒店。

Chapter Two Reservation Desk Service
客房预订部服务

Unit Three Room Reservation
单元 3 客房预订

Unit Four Revising the Reservation
单元 4 预订变更

Service Position 服务岗位

The Reservation Desk/Room Reservation(s)/Reservations(客房预订部/订房部/预订部) is another very important position of the Front Office Department. Sometimes it is also called "the Back Office", for most of the room reservations are always carried out in the "back place" where no guest appears. Its responsibility includes receiving, charting and storing the guests' room reservations and assigning the rooms.

Skills and Attainments 服务技能与素养

The reservationists are responsible for answering questions about room reservation, accepting the room reservations (the FIT reservation, the group reservation), changing the reservation, extending the reservation, cancelling the reservation; writing and sending out the hotel's letters of confirmation.

The reservationists must have the excellent English ability in communication. Because they often need to talk with the guests by telephone, it will be very good for them to have a nice voice, fluent and clear English and a friendly attitude. Certainly, they need to know well about the hotel (for example, the room rate, the type of the room, the services and the facilities), the nearby places and the city very well and can answer every question from the guests.

Key Words and Expressions

Room Reservation	客房预订部
room reservation	客房预订
responsibility (n.)	责任;责任心;职责,义务;负担
extend the reservation	延长预订
cancel the reservation	取消预订
chart (vt.)	制订……的计划
assign (vt.)	分配,派给
the FIT (Free Individual Travelers) reservation	散客预订

Unit Three Room Reservation
单元 ❸ 客房预订

Procedure of Service 服务流程

- Greet the guest.
- Get the following reservation information from the guest:
  The dates of arrival and departure.
  The number of the people.
  The room type and the number of the room.
- Search for the vacancy needed in the computer.
- Get the following information from the guest:
  The name of the guest or the name of the group.
  The guest's telephone number.
  (*If the reservation is made for the other persons instead of himself, get the contact name and his telephone number.*)
- Confirm the reservation.
- Make up the record of the reservation in the computer.
- Express your wishes to the guest.

Full house

- Greet the guest.
- Get the following reservation information from the guest:
  The dates of arrival and departure.
- Tell the guest why the reservation can't be made.
- Give the suggestion.
- Express your wish to have another chance to serve him.

Points of Service Language 服务语言要点

1. **Polite expressions**　礼貌用语

   Good morning/afternoon/evening. Room Reservations. May I help you?

早上好/下午好/晚上好。客房预订部。能为您服务吗？
Just a moment, please. I'll check the room available.
请稍等，我查一下房间预订情况。
Please wait a moment, sir. Thank you for your waiting.
请稍等，先生。让您久等了。
Sorry to have kept you waiting so long, sir.
对不起，先生，让您久等了。
It's my pleasure. We look forward to your arrival.
很高兴为您服务。我们恭候您的光临。
You're welcome. We look forward to serving you.
不用谢。我们期待为您服务。
We look forward to having another chance to serve you.
我们期待能再有机会为您服务。

2. **Finding out what the guest wants　了解客人需求**

What/which date would that be?
For when/which date?
请问订在什么时间？
When would you like your room?
您什么时间来住？
How long will you be staying?
请问您住多久？
For how many nights?
您准备住几个晚上？
What/which room would you prefer/like?
请问需要什么样的房间？
What type of room would you like?
您需要什么样的房型？
A double room or a standard room?
双人间还是标准间？
How many people?
几位客人？
How many rooms would you like?
您需要几间房？
May I have/know your name and your telephone number?
您能留下您的姓名和电话号码吗？

3. **Confirming　确认**

Mr. Smith, you've booked/reserved a double room from the 14th to the 15th of May, and your telephone number is…
Smith 先生，您预订了5月14日至15日的一个双人间，您的电话号码是……

Chapter Two Reservation Desk Service
客房预订部服务

I'm afraid that we have no record of the reservation (for the date) in your name. Shall I make a reservation for you now?

没有您的预订记录，我现在可以为您预订吗？

4. Giving the information about the room rates 告知客人房价

The standard room costs 956 yuan per night.

标准间每晚 956 元。

One hundred and sixty(160) US dollars per night including/with breakfast.

包括早餐，每晚 160 美元。

A double room facing south is 170 US dollars.

向南的双人间 170 美元。

There is a 15 percent deduction for a group reservation.

团队预订 8.5 折。

5. The Reservation can not be made 不能预订

Unfortunately, we're fully booked for (date) but you can reserve…

很遗憾，……日的客房都已订满，但您可以预订……

I'm sorry. I can't book you a room for the 17th of June. Is it possible for you to change your reservation date?

对不起，我不能为您订 6 月 17 日的客房。可不可以改变预订日期呢？

We don't have a single room available. Would you mind a standard room?

我们没有单人间了。如果是个标准间您介意吗？

Sorry, we won't have any vacancy today. But we can recommend nearby hotels for you if you like.

对不起，今天我们没有空房了。如果您愿意，我们可以为您推荐附近其他的酒店。

Accepting a Reservation

03-05 Accepting a Reservation. mp3

R：Receptionist

G：Guest

R：Good morning. Beijing Hotel, Room Reservations. May I help you?

G：Yes, I'd like to reserve a room at your hotel.

R：What date will that be?

G：From May 14th to 15th.

R：What kind of room would you prefer?

G: A double room.

R: Please wait a moment, sir. Thank you for waiting. We have the room you need.

G: What's the room rate per night?

R: 1,200 yuan. Will that be all right?

G: Yes, that will be fine. Thank you.

R: With pleasure! May I have your name and your telephone number?

G: Certainly. My name is Tom Davis and my phone number is 00490347620598.

R: Thank you, Mr. Davis. You've booked a double room from the 14th to the 15th of May, and your telephone number is 00490347620598. Is that right?

G: Yes, that's right. Thank you. Goodbye.

R: Thank you for calling, Mr. Davis. We look forward to your arrival.

Practice Answer the questions according to the service conversation.

1. When will the guest arrive and how long will the guest be staying in the hotel?
2. What type of the room does the guest want?
3. How much is the room rate?

Service Conversation 6

Recommending Other Hotels

03 – 06 Recommending Other Hotels. mp3

R: Reservationist

G: Guest

R: Good morning. This is Room Reservations. What can I do for you?

G: Yes, I'd like to reserve five standard rooms at your hotel.

R: What date will that be?

G: From June 15th to 19th.

R: Please wait a moment, sir. I'm very sorry, sir. We're fully booked at that time.

G: Oh, that's too bad.

R: Would you like us to put you on our waiting list and call you in case we have a cancellation?

G: Thank you. You are very kind. Could you give any other suggestions?

R: Certainly, could you change the time of the reservation?

G: No, we can't because we're attending an important international conference in

Beijing.

R: Would you like me to recommend nearby hotels that won't be full up?

G: That's great.

R: Grand Hyatt Beijing, Beijing Hotel and Beijing International Hotel.

G: I appreciate your kindness.

R: With pleasure. We look forward to having another opportunity to serve you.

Practice Answer the questions according to the service conversation.

1. The guest changes the date of arrival, doesn't he? Why?
2. What suggestion does the reservationist give?
3. Which one does the guest prefer?

Key Words and Expressions

recommend (v.)	推荐
reservationist/reservation clerk	预订员
prefer (v.)	更喜欢,宁愿选择
reserve/book a room	订房
confirm the reservation	确定预订
look forward to	期盼,盼望
standard room	标准间
cancellation (n.)	取消,撤销
appreciate (v.)	感激,感谢

Points of Service Performance 服务演练要点

- When handling the reservations, use the polite language.
  预订中注意使用礼貌服务用语。
- After we get all of the information about the reservation, be sure to confirm.
  在获取所有的预订信息之后,一定要确认。
- You should get the contact name and his telephone number if the reservation is made for the other person.
  如果是代订,还要留下代订人的姓名及电话号码。
- If the reservation can not be made, recommend other type of room/date/hotel.
  如果不能预订,可以推荐其他房型/日期/酒店。

Performance for Service 模拟演练

Task A

Performance in pairs according to the following two cards.

Guest Card	Guest name:	Tom Smith
	Arrival date:	May 15th
	Departure date:	May 23rd
	Room Type Required:	one family suite
	Persons:	a couple and their child
	Room Rate:	980 yuan with breakfast
	Way of reservation:	telephone
	Special request:	to buy a birthday cake for the child on May 15th
	Telephone number:	0044-0376-830476

Receptionist Card	Greet the guest
	Name of the guest
	Telephone number of the guest
	What kind of room
	Arrival and departure dates
	Introduce the room rate
	Any special request
	Express the wishes

Task B

Mr. Jenny Brown is walking to the Front Desk. He will reserve 20 standard rooms from the 14th to the 21st of June for the professors of London University. The room rate is 198 US dollars. He also wants to book a convention room. The receptionist Wang Juan will make the reservation for him.

> **Position Knowledge 岗位知识**

- We should remember: excellence is our service standard, and the service quality is the lifeblood of our business.
  我们要记住:尽善尽美是我们的服务规范,服务质量是我们行业的生命线。
- The main ways of room reservation:
  客房预订的基本方式:
  talk　前台预订　　telephone　电话预订
  computer network　计算机网络预订
- The names of the room types:
  房型名称:
  standard room　标准间　　　　　　　　double room　双人间/大床间

Chapter Two　Reservation Desk Service
客房预订部服务

triple room　三人间
suite　套间
deluxe suite　豪华套间

deluxe single room　豪华单人间
family suite　家庭套间
presidential suite　总统套间

Ⅰ. **Topics for discussion.**

1. In what way have you ever made a reservation?
2. Introduce the service procedure of the room reservation in English.
3. Please speak out some names of the room types.

Ⅱ. **Write out the questions in room reservation according to the answers.**

1. _____
   I'd like to book a family suite.
2. _____
   For four nights.
3. _____
   Just my wife and I.
4. _____
   160 US dollars per night per room including breakfast.
5. _____
   John Smith.

Ⅲ. **Translate the following sentences into English.**

1. 我们没有单人间了。如果是个标准间您介意吗?
2. 我想预订一个面湖的家庭套间。
3. 我们会为您延长预订。
4. 为您服务是我们的荣幸。我们恭候您的光临。
5. 对不起,今天我们没有空房了。如果您愿意,我们可以为您推荐附近其他的酒店。
6. 团队预订8.5折。

Unit Four Revising the Reservation

单元 ④ 预订变更

Procedure of Service 服务流程

Changing the Reservation

- Greet the guest.
- Ask the guest in whose name the reservation has been made.
- Check in the computer and confirm the reservation.
- Ask the guest how to change.
- Introduce the information that he wants to get.
- Confirm the changed reservation.
- Express your wishes to the guest.

Cancelling the Reservation

- Greet the guest.
- Ask the guest in whose name the reservation has been made.
- Check in the computer.
- Confirm and cancel the reservation.
- Express your wish to have another chance of serving the guest.

Points of Service Language 服务语言要点

1. **Polite expressions   礼貌用语**

   Good morning. Room Reservations.
   早上好。客房预订部。
   How can I help you?/What can I do for you?
   能为您服务吗?
   It's my pleasure. Mr. Davis, we look forward to your visit.

Chapter Two Reservation Desk Service
客房预订部服务

很高兴为您服务。Davis 先生,我们期盼您的光临!

We look forward to another chance to serve you/of serving you.

We look forward to having another chance/opportunity to serve you.

我们期待能再有机会为您服务。

2. **Checking the reservation that has been made   查找预订**

   In whose name was the reservation made?

   请问是用谁的名字预订的?

   When was the reservation made?

   请问是何时预订的?

   In what way was the reservation made?

   预订是用什么方式做的?

   Was the reservation made in John Smith?

   是用 John Smith 的名字预订的吗?

   What was the date of the reservation?

   预订在何时?

3. **Asking the guest how to revise   询问客人怎样变更**

   How would you like to change/revise?

   怎样变更?

   How would you like to change your previous reservation?

   怎样变更您的预订?

4. **Confirming and extending/cancelling/changing for the guest   确认并为客人延长/取消/改变预订**

   Would you like to cancel the reservation from July 6th for 3 nights altogether?

   您要取消 7 月 6 日起共 3 个晚上的预订吗?

   Would you like to extend your stay for two more days?

   您需要将预订延长两个晚上?

   You'd like to extend your reservation for one more night, is that right?

   您需要将预订延长一个晚上,是这样吗?

   I will cancel/change /extend your reservation for... for you.

   我为您取消/改变/延长……的预订。

   Mr. John Berry, I'll cancel your reservation from May 6th for 5 nights altogether. My name is Zhao Li. We look forward to another chance to serve you.

   John Berry 先生,我为您取消 5 月 6 日起共 5 个晚上的预订。我叫赵莉,我们期待能再有机会为您服务。

   Certainly, sir. We'll make the change/cancellation for you.

   当然可以,先生。我们为您改变/取消预订。

Service Conversation 7

Changing a Reservation

04-07 Changing a Reservation. mp3

R: Receptionist

G: Guest

R: Good morning. Great Wall Hotel. Room Reservations. Can I help you?

G: Yes. I have to change a reservation.

R: In whose name has the reservation been made?

G: In my name, Tom Davis.

R: Please wait a minute. I'll check the computer. Thanks for waiting. You've booked a double room for the 14th and 15th of May. How would you like to change it?

G: We'll be arriving in Beijing on the 17th of May as it turns out.

R: We only have a standard room available for the 17th and the 18th.

G: How much do you charge?

R: 160 US dollars per night, including breakfast.

G: OK, I'll take it. Sorry to have caused you such trouble.

R: Not at all. Can I confirm those details, Mr. Davis? You require a standard room from the 17th to 18th of May. The room rate is 160 US dollars per night including breakfast.

G: Yes, that's right. Thank you.

R: It's my pleasure. Mr. Davis, we look forward to your visit.

Practice Answer the questions according to the service conversation.

1. Who wants to change the reservation?
2. Please tell us the room rate.
3. Could you repeat the confirmation of the changed reservation in the conversation?

Chapter Two　Reservation Desk Service
客房预订部服务

Canceling a Reservation for the Guest

04 - 08　Canceling a Reservation for the Guest. mp3

R：Receptionist

G：Guest

R：Good morning. Room Reservations. How can I help you?

G：I'd like to cancel a reservation.

R：In whose name was the reservation made?

G：John Berry.

R：Wait a moment, please. What was the date of the reservation?

G：From July 6th, for 5 nights altogether.

R：Mr. John Berry, I'll cancel your reservations from July 6th, for 5 nights altogether. My name is Zhao Li. We look forward to another chance to serve you.

Practice　Answer the questions according to the service conversation.

1. What does the guest want to do?
2. In whose name was the reservation made?
3. What does the receptionist cancel?

cancel the reservation	取消预订
revise the reservation	改变/变更预订
standard room available	标准间空房

Points of Service Performance 服务演练要点

- When revising the reservations, use the polite language.
  预订变更中注意使用礼貌服务用语。
- After finding out the record in the computer, be sure to confirm the previous reservation.
  在计算机上找出记录之后,一定要确认先前的预订。
- Confirm the changed reservation.
  确认已变更的预订。

Performance for Service 模拟演练

Task A

Performance in extending the reservation in pairs according to the following cards.

Guest Card	Guest name: Anne Previous reservation: May 15th to 17th Demand: two more days

Receptionist Card	Greet the guest Ask in whose name Confirm the previous reservation Get the demand of the guest Express the wishes

Task B

John Berry wants to cancel the reservation from June 9th, for 3 nights altogether. The receptionist Zhao Li cancels the reservation for John Berry.

Position Knowledge 岗位知识

Martin W. B. once pointed out that the ability of building up the sound and friendly relationship between the clerk and the guest contains the following 9 points.

Martin W. B. 指出，服务人员与客人建立良好而友善的关系的能力包括以下九点。

(1) Attitude　友善的态度；

(2) Attentiveness　无微不至的关照；

(3) Tone of voice　悦耳的声音；

(4) Body language　得体的肢体语言；

(5) Naming names　叫出客人的姓名；

(6) Guidance　准确的指引；

(7) Suggestion selling　建议性销售；

(8) Problem solving　解决问题；

(9) Tact　灵活机智。

Chapter Two Reservation Desk Service
客房预订部服务

Exercises

Ⅰ. **Topics for discussion.**

1. Tell us how to make a reservation.

2. If there is no vacancy, how to deal with it?

3. Speak out the polite sentences of reservation.

Ⅱ. **Write out the questions in room reservation according to the answers.**

1. _____

   John Berry.

2. _____

   Over/By telephone.

3. _____

   From July 24th, for 6 nights altogether.

4. _____

   Three more nights.

5. _____

   200 US dollars per night including breakfast.

6. _____

   We'll have to arrive in Beijing on April 24th for some reasons.

Ⅲ. **Translate the following sentences into English.**

1. 很高兴为您服务。Davis 先生,我们期盼您的光临!

2. 我想将预订延长 3 个晚上。

3. 你认为我们能够改变预订吗?

4. 是以谁的名字,什么方式预订的?

5. Ramsay 先生,5 月 7 日至 9 日您共需要 20 个标准间和 1 个商务套间,是这样吗?

6. Rose Berry 小姐,我为您取消 5 月 6 日起共 3 个晚上的预订。我叫李海,我们期待能再有机会为您服务。

Ⅳ. **Translate the following sentences into Chinese.**

1. The rooms will be kept to six o'clock in the evening for the reservation without

guarantee, and blocked for twenty-four hours for the guarantee reservation in most hotels.
2. We'll send you a fax to confirm the reservation as soon as possible.
3. Sorry, but we have no vacancy at this time.
4. This is Marcus Ramsay calling from New York. I have to change the dates of the reservation.

Chapter Three Concierge Desk Service
礼宾部服务

Unit Five   Luggage Service
单元 5   行李服务

Unit Six   Car Reservation Service
单元 6   车辆预订服务

Service Position 服务岗位

In hotels, the Concierge Desk is a position of the Front Office Department. It is mainly in charge of the luggage and car rental services of the guest who stays at the hotel.

The guest always turns to the Concierge Desk for help when he meets some trouble or wants to enjoy himself during his stay at the hotel. Therefore the service of the Concierge Desk can give the guest the most important impression on hotel's fame and image.

Skills and Attainments 服务技能与素养

The Concierge Desk is responsible for meeting the guest at the door, helping him with his luggage when he firstly goes into the hotel, and then assisting him with every detail during his stay: introducing the hotel facilities and room services, arranging cars to meet the guest at the airport, railway station or dock; introducing distinctive restaurants and shopping areas in the city; making contact with travel agency to find a tour guide for the guest; and so on. Finally, when he leaves, the Concierge Desk should book tickets of vehicle for him, and help him consign the luggage.

The clerks in the Concierge Desk should be familiar with many kinds of knowledge, such as the hotel facilities and procedures of hotel service; also scenic spots, entertainment and shopping areas in the city; then provide information for the guest to make decision. The clerks should also have a good ability of communication and be able to serve the guest politely and appropriately.

Key Words and Expressions

Concierge Desk	礼宾部
luggage (n.)	行李
fax (n.)	传真
package (n.)	包裹, 邮包
reserve (v.)	预订
travel agency	旅行社
dock (n.)	码头
tour guide	导游
vehicle (n.)	交通工具
consign (v.)	运送
fame (n.)	声誉
scenic spots	景点

Unit Five Luggage Service

Procedure of Service 服务流程

Luggage service when the guest firstly comes to the hotel

Doorman(门童)should do the following:

- Greet the guest.
- Open the car door for the guest.
- Remind the guest with "Mind your head, please".
- Move the luggage off with the help of the bellboy.
- Check whether there is something left in the car.
- Close the car door and thank the driver.

Bellboy(行李员)should do the following:

- Move the luggage off from the car.
- Count the number of luggage and confirm it with the guest.
- Ask the guest whether there is reservation and lead him to the Front Desk.
- Wait for the guest till he finishes check-in.
- Deliver the luggage to the guest's room.
- Greet the guest again.

Luggage service when the guest is going to check out

Bellboy should do the following:

- Receive the call from the leaving guest.
- Confirm the number of luggage with the guest.
- Help the guest with his luggage downstairs.
- Wait for the guest till he finishes check-out.
- Put the luggage into the car trunk.

- Greet the guest and thank him for coming to the hotel.

Doorman should do the following：

- Arrange cars for the guest in advance.
- Pack the luggage with the help of the bellboy.
- Make the guest look over and check the luggage.
- Greet the guest a good trip when he gets on the car and thank the guest's coming.

Points of Service Language 服务语言要点

1. **Polite expressions** 礼貌用语

    Don't worry, your luggage will be sent up at once.
    别担心，您的行李很快就会送上去的。

    Do you mind if I put your luggage here?
    我把您的行李放在这里好吗？

    We hope you have a pleasant/an enjoyable stay, sir/madam.
    希望您在这儿住得愉快，先生/夫人。

    We look forward to serving you again.
    我们期待再次为您服务。

2. **Delivering luggage** 运送行李

    Let me help you with the luggage.
    请让我来帮您拿行李。

    How many pieces of luggage do you have?
    您一共有几件行李？

    Is there anything valuable or breakable in your bag?
    您的袋子里有什么贵重或易碎的物品吗？

    Just a moment, please. I'll bring a trolley/baggage cart.
    请稍候。我去推一辆行李车来。

    Shall I put your suitcase here?
    我把您的旅行箱放在这儿好吗？

    I'll send the luggage up by another lift.
    我乘另一部电梯把行李送上去。

    When you check out, please call No. 6001 and we'll help you with your luggage immediately.
    如果您要退房，请打电话6001，我们会马上帮您运送行李。

3. **Special luggage service** 特殊行李服务

    You may/can leave your luggage in the Concierge.
    您可以把行李放在礼宾部。

    I wonder if you could look after my luggage for a while.
    我想让您帮我照看一下行李。

    You may/can claim your luggage with the tag.

您可以用行李标签领回您的行李。

Could you please show me the luggage tag?

您能出示行李标签吗？

05-09 Welcome to the Great Wall Hotel. mp3

Welcome to the Great Wall Hotel

Part 1   Greeting the guest at the gate of the hotel

D：Doorman

G：Guest

D: Good evening, sir and madam. Welcome to the Great Wall Hotel.

G: Good evening.

D: Excuse me, sir. So you have four pieces of luggage altogether?

G: Yes.

D: OK. Leave it to me, sir. I'll take care of your luggage.

G: Thank you.

D: Not at all. The Reception Desk is straight ahead. This way, please.

Part 2   Leading the guest to the room

B：Bellboy

G：Guest

B: Is this everything, sir?

G: Yes, that's everything.

B: May I have a look at your room card?

G: Oh, yes. It's 1101.

B: I see. Now please follow me. I'll show you to your room.

G: Is there a coffee shop in your hotel?

B: Yes. It's on the first floor. Get out of the lift and turn right, sir.

G: When will it be open?

B: The hours are 6:30 a.m. to 10:00 p.m.

G: OK. Do you have car rental service?

B: Yes. You can call the Concierge Desk for detailed information.

G: That's fine.

B: Here we are, sir. Room 1101. Let me help you open the door.

(*The door is opened.*)

B: After you, sir. Do you mind if I put your luggage here?

G: That's OK. Thank you very much.

B: That's my job. How do you like this room?

G: It is very cozy. I like it very much.

B: If you have any special requirements or have some difficulties, there is a hotel service brochure on the desk.

G: That's great.

B: Right, is there anything else I can do for you?

G: No, thank you.

B: Good night.

Practice Answer the questions according to the service conversation.

1. How many pieces of luggage does the guest have?
2. When the guest comes to the hotel, who serves him first?
3. What should a bellboy do when the guest comes to the hotel?

Service Conversation 10

Is It Charged or Free

05-10 Is It Charged or Free. mp3

C: Clerk in Concierge Desk

G: Guest

C: Good morning, the Concierge Desk. Can I help you?

G: Yes. I'm calling because I have to check out in 25 minutes and go out for something urgent but I don't know how to deal with my luggage after I check out.

C: Don't worry, ma'am. We can look after your luggage. May I have your name and your room number, please?

G: John Carter, Room 166.

C: Ms. Carter, I'll send a bellboy to Room 166 to fetch your luggage at once. Please be sure to put your name tag on your suitcases.

G: Is it free or is there a charge?

C: It's free for 24 hours. Would you like to tell me when you come back to our hotel for the luggage?

G: At 5 this afternoon.

C: My name is Li Ming. We'll take good care of your luggage until you come back to our hotel for it.

G: Thank you very much indeed. And where shall I collect my luggage at that time?

C: At the Concierge Desk beside the general service counter. You can claim your luggage with your ID.

G: It's very kind of you. See you.

C: See you then.

Practice Answer the questions according to the service conversation.

1. How does the guest deal with his luggage after checking out?
2. Who would serve the guest with his luggage?
3. Will the guest pay for the luggage look-after service?
4. What information should the guest provide when he wants to collect luggage?

Key Words and Expressions

rental(*n.*) 出租

cozy(*adj.*) 舒适的

brochure(*n.*) 手册

emergent(*adj.*) 紧急的

tag(*n.*) 标签

suitcase(*n.*) 行李箱

charge(*v.* & *n.*) 收费

Points of Service Performance 服务演练要点

- When the guest comes, the doorman should open the door of the car with the right hand, cover the frame of the car with the left hand, preventing the guest's head from knocking at the door and then remind the guest with "Mind your head, please".
  客人抵达时,门童应右手拉开车门,左手遮挡于车门框上沿,以防客人头部与车门框相碰,并提醒客人注意。

- Before helping the guest with his luggage, the bellboy should confirm the pieces of the luggage.
  在帮客人运送和收集行李之前,行李员都应确认行李件数。

- When the guest checks in, the bellboy should wait two or three steps behind the guest.

客人办理入住手续时,行李员应站立在客人身后两三步处等候。
- When taking the lift, the bellboy should go into the lift first with luggage, then let the guest in. When arriving at the floor, the bellboy should let the guest out first and then the luggage.

  乘电梯时,行李员带行李先行进入,然后请客人进入。电梯到达要去的楼层后,关照客人先出电梯,然后将行李运出。

- When accompanying the guest to his room, the bellboy can introduce the facilities and services of the hotel to him.

  陪送客人到房间的途中,行李员可以介绍酒店的设施和服务。

Performance for Service 模拟演练

Task A

Perform the conversation about luggage look-after service in pairs according to the following two cards.

Guest Card		
	Guest name:	Tom Smith
	Room number:	Room 1206
	Pieces of luggage:	3
	Time of keeping luggage:	1 day
	Fee of luggage look-after:	2 yuan

Clerk Card	
	Guest name
	Room number
	How many pieces of luggage?
	How long to keep luggage?
	How much is the fee of luggage look-after?

Task B

Mary White in Room 516 of Beijing Hotel is going to check out at 12 a.m., but she plans to visit Tianjin and returns to Beijing the next day. Mary doesn't want to take so many suitcases, so she calls the Concierge Desk asking for luggage service. The clerk Lily in the Concierge Desk receives the call and explains the details about luggage service and then sends the bellboy Xiao Ping to fetch Mary's 4 pieces of luggage.

Position Knowledge 岗位知识

- When the guest comes, the doorman and the bellboy should greet the guest with

polite language and help him to carry luggage and confirm the pieces of luggage.
客人抵达时，门童和行李员应使用礼貌用语问候客人，帮助其提携行李并确认行李件数。

- Some useful expressions when introducing hotel facilities to the guest：
  在介绍酒店设施时经常用到的词汇：

  Foreign Exchange　外币兑换　　　　　Cafe　咖啡厅
  Business Center　商务中心　　　　　　Parking　停车场
  Beauty Parlor/Salon　美容院　　　　　Pub　夜总会
  Shopping Arcade　购物中心　　　　　Health Club　健身俱乐部

Exercises

Ⅰ. Topics for discussion.

1. How should a doorman serve the newly-come guest better?
2. What service can a bellboy provide to the guest?
3. What service can the Concierge Desk provide for the guest?

Ⅱ. Write out the questions according to the answers.

1. _____
   There are 30 pieces of luggage totally in my team.
2. _____
   I wonder if you can look after my luggage for one day.
3. _____
   My room is 1105.

Ⅲ. Translate the following sentences into English.

1. 请问您要寄存行李吗？
2. 您可以凭行李标签取回您的行李。
3. 您可以把行李放在礼宾部。
4. 请稍候。我去推一辆行李车来。
5. 您的袋子里有什么贵重或易碎的物品吗？

单元 6 车辆预订服务

Procedure of Service 服务流程

Car reservation at the Concierge Desk

- Provide information about the car reservation, such as type of car, charge of car rental, etc.
- Ask for the guest's information, such as the guest's name, room number, type of car, destination, departure and return time, etc.
- Confirm the guest's information.
- Thank the guest for calling.

Car arrangement at the door

- Ask the guest whether he wants a taxi.
- Arrange a taxi waiting at the gate of the hotel.
- Tell taxi driver the destination of the guest.

Points of Service Language 服务语言要点

1. **Accepting car reservation**　接受车辆预订

    Would you like me to call a taxi for you?
    您需要我为您叫一辆出租车吗?
    Would you like to reserve a car?
    您要预订车辆吗?
    What kind of car would you like to reserve?
    您想要预订什么样的车?
    There are compact car, sports car, jeep and coach to rent in our hotel.

我店有小轿车、跑车、吉普车和大客车供出租。

What time would you like to use the car?

您想什么时候用车？

Where would you like to go and when will you leave and return?

您想去哪里、何时离开、何时返回？

How many people will take the car?

有多少人乘车？

The rental charge of 5-seat car in our hotel is 500 yuan per day.

我店五座汽车的租车费用是每天 500 元。

2. **The Reservation can not be made 不能预订**

Unfortunately，we are fully booked for (some car) but you can reserve…

很遗憾，……样的车都已订满,但您可以预订……

I'm sorry. I can't book you any car for the 8th of August. Is it possible for you to change your reservation date?

对不起。我不能为您订 8 月 8 日的车。可不可以换一个预订日期呢？

We don't have a coach available. Would you mind a jeep?

我们没有大客车了。如果是辆吉普车您介意吗？

Sorry，we won't have any cars that can be booked today. But we can recommend another car rental company if you like.

对不起,今天我们没有可以预订的车辆了。如果您愿意,我们可以为您推荐其他的租车公司。

Calling a Taxi at the Hotel Gate

06－11 Calling a Taxi at the Hotel Gate. mp3

D：Doorman

S：Mr. John Stevens

D：Would you like me to call a taxi for you?

S：Yes，thanks.

D：Where to，sir?

S：To T3，Beijing International Airport.

D：OK，just a moment，please.

(*The taxi is coming…*)

D: Sorry to have kept you waiting, sir. Are there four pieces of luggage in all?

S: Yes.

D: Let me put them into the trunk.

S: OK, thank you very much.

D: You're welcome, sir. Hope to see you again. Good luck.

Practice Answer the questions according to the service conversation.

1. Where will the guest go?
2. What should the doorman do when the guest is leaving the hotel?
3. How should the doorman deal with the luggage that the guest takes?

Service Conversation 12

Car Reservation at the Concierge Desk

C: Concierge

S: Mr. John Stevens

06 – 12 Car Reservation at the Concierge Desk. mp3

C: Good morning, this is the Concierge Desk, what can I do for you?

S: Is there car rental service in your hotel?

C: Yes, sir. We have many kinds of cars to rent.

S: Is there an SUV or jeep for rent? My wife and I want to go for an excursion in the Beijing suburbs.

C: Yes. There is a 5-seat Beijing Jeep for rent.

S: How much is the rental charge?

C: It is 450 yuan per day excluding fuel.

S: Well, the price is reasonable. I'll rent one jeep.

C: May I have your name and room number, sir?

S: No problem. My name is John Stevens, and my room number is 1106.

C: Would you mind telling me when you will use the jeep and where you would like to go?

S: No. We are going to Huairou County at 6 o'clock on Friday morning.

C: May I know when you will return to the hotel?

S: Yes. We plan to return in the evening, about 7 o'clock that day.

C: OK, sir. Let me confirm your rental information: Mr. John Stevens and his wife in Room 1106, a Beijing Jeep from 6 a. m. to 7 p. m. on Friday, that is, on August 15th; your destination is Huairou County. Is that all right?

S: Yes, that's right.

C: OK, sir. We'll arrange for one jeep to be waiting for you at the gate at 6 on Friday morning. The rental charge will be taken when you check out.

S: OK, I'll be waiting right there. Thanks.

C: Thank you for calling, sir.

Practice   Answer the questions according to the service conversation.

1. Where will the guest go?
2. When will the guest leave from and return to the hotel?
3. What kind of vehicle will the guest rent?

Key Words and Expressions

SUV (sport-utility vehicle) (n.) 运动型多功能车
jeep (n.) 吉普车
charge (n.) 收费, 要价
rent (v. & n.) 出租
rental (n.) 出租
fuel (n.) 燃料
reasonable (adj.) 公道的, 合理的

Points of Service Performance 服务演练要点

- When handling the car reservations, use the polite language.
  车辆预订中注意使用礼貌服务用语。
- Ask for the guest's information, such as the guest's name, room number, kind of car, destination, departure and return time, etc.
  询问客人的租车信息, 如客人的姓名、房间号、车型、目的地以及往返时间等。
- After finishing the car reservation, make sure to confirm all of the information.
  在完成车辆预订工作之后, 一定要确认所有的信息。

Performance for Service 模拟演练

Task A

Performance in pairs according to the following two cards.

Guest Card	Guest name: Tom Smith
	Room number: Room 1123
	Car rental date: August 23
	Departure time: 6 a.m.
	Return time: 7 p.m.
	Destination: the Great Wall
	Persons: 15
	Vehicle type: a coach with 20 seats
	Way of reservation: telephone
	Telephone number: 159＊＊＊＊5036

Concierge Receptionist Card	Greet the guest
	Name of the guest
	Room number of the guest
	Telephone number of the guest
	Car rental date
	Departure and arrival time
	Destination
	Persons
	Vehicle type
	Car rental charge: 980 yuan RMB a day
	Confirm the information
	Express the wishes

Task B

Mr. Robin Williams and his colleagues are going to visit Yizhuang Economy and Technology Developing Zone on Tuesday April 22, at 10 a.m. and will return to the hotel at 6 p.m. that day. They plan to rent a business car from the hotel. The clerk Liu Ming at the Concierge Desk receives his call and explains the details of car rental service. Make a dialogue and try to fill in the following form according to the above information.

Car Rental Form

SERIAL NO.	1	2	3	4	5
GUEST NAME					
ROOM NO.					
PHONE NO.					
CAR TYPE					

续表

SERIAL NO.	1	2	3	4	5
CAR NO.					
LEAVING DATE					
LEAVING TIME					
ARRIVAL DATE					
ARRIVAL TIME					
DESTINATION					
RENTAL FEE					
CLERK SIGNATURE					
REMARKS					

Position Knowledge 岗位知识

The main types of the cars:
车辆的基本类型:

compact car　小轿车　　　　sports car　跑车　　　　　　　　jeep　吉普车
coach　大客车　　　　　　　SUV(sport-utility vehicle)　　　运动型多功能车

Exercises

Ⅰ. **Topics for discussion.**

1. How to confirm a car reservation?
2. What information should be confirmed in car reservation?
3. What should a doorman do when the guest wants a taxi?

Ⅱ. **Write out the questions according to the answers.**

1. _____
   I'd like to reserve a coach with 30 seats tomorrow.
2. _____
   I plan to return at 7 p.m.
3. _____
   I'd like to go to the Great Wall.

Ⅲ. **Translate the following sentences into Chinese.**

1. It's good for you to book a return tour by taxi.
2. Please wait a moment. The taxi is expected to come in 15 minutes.
3. We have a car in our hotel parking lot to take you to the airport.

Chapter Four Cash Desk Service
收银台服务

Unit Seven   Foreign Currency Exchange
单元 7   外币兑换

Unit Eight   Check Out
单元 8   结账退宿

Unit Nine   Solving Problems with the Bill
单元 9   解决账单问题

Service Position 服务岗位

The cashiers are actually the staff of the Finance Department. But their working position, the Cash Desk/Cashier Counter(收银台/收银处), is in the Front Office Department and their work is closely contacted with many positions of the Front Office Department, so the manager of the Front Office Department is responsible for its management and control on a day-to-day basis. The main work of this position is to deal with the guests' accounts and the business of changing the foreign currencies.

As has been repeatedly stressed, first and last impressions carry the most weight. The last is probably even more important. That is the impressions the guests carry home and is most apt to remember. It probably affects their attitude in later discussing the service and facilities of the hotel with their friends and business associates. It is the staff of the Cash Desk that gives the last impression to the guests.

Skills and Attainments 服务技能与素养

The cashiers of the Cash Desk typically post some revenue center charge to the guests' accounts; exchange foreign currencies, give the reason to a guest when he isn't allowed to change; cash traveler's checks; when the guests come to check out, handle promptly various settlement, including credit card, cash, checks, and foreign currency, explain the questions that the guests raise and deal with the complaints about the bill.

In order to do the work well and gain the last good impression for the hotel, the cashiers must have both good service skill in finance and the excellent quality. Moreover, they are good at computer technology. Certainly, they also can communicate effectively with the guests answer the guests' questions and deal with the complaints in English.

Key Words and Expressions

cashier(*n.*)	收银员,出纳员
the Finance Department staff	财务部员工
the Cash Desk	收银台
as has been repeatedly stressed	正如反复强调的那样
exchange the foreign currency	兑换外币
cash traveler's checks	兑现旅行支票

Notes

1. The cashiers of the Cash Desk typically post some revenue center charge to the guests' accounts.
   收银台的收银员负责将客人在各营业点的实际消费记入客人账单。
2. carry the most weight 非常重要
3. handle promptly various settlement 迅速办理各种结账

 Foreign Currency Exchange

Procedure of Service 服务流程

- Greet the guest.
- Introduce today's exchange rate to the guest.
- Ask the guest how much he wants to change and receive the money from the guest.
- See the passport of the guest.
- Fill in the exchange memo.
- Tell the guest about the amount of money of exchange.
- Give the money to the guest, and ask him to count.
- Give the receipt to the guest, and ask him to keep it well.

Points of Service Language 服务语言要点

1. **Polite expressions   礼貌用语**

    Here is 2,000 yuan. Please count it.
    这是2,000元。请清点一下。
    Please check it, and keep the memo.
    请您查一下,保存好水单。
    You're welcome. Glad to have served you.
    没什么。很高兴为您服务。

2. **Changing the foreign currency   兑换外币**

    We change foreign currencies according to today's exchange rate.
    我们根据今天的牌价兑换外币。
    The exchange rate of US dollar to RMB is 1∶6.70.
    美元兑换人民币为1∶6.70。
    How much would you like to change, sir?
    先生您想兑换多少?

According to today's rate of exchange, every 100 US dollars in cash comes to 670 yuan RMB.

根据今天的兑换率,100美元兑换670元人民币。

200 Euros is equal to 2,050 yuan RMB.

200欧元兑换2,050元人民币。

The exchange rate of US dollars to RMB is 100∶680, that will give you 3,350 yuan RMB.

美元兑换人民币的兑换率是100∶680,那就是说该给您3,350元人民币。

500 US dollars. The exchange is 3,350 yuan RMB.

500美元。可兑换3,350元人民币。

Please fill in your passport number, the total amount, your room number or permanent address, and sign your name here as well.

请您仔细填写护照号、兑换金额、房间号或永久性地址,并在这里签字。

What denominations would you like?

How would you like your money?

您要什么面值的货币?

3. **Drawing the guest's attention　提醒客人注意**

You can change the RMB left back into Euros at the Bank of China or at the Airport Exchange Office, and there you are required to show the memo.

您可以在中国银行或机场外币兑换处将剩余的人民币兑换成欧元,兑换时您还得出示这张兑换水单。

Here's your memo. Please hold onto it. You're required to show it at the Customs when you go back to your country.

这是您的水单,请妥善保存,当您回国时,在海关需要出示它。

4. **Unable to change the foreign currency for the guest　不能为客人兑换外币**

I'm afraid that you'd better go to change KRW in a specialized foreign exchange bank, for we can't change KRW.

恐怕您得到一家外汇专业银行兑换韩元,因为我们酒店不能兑换韩元。

I'm afraid that we only offer one-way change in our hotel.

我们只能进行单向兑换。

But you can change the RMB left back into Euros at the Bank of China or at the Airport Exchange Office.

但是您可以到中国银行或机场外币兑换处将剩余的人民币兑换成欧元。

We have a change limit of US between 9 p.m. to 8 a.m.

在晚上9点到早上8点之间,我们有……美元的兑换限制。

We hope you can understand.

希望您能谅解。

Chapter Four　Cash Desk Service
收银台服务

Service Conversation 13

Exchange US dollars into Chinese yuan

07 - 13　Exchange US dollars into Chinese yuan. mp3

C: Cashier

G: Guest

C: Good morning. Is there anything I can do for you?
G: I want to change some foreign currency for souvenirs.
C: What kind of foreign currency would you like to change?
G: US dollars.
C: According to today's rate of exchange, every 100 US dollars in cash comes to 680 yuan. How much would you like to change, sir?
G: $400. Here you are.
C: The exchange is 2,720 yuan. May I see your passport?
G: Sure. Here you are.
C: Please fill in the exchange memo. Be careful to fill in your passport number, the total amount, your room number or permanent address, and sign your name here as well.
G: Here you are. Is that all right?
C: That's all right. Thanks. What denominations would you like?
G: Any kind will be OK.
C: Here is 2,720 yuan. Please count it. Here's your memo. Please hold onto it. You're required to show it at the Customs when you go back to your country.
G: No problem. By the way, how can I change my remaining RMB back into US dollars when I go back to my country?
C: You can change it back into US dollars in the specialized foreign exchange bank or the Airport Exchange Office, and you're required to show the memo there, too.
G: Thanks for your help.
C: You're welcome. Glad to have served you.

Practice　Answer the questions according to the service conversation.

1. What does the guest want to change?
2. What is today's rate of exchange?
3. How much does the guest change?

Service Conversation 14

Changing at the Airport Exchange Office

C: Cashier
G: Guest

C: Good morning, sir. Can I help you?
G: Good morning, I'd like to change some KRW into Euros.
C: I'm afraid that you'd better go to change KRW in the Bank of China. We can't change KRW for you in our hotel.
G: Can I change my RMB left back into Euros in the hotel because I'll go back to my country at 2 this afternoon?
C: I'm very sorry, sir.
G: Why?
C: I'm afraid that we only offer one-way change in our hotel. But you can change your RMB left back into Euros at the Airport Exchange Office.
G: Good idea. Thanks a lot. Good bye.
C: Good bye.

07-14 Changing at the Airport Exchange Office. mp3

| Practice | Answer the questions according to the service conversation. |

1. What does the guest want to do?
2. Why does the guest want to change the RMB left back into Euros?
3. Why doesn't the cashier change the money for the guest?

foreign currency	外币
souvenir(*n.*)	纪念品,礼物
exchange memo	外汇兑换水单,水单
rate of exchange/rate of foreign exchange/foreign exchange rate	外汇兑换率
the Customs	海关
permanent address	永久性地址
the Airport Exchange Office	机场外币兑换处
specialized foreign exchange bank	外汇专业银行
change...into...	把……兑换成……

denomination (*n.*)　　　　　　　　　　票面金额
KRW (*n.*)　　　　　　　　　　　　　　韩元
Euro (*n.*)　　　　　　　　　　　　　　欧元

Points of Service Performance 服务演练要点

- Since the rate is changing every day, firstly you should explain today's exchange rate very clearly to the guest.
  由于汇率每天都在变,所以首先你需要向客人清楚地介绍当天的汇率。
- If you can not exchange for the guest, you should explain the reason and give him your suggestion.
  如果不能给客人兑换,你要向客人解释原因并提出建议。

Performance for Service 模拟演练

Task A

Performance in changing the currency according to the following card.

Guest Card	Aim: Change Euros into RMB Amount: 200 Euros

Cashier Card	The exchange rate of Euros to RMB:100∶1,025 Exam his passport Ask the guest to fill in the memo Give the RMB and the memo to the guest

Task B

It's 9 p.m. A guest wants to change 2,000 US dollars into RMB. But there is a change limit of 500 US dollars between 9 p.m. to 8 a.m. You can't change for him. You will explain the reason and give him some suggestions.

Position Knowledge 岗位知识

- The three sentences of the benediction that the clerks in the hotel often use:
  酒店工作人员常用的三句祝福语:
  ◆ We hope you will enjoy your stay in the hotel.
  　希望您会对我们的服务感到满意/祝您入住愉快。
  ◆ We hope you are enjoying your stay in the hotel.
  　希望我们现在的服务让您满意。

◆ We hope you have enjoyed your stay in the hotel.
希望您对我们的服务满意。

● 在书写时把货币单位写在金额之前,但在口头表达时却要先说金额,再说货币。例如,＄50 读作 fifty dollars(50 美元),￡90 读作 ninety pounds(90 英镑)。另外,有些国家和地区使用"＄"这个符号代表当地货币,例如,HK＄表示港元(中国香港),A＄表示澳大利亚元。

Ⅰ. Topics for discussion.

1. What does the cashier begin with to exchange the foreign currency?
2. Why does the cashier ask the guest to keep the memo well?
3. What will you do if you can't change the foreign currency for the guest?

Ⅱ. Write out the Chinese names of the following currencies and then fill in their codes.

(JAN ¥   ￡   RMB ¥   S＄   US＄   ZN＄   HK＄   Can＄   A＄   EUR)

1. Australian dollar   _____   _____
2. Canadian dollar   _____   _____
3. Hongkong dollar   _____   _____
4. New Zealand dollar   _____   _____
5. Singapore dollar   _____   _____
6. US dollar   _____   _____
7. British pound   _____   _____
8. Renminbi yuan   _____   _____
9. Japanese yen   _____   _____
10. Euro   _____   _____

Ⅲ. Answer the questions.

1. What denominations would you like?
2. Can I change my RMB left back into Euros in the hotel?
3. How can I fill in the memo?
4. Why is the guest required to keep the memo well?
5. If a guest wants to change 2,600 US dollars into RMB, how much RMB can he get according to today's rate?

Ⅳ. Decide whether the following sentences are true or false.

1. There is no limit to the foreign currencies in the hotel.
2. The foreign exchange memo can help a guest exchange the Chinese currency back to the foreign currency before he leaves China.
3. A guest can exchange traveler's checks into US dollars in any hotel in China.
4. The cashier can't tell the exchange rate to the guest.
5. If the cashier can't exchange for the guest, he will explain the reason and give the guest some suggestions.
6. The cashier will shake hands with the guest before exchanging the foreign currency.

Ⅴ. Translate the following sentences into English.

1. 先生，您想兑换多少？
2. 我们根据今天的牌价兑换外币。
3. 美元兑换人民币汇率为 1∶6.70。
4. 600 美元可兑换人民币 4,080 元。
5. 希望您对我们的服务已经满意。
6. 根据今天的兑换率，100 美元兑换 680 元人民币。
7. 顺便问一下，我回国时怎样将剩下的人民币兑换成加拿大元？
8. 这是您的水单，请妥善保存，当您回国时，在海关需要出示它。
9. 查看客人护照时，你需要关注客人的姓名、国籍、护照号码和有效期。
10. 填写兑换水单时，要求客人填写护照号码、兑换金额、房间号或永久性地址并签名。

Unit Eight Check Out

Procedure of Service 服务流程

- Greet the guest.
- Get the name and the room number of the guest.
- Ask the guest to give you the room keycard.
- Draw up the bill.
- Tell the guest the total and give the bill to the guest for checking.
- Explain the items if necessary.
- Ask the guest how to pay?
- Form the record of checkout in the computer.
- Bid farewell to the guest.

Points of Service Language 服务语言要点

1. **When you recognize the guest   当你认出客人时**

    May I be of help(service), Miss Wood?
    Wood 女士,需要我为您服务吗?
    Are you checking out today, Miss Wood?
    Wood 女士,您今天退房吗?
    Would you like to vacate the room now, Mr. Wood?
    Wood 先生,您打算现在退房吗?

2. **If you can't recognize the guest   如果你不能认出客人时**

    Would you please tell me your name and your room number?
    What's your name and room number, please?
    Could I have your name and room number?
    能告诉我您的姓名和房间号吗?

Chapter Four Cash Desk Service
收银台服务

3. Don't forget to ask   别忘了询问

May I have your keycard?

请把房卡给我,好吗?

Did you have breakfast this morning?

您今天早晨用过早餐了吗?

Did you make any phone call from your room?

您今天在房间打过电话了吗?

Have you used any hotel services, Mr. Wood?

Wood 先生,您用过酒店的服务了吗?

4. Calculating and presenting the bill   结账并出示账单

Please wait a moment. I'll figure it out.

请等会儿,我来跟您加总账。

I'll draw up/add up/draft/calculate/settle your bill.

我跟您结算一下账单。

It totals 3,500 yuan.

Your bill comes/amounts to 3,500 yuan.

Your bill makes a total of 3,500 yuan.

您的账单总额是 3,500 元人民币。

Thanks for waiting so long. Here's your bill. It totals 3,500 yuan. Is that correct?

谢谢您,让您久等了。给您账单,总计 3,500 元人民币。您看对吗?

Would you like to check and see if the amount is correct?

您检查一下,看看数额是否正确?

5. How to pay   怎样付款

How will you be paying, sir?

How would you like to make your payment, sir?

先生,您用什么方式付款?

How do you wish to settle your account, sir? In cash, by credit card or by/with traveler's check?

先生,您用什么方式付款? 现金、信用卡还是旅行支票?

What kind of credit cards do you honor?

你们接收什么信用卡?

We accept American Express, Visa and Federal Card.

我们接收美国运通卡、维萨卡和联邦卡。

There's a 5% merchant commission you have to pay if you use a credit card.

如果您用信用卡买单要付 5% 贸易商委托费。

6. Bid farewell to the guest   向客人道别

We hope you'll be staying with us again. Have a good trip!

欢迎您下次光临我们酒店。祝您旅途顺利!

You're welcome. We hope you've enjoyed your stay in the hotel. We hope we will have another opportunity to serve you.

没什么,希望您对我们的服务满意。我们希望能再有机会为您效劳。

59

It's my pleasure. Hope you will enjoy your journey.

为您服务是我的荣幸。祝您旅途愉快。

Checking Out in Cash

08 – 15 Checking Out in Cash. mp3

C: Cashier

G: Guest

C: Good morning, sir. Can I help you?

G: Good morning. I'd like to check out.

C: Would you please tell me your name and your room number?

G: George Wright, Room 576.

C: Please give me the keycard.

G: Here you are.

C: Thank you. Have you had any bills in the restaurant?

G: No, I haven't.

C: Please wait a moment, Mr. Wright. I'll draw up your bill for you. Here is your bill, 3,447 yuan in all. Please check it.

G: That's correct.

C: May I have your receipt of deposit?

G: OK. Here you are.

C: Thank you, Mr. Wright. You paid a deposit of 4,000 yuan.

G: Yes.

C: Here is the invoice and your change, 553 yuan. Please check it.

G: It's correct. Thank you.

C: You're welcome. We hope you've enjoyed your stay in the hotel. We hope we will have another opportunity to serve you.

Practice Answer the questions according to the service conversation.

1. Has Mr. Wright had any bill in the restaurant?
2. What's the total of the bill?
3. How much has Mr. Wright paid as deposit?

Chapter Four Cash Desk Service
收银台服务

Service Conversation 16

Checking Out by Credit Card

08-16 Checking Out by Credit Card. mp3

C: Cashier

G: Guest

C: Good morning. Are you checking out today, Mr. Smith?

G: Yes, I'm checking out. Here is the room keycard.

C: Thank you, Mr. Smith. Just a moment, let me figure it out. Did you make any phone calls from your room this morning?

G: Yes, I did, to the United States.

C: Thanks for waiting so long. Here's your bill. It totals 6,500 yuan. Your international call is included in the bill. Is that correct?

G: Correct.

C: How will you be paying this time, by traveler's check like last time?

G: By credit card. What kinds of credit cards do you honor?

C: We accept American Express, Visa and Federal Card.

G: American Express. Here you are.

C: Thank you, Mr. Smith. By the way, there's a 5% merchant commission you have to pay if you use a credit card.

G: I see.

C: If you could just sign here, please, sir. Thanks. Here's your card and your receipt.

G: Thank you.

C: We hope you'll be staying with us again. Have a good trip!

Practice Answer the questions according to the service conversation.

1. How much does the bill total?
2. How does the guest pay?
3. Is there any merchant commission if the guest uses a credit card to pay?

Key Words and Expressions

bid farewell	道别
figure out	算出
merchant commission	贸易商委托费

61

credit limit	信用卡限额
deposit(*n.*)	押金
IOU (I Owe You)(*n.*)	欠单
service charge(*n.*)	服务费
receipt(*n.*)	收据
invoice(*n.*)	发票
rental(*n.*)	租金
check(*n.*)	支票

Notes

1. We accept American Express, Visa and Federal Card.
   我们接收美国运通卡、维萨卡和联邦卡。
2. By the way, there's a 5% merchant commission you have to pay if you use a credit card.
   顺便说一下,如果您用信用卡买单要付 5% 贸易商委托费。
3. Your international call is included in the bill.
   您的国际长途电话包含在账单中。
4. If you could just sign here, please, sir. Thanks. Here's your card and your receipt.
   先生,请您在这里签字。谢谢,这是您的卡和收据。

Points of Service Performance 服务演练要点

- When the guest is walking to you for check out, greet the guest firstly, and then ask about the name and the room number. Certainly, you also need to ask the guest to give you the room keycard.
  当客人走向你结账退宿时,首先是问候客人,接着询问客人的名字和房号。当然还需要求客人交回房卡。
- Tell the guest the total and give the bill to the guest for checking. If necessary, you ought to explain the items to the guest.
  告知客人消费总额,并把账单给客人核查。如果需要,还要向客人解释账目。
- Ask the guest how to pay and handle making the payment.
  询问客人怎样付款并办理付款手续。
- Be sure to bid farewell to the guest warmheartedly.
  别忘了向客人热情地道别。

Performance for Service 模拟演练

Task A

Performance in checkout with the Federal Card in pairs according to the following two cards.

Chapter Four Cash Desk Service
收银台服务

Guest Card	Name:	Grand Wood
	Room number:	Room 2045
	Hotel services:	1. a couple of calls to his New York office
		2. three meals in the Chinese Restaurant
	Payment:	Federal Card

Cashier Card	Ask the name and the room number
	Ask the guest whether he has used the hotel services or not
	Tell the total of the bill, 5,378 yuan
	Ask how to pay

Task B

Miss Rose White is going to the Front Desk for check out. She had three suppers in the Chinese Restaurant and signed a brandy at the lobby bar.

Miss Rose White pays in cash. She has paid a deposit of 5,000 yuan. The total in the bill is 5,000 yuan.

Position Knowledge 岗位知识

- 结账须知：
  - 用现金结账的时候,要客人把交押金的收据给你,并核对押金数额。
  - 用信用卡结账的时候,首先要确定酒店是否能接收这种信用卡。还要特别留意信用卡的有效日期和信用额度。
  - 用旅行支票结账的时候,首先要检查支票是否完好,要求客人在正确的位置签名。如果客人签名签错地方,酒店将无法兑现这张支票。
- Some international credit cards： 几种国际上常用的信用卡：
  American Express　美国运通卡　　　　　　Visa　维萨卡
  Federal Card　联邦卡/发达卡　　　　　　　Master　万事达卡
  International Dinner's Club　国际大来俱乐部卡　International Great Wall　长城卡

Exercises

Ⅰ. **Topics for discussion.**

1. Name some of the credit cards.
2. The procedure of paying in cash or by credit card.

3. Why is the last impression very important?

Ⅱ. Speak English fluently according to the Chinese situations. Some situations can be expressed in many ways.

1. 向客人介绍退房时间是在 12 点之前。
2. 询问客人是付现金还是用旅行支票结账。
3. 告知客人账单是 4,567 元。
4. 向客人道别。

Ⅲ. Translate the following sentences into English.

1. White 小姐，请稍等，我帮您结算账单。您的消费金额为 6,500 美元。请您查看一下。
2. 您已预交 1,000 美元，请把收据给我。
3. 你们收什么信用卡？
4. 欢迎您用旅行支票付账。
5. 如果您用信用卡买单，要付 5% 贸易商委托费。

Ⅳ. Fill in the blankets and then translate the passage into Chinese.

When ___1___ for the guest, we ___2___ pay special attention to the following:

Checking out ___3___, ask the guest to give you the ___4___.

Checking out ___5___, firstly you should make sure ___6___ the credit card can be accepted or not in the hotel. Secondly you must pay special attention to the valid date and ___7___.

Checking out ___8___, first exam whether the check is good; pay more attention to ___9___ the guest to sign his name in ___10___ place. If the guest signs his name in wrong place, the hotel can not cash the check.

Unit Nine Solving Problems with the Bill
单元 9 解决账单问题

Procedure of Service 服务流程

- Greet the guest.
- Be patient to listen to what the guest says.
- Repeat the points of what the guest says to you for confirmation.
- Say "sorry" or make an apology to the guest.
- Find out the mistake and correct it.
- Bid farewell to the guest.

Points of Service Language 服务语言要点

1. **Repeating the points of what the guest says for confirmation   复述客人说话要点以确认**

    So you've been overcharged. There is something wrong with our bill.

    也就是说,账单有错,我们多收了您的钱。

    So the total of the bill is more than the total you calculate.

    也就是说,账单总额要多出您所计算的总额。

2. **Finding the mistake   查找错误**

    Please wait a moment, Mr. Johnson. I'll check it.

    请稍等,Johnson 先生。我查一下。

    I'll check it with the department concerned, Would you mind waiting for a minute?

    我跟有关部门核对一下,您介意等一会儿吗?

3. **Saying "sorry" or making an apology to the guest   向客人道歉**

    I must apologize for the inconvenience.

    给您带来了不便向您道歉。

    We're terribly sorry for overcharging you.

    非常抱歉向您多收了钱。

    I'm sorry to hear that.

听到您这么说,我很抱歉。
There has been an error.
是我们错了。
Please accept my apologies for our mistakes.
让我为我们所犯的错误向您道歉,请您接受。

4. **Correcting the mistake** 改错

We'll correct your bill by deducting 228 yuan from the total. I'll return the money you've overpaid.
我们将把账单更正过来,从总额中减去 228 元人民币。我把您多付的钱还给您。
I must apologize for the inconvenience. Here is the money you've overpaid.
给您带来了不便向您道歉。这是您多付的钱。

Service Conversation 17

Explaining the Bill

09 – 17 Explaining the Bill. mp3

C: Cashier

G: Guest

C: Is there anything else I can do for you?

G: The total of the bill is more than I calculate.

C: So the total of the bill is more than the total you calculate. Please wait a moment, Miss White, I'll check it for you. It all seems right. Thank you for waiting so long. Could you tell me where the errors are?

G: The total of the bill is 40 US dollars more than the total that I calculate.

C: I'm very sorry I didn't explain it to you just now. There's a 5% merchant commission if the guest uses a credit card. 40 US dollars is the merchant commission.

G: Oh, I see. Thank you.

C: Have a good trip.

Practice Answer the questions according to the service conversation.

1. Why is the total of the bill more than the guest calculates?
2. How does the cashier explain to the guest?

Chapter Four　Cash Desk Service
收银台服务

Service Conversation 18

Here Is the Money You've Overpaid

09 – 18　Here Is the Money You've Overpaid.mp3

C：Cashier
G：Guest

C：What else can I do for you?
G：I think there's something wrong with the bill. You've overcharged me.
C：So you've been overcharged. There's something wrong with our bill. Please wait a moment, Mr. Johnson. I'll check it. It's all correct.
G：What do they mean?
C：L means laundry, while RESTR stands for restaurant.
G：The restaurant is 360 yuan, but I've never been to the restaurant except for the free breakfast.
C：Don't worry. Please wait a moment, Mr. Johnson. I'll have to check it. We've charged to your account by mistake. We're terribly sorry for overcharging you. I must apologize for the inconvenience. Here is the money you've overpaid.
G：Thank you.
C：Have a good trip.

Practice　Answer the questions according to the service conversation.

1. What do L and RESTR mean?
2. What did the cashier say to the guest when he found the error?

Notes

1. Here is the money you've overpaid.
   这是您多付的钱。
2. charged to your account　记入您的账下

Points of Service Performance 服务演练要点

When a guest makes a complaint against the bill to you, be sure to repeat the points of what the guest says to you in order to confirm.
当客人因账单向你投诉时，一定要重复客人所说的要点以确认。

Performance for Service 模拟演练

Task A

Perform in explaining the bill according to the following card.

Guest Card	Aim: check out Question: don't understand what the following mean 1. T 2. L. DIST 3. RESTR
Cashier Card	Task: check out Explanation: T＝ Telephone Call Charge L. DIST＝ Long Distance Call RESTR＝ Restaurant

Task B

Tom Johnson has never been to the bar, but he has been charged 315 yuan for the bar. He comes to the Cash Desk for it. The cashier Xiao Ling receives him.

Position Knowledge 岗位知识

Some abbreviations in the bills:
账单上的一些缩写词：

Room ＝ Room Charge　房费　　　　T＝ Telephone Call Charge　电话费

RESTR＝ Restaurant　餐饮费　　　　L. DIST＝ Long Distance Call　长途电话费

L＝ Laundry　洗衣费　　　　　　　MISC＝ Miscellaneous　杂费

TR. CH＝ Transfer Charge　转出　　TR. CR＝ Transfer Credit　转入

PD. OUT＝ Paid out　代付　　　　　PAID＝ Paid　付现

C. I. A(Cash In Advance)　预付　　P. I. A(Paid In Advance)　已预付

C. O. D(Cash Payment on Departure)　离店时现付　　BND(Bill Not Paid)　未结账

Exercises

Ⅰ. Topics for discussion.

1. Speak out some sentences to make an apology to the guest.

2. How to deal with the guest's complaint against the bill.

Ⅱ. **Translate the following sentences into English.**

1. 给您带来了不便,向您道歉。
2. 这是您多付的钱。
3. 当客人因账单向你投诉时,一定要重复客人所说的要点以确认。
4. 我认为账单有错,你多收了钱。

Ⅲ. **Fill in the blanks.**

The Hotel Doesn't Accept Personal Checks

C:Cashier

G:Guest

C:Good afternoon, sir. Can I help you?
G:Good morning. _____1_____ My name is Harry Carpenter.
C:Mr. Carpenter, _____2_____
G:Here you are.
C:Thank you. _____3_____
G:No, I haven't.
C:Please wait a moment, Mr. Wright. _____4_____ Here is your bill, 2,678 US dollars in all. Please check it.
G:That's correct.
C:_____5_____
G:_____6_____
C:_____7_____, we don't accept personal check.
G:Would you accept Visa Card?
C:Visa Card is welcome. _____8_____
G:Here you are.
C:Thank you. _____9_____
G:Thanks a lot.
C:_____10_____ _____11_____ _____12_____

Chapter Five Telephone Desk Service
总机服务

Unit Ten   Telephone Operator
单元 10   转接电话

Unit Eleven   Other Service
单元 11   其他服务

Service Position 服务岗位

Switchboard plays an important role in the whole hotel. It handles telephone traffic for guests and the rest of the operation. How polite the switchboard operators are, how well they speak and how well they present on the phone will influence the guests' impression of the hotel!

Unlike the face-to-face talk, speaking on the phone is easy to cause misunderstanding if the switchboard operators' response is not appropriate. So some telephone skills and abilities of dealing with varied situations are especially essential for the professional operators.

Skills and Attainments 服务技能与素养

The operators in the hotel need to complete the following services in English: connect calls for guests, provide wake-up and messages services, show guests how to use IDD and DDD, answer guests' inquiries, page a guest, etc.

As operators in a hotel, they must be familiar not only with their professional knowledge but also with English on telephone. And moreover, for a good telephone conversation, operators must also pay attention to their tone of voice. Be polite and responsive. Speak clearly and answer courteously. Don't use slang and always be mindful of the guest. At the moment when operators pick up the handset, they're the hotel's representatives, so giving the guests their full attention is an important quality, operators should demonstrate in their work.

Key Words and Expressions

switchboard (n.)	电话总机
handle (v.)	应付,处理
impression (n.)	印象
response (n.)	回答,应对
appropriate (adj.)	适当的,适合的
essential (adj.)	极为重要的
inquiry (n.)	询问,查问
page (v.)	(在旅馆等用广播)呼叫找人
responsive (adj.)	有回应的
courteously (adv.)	有礼貌地
slang (n.)	俚语
handset (n.)	话筒
representative (n.)	代表
demonstrate (v.)	展示,示范

Unit Ten Telephone Operator

Procedure of Service 服务流程

- Get to know what kind of the call that the guest wants to make.
- Explain to the guest in detail how to dial it if the guest wants to call directly from his room.
- Place the call for the guest after you have got the following information:
  Which country the guest is calling.
  What number the guest is calling.
  To whom the guest would like to speak.
  A pay call or a collect call.
  The guest's name and room number.
- Tell the guest whether the line is busy or free.

Points of Service Language 服务语言要点

1. **Polite expressions on the phone**　电话礼貌用语

   Good morning. This is ×× Hotel. May I help you?
   早上好。这是××酒店。能为您效劳吗？
   Thanks for calling.
   谢谢您的来电。
   We're sorry that we couldn't help you, sir.
   很抱歉没法为您服务。
   We look forward to another chance to serve you, sir.
   希望下次有机会能为您效劳。

2. **Placing the call for the guest**　为客人转接电话

   Just a moment please, I'll put you through.
   请稍等，我马上帮您转接。

Please hold the line a moment, I'm putting you through to…

请别挂电话,我这就给您接过去……

Thank you for waiting, sir. Please go ahead, you're through.

让您久等了,先生。您的电话已接通,请讲。

This is the Hotel Operator, I have a collect call from Mr. Smith in America, will you accept the charges?

这里是酒店总机,有一位史密斯先生从美国打来的接听人付费电话,您愿意付款吗?

3. Receiving a telephone call with wrong number 当对方拨错号码时

I'm afraid you have the wrong number. This is the Beijing Hotel.

您恐怕拨错号码了。这里是北京饭店。

Outgoing Calls

10 – 19 Outgoing Calls. mp3

O: Operator

G: Guest

O: Good morning. This is the hotel operator. May I help you?

G: Yes. This is John Smith in Room 402. I'd like to make an international call.

O: Mr. Smith, we offer IDD and DDD services in our hotel. So you may call directly from your room. It's cheaper than going through the operator.

G: Oh, would you please tell me how to dial?

O: Certainly, sir. Please dial the country code, the area code and the number you want. The country codes are listed in the services directory in your room.

G: I see. Well, what about domestic calls?

O: For calls outside Beijing, please dial 0 first and then the area code and the number you want. For calls inside Beijing, please dial 0 first and then the number you want.

G: Fine. Thanks a lot.

O: You're welcome, sir.

Practice Answer the questions according to the service conversation.

1. If you are an operator in a hotel, how can you tell the guest the way to make an international call?

2. What kinds of calls are mentioned in this conversation?

Chapter Five Telephone Desk Service
总机服务

3. Why does the operator advise the guest to use IDD and DDD services instead of going through the operator?

Service Conversation 20

Incoming Calls

10-20 Incoming Calls. mp3

G: Guest
O: Operator

G: Is this Beijing Hotel?
O: Yes, it is. May I help you?
G: Yes. Could you put me through to Room 213, please?
O: Certainly, sir. Just a moment, please.
   (*After a while*)
O: I'm sorry. The line is busy. Would you like to hold on or call back?
G: OK, I'll call back later. Thank you.
O: You're welcome, sir.
   (*An hour later*)
G: I'd like to speak with Mr. Winston in Room 213. Could you try again, please?
O: Please hold the line, and I'll put you through.
O: Thank you for waiting, sir. Please go ahead, you're through.

Practice Answer the questions according to the service conversation.

1. If the line is busy (engaged), what would you say to your guest?
2. If the call is connected, what would you say to your guest?

Key Words and Expressions

put sb. through	帮某人接通电话
be busy(engaged)	电话占线
call back	回拨或重打
hold on, hold the line	请不要挂断,稍候
go ahead	(接通后)请讲

75

Points of Service Performance 服务演练要点

- If a guest wants to make a long distance call in the hotel, he can either call directly from his room or go through the operator. Calling directly is cheaper than the latter one, so the operator should get clear about the guest's request when answering his phone.
  在饭店打长途电话,可以直接拨打,也可以让总机帮助拨通电话。一般情况下,采用直接拨打的方式比较便宜。接线员在接受咨询时应该问清楚客人的要求。
- When the operator is connecting an incoming collect call from overseas, be sure to inform the guest first and then confirm whether he would like to answer or not.
  当总机为客人转接越洋接听人付费电话时,应先告知接听人并确认其是否愿意接听。

Performance for Service 模拟演练

Performance in pairs according to the information given below.

Task A

Mike Smith wants to make a long distance call to his friend in Guangzhou, so he asks the hotel operator for help. The operator explains to him in detail how to call directly from his room.

Task B

Mr. Wang calls switchboard operator of the Holiday Hotel to speak with Mr. Hubert in Room 401. The operator should deal with two situations.
(1) The line is busy.
(2) This incoming call is connected well.

Position Knowledge 岗位知识

- Some Main Calls in the Hotel:电话服务常用术语:
  IDD (International Direct Dial)　国际直拨电话
  DDD (Domestic Direct Dial)　国内直拨电话

  station-to-station call　叫号电话　　　　outside call　外线电话
  person-to-person call　叫人电话　　　　internal call　内线电话
  morning call/wake-up call　叫醒电话　　local call　市内电话
  collect call　对方付费电话　　　　　　long distance call　长途电话
  pay call　打电话人付费电话　　　　　　coin call　投币电话
  international call　国际电话　　　　　domestic call　国内电话
  credit card call　信用卡电话　　　　　emergency call　急救电话

- Some guidelines for good telephone conversation:
  总机在接听客人电话时的注意事项:

Chapter Five　Telephone Desk Service
总机服务

- Try to visualize the person you are talking to. It is necessary to maintain a pleasant tone. Put a smile in your voice.
  试着想象和你通话的客人就在面前,说话时如平常般殷勤、恳切。
- Listen attentively and, if necessary, ask the caller to repeat.
  认真接听电话内容,如果有必要,请客人再重复一遍。
- Be patient and attentive.
  接听电话时既要耐心又要专心。
- Always answer the phone promptly before the second ring.
  通常电话铃响第二声之前就要快速拿起电话。
- Afterwards, hang up gently (don't bang down the phone abruptly).
  通话结束后,轻轻地挂断电话(切忌很生硬地摔电话)。

Exercises

Ⅰ. **Topics for discussion.**

1. If you are an operator in a hotel, how can you tell the guest the way to make the domestic calls? (Including a local call and a long distance call)
2. If you are an operator in a hotel, a guest wants you to place an international call for him, what information should you confirm first from the guest?

Ⅱ. **Write out the questions according to the answers.**

1. _____
   Yes. I'd like to make an international call to Switzerland. Could you place the call for me?
2. _____
   The Number is Lausanne 85027.
3. _____
   Yes, it's Grace Perira.
4. _____
   A pay call, please.
5. _____
   Yes, my name's Robbins and I'm in Room 102.
6. _____
   Fine. Thanks a lot.

III. Translate the following sentences into English.

1. 要我帮您打通这个电话吗？
2. 您可以直接由客房打出去。这样比经由总机打出便宜一些。
3. 抱歉，电话占线。等线路畅通后，我请他给您回电话，好吗？
4. ——请帮我接通 103 号房间，好吗？
   ——好的，先生。您想找哪一位？
5. 让您久等了，先生。您的电话已接通，请讲。

IV. Read the following passage and answer the questions.

Making a Call in America

The way to make a call abroad is almost the same as that at home.

If you don't know the number you want, you can look it up in the phone book. There are two kinds of phone books. One is called the "White Pages", which lists in alphabetical order with the last name first. The list includes the names, addresses, and telephone numbers of people in the area. The other is the "Yellow Pages", which lists all the businesses, hotels, restaurants, shops, theaters, and services in the area. This listing is arranged in alphabetical order according to the type of establishment. Emergency numbers are usually printed inside the front cover of the phone book.

The charges for public phones are different in different cities in the United States.

Long distance calls can be "collect". Person-to-person calls and collect calls are operator assisted and more expensive. You first dial "0", then the area code and the telephone number. The call can only be received by the particular person you want. After dialing the number, an operator will come on the line to help. She will ask you who you want, your name and your number. For person-to-person calls the operator will tell you when to drop in your coins, while for collect calls, you may hear the operator say: "I have a collect, person-to-person call for ×× from ××. Will you accept the charges?" If the person says "Yes", you may begin to speak and charges for the call start at that time. There is no charge for a call that is refused.

Questions：

1. What does the list of "White Pages" include?
2. What does the list of "Yellow Pages" include?
3. If you are looking for an emergency number in the phone book, where can you find it?
4. Who will help you on the line when you make a person-to-person call? And is this call expensive or not?

Unit Eleven Other Service
单元 11 其他服务

Procedure of Service 服务流程

The morning call

- Find out what the guest's request is.
- Ask what kind of wake-up call the guest wants.
- Give instructions if the guest is to use computer wake-up service.
- Confirm the time, the guest's name and the room number if the guest prefers operator wake-up service.
- Express your wishes.

Leaving the message

- Put the caller through to the guest to whom the caller wants to speak.
- Make sure nobody answers the phone.
- Ask the caller if he wants to leave a message.
- If the caller would like, please confirm the following information: the caller's name, address, telephone number and message.
- Promise the caller to take the message as soon as possible.

Points of Service Language 服务语言要点

1. **How to call** 电话中怎样称谓

   在电话中,要表达"我是……"时,是用"This is…",而不是"I am …"。同样的道理,问对方是谁时,也是用"Who is that?"而不用"Who are you? "。

2. **Refusing the caller's inquiry about the guest's information** 拒绝来电者对客人信息的查询

   I'm afraid I can't help you due to the regulations.

很抱歉,按规定我不能帮您这么做。

3. **Taking a message for the guest 为客人提供留言服务**

   I'm afraid Mr. Black is not in his room now. Would you like to leave a message for him?
   恐怕 Black 先生不在房间内。您需要给他留言吗?

   I'm afraid there is still no reply. Can I take a message, please?
   恐怕还是没有人接听,我能帮您留言吗?

   Sorry, there is no answer. Would you like to leave a message?
   很抱歉,房间没有人接听。您想留言吗?

   I'll pass your message to Mr. Black.
   我会把您的留言转给 Black 先生的。

   I'll make sure she gets the message.
   我一定会把您的留言转给她的。

4. **The guest asks the operator for the morning call 酒店客人向总机要求叫醒服务**

   Will you please give me a wake-up call in the morning?
   早上请用电话叫我起床,好吗?

   I'd like to be woken up at 7:00 tomorrow morning.
   明天早上 7 点想请你叫我起床。

   I want to have a morning call at 7:00.
   我需要一个早晨 7 点的叫醒服务。

5. **Responding to the guest's request for the morning call 总机对客人要求的应答**

   What time would you like?/At what time?
   几点叫您呢?

   We have a computer wake-up service. Please dial…and our computer will record the time and your room number.
   我们有计算机叫醒服务。请拨……,我们的计算机将会记录您的叫醒时间和房间号码。

   What kind of call would you like, by phone or by knocking at the door?
   您要哪种叫醒服务,电话叫醒还是敲门叫醒?

Service Conversation 21

The Wake-up Call

11-21 The Wake-up Call.mp3

G: Guest
O: Operator

G: Operator. I wonder if your hotel has the wake-up call service.

O: Yes. Anyone who stays in our hotel can ask for the service. Would you like a wake-up call?

G: Yes. I'd like to be woken up at 6:30 tomorrow morning.

O: What kind of wake-up call would you like, by computer or by phone?

G: But I don't know how to use a computer wake-up service.

O: Please dial 5 first and then 0630 for the time. There must be five digits in the final number.

G: 50630. I see.

O: That's all right, sir. Our computer will record the time and your room number.

G: Thank you.

O: You're welcome, sir. Have a good night.

Practice Answer the questions according to the services conversation.

1. What kinds of the morning call services are mentioned in this conversation?
2. How can a guest use the computer wake-up service?
3. Does the operator need to record the time and the guest's room number?

11 - 22 Leaving the Message.mp3

Leaving the Message

O: Operator

G: Guest

O: Good afternoon. Hilton Hotel. May I help you?

G: Yes. I'd like to speak to Mr. Brown in Room 1532, please.

O: Please hold the line, and I'll put you through.

(One minute later)

O: I'm sorry, sir. Nobody answers the phone. Would you like to leave a message for him?

G: OK. Please tell him I'm going to call on him this evening at about 9:30.

O: May I have your name?

G: Yes, this is Tom Miles.

O: Would you like to give me your phone number, so he can call you back if necessary?

G: Yes, my number is 6632-4564.

O: 66324564. Thank you. We'll inform him as soon as possible when he comes back.

G: Thanks a lot.

O: You're welcome, sir.

> **Practice** Answer the questions according to the service conversation.

1. For whom does Tom Miles want to leave a message?
2. In this conversation, what information has the operator got from the caller?
3. What's the message that Tom Miles has left?

Points of Service Performance 服务演练要点

For a complete telephone message, the following information should be recorded:
记录完整的电话留言应该注意以下信息:

- Name of the person called and his room number.
  客人(即接电话人)的姓名和房间号。
- Name of the caller, and company.
  打电话人的姓名及其公司名称。
- The caller's telephone number including extension.
  打电话人的电话号码包括分机号。
- The caller's city.
  打电话人所在城市。
- The message.
  留言内容。
- The action requested and promised.
  打电话人要求的注意事项。
- The date and time of the call.
  打电话的日期及具体时间。

Performance for Service 模拟演练

Task A

Performance in pairs according to the following two cards.

Guest Card		
	Guest name:	Billie Brandy
	Room number:	Room 1523
	Request:	a morning call at 7:15
	Arrangement:	attend an important meeting at 8:00

Chapter Five Telephone Desk Service
总机服务

Operator Card	Suggestion: use the operator wake-up service
	Confirm the time
	Record the guest's name and room number

Task B

Tom Miles wants to speak to Mrs. Chen in Beijing Hotel. But Mrs. Chen happens to be out. So the operator asks Mr. Miles if he wants to leave a message for her. Mr. Miles says that they will hold a conference in Xiyuan Tower the next Tuesday and Mrs. Chen is expected to attend it. So he wants Mrs. Chen to call him back at 66324564.

Position Knowledge 岗位知识

- Morning Call/Wake-up Call:
  叫醒电话:
  There are three ways of wake-up call. Wake-up service by operator, Wake-up service by computer, Wake-up service by knocking at the door.
  叫醒电话一般有三种方式:总机人工叫醒服务、计算机自动叫醒服务、在特殊情况下的服务员敲门叫醒服务。
- The operator should remind the guest that while dialing IDD, he had better pay attention to dial the hotel code, international prefix, country code, area and subscriber number continuously, with no pause (exceeding 10 seconds), making him ensure that his dialing will not be interrupted.
  总机应提醒客人打国际电话时,要将酒店代号、国际字冠、国家代号、地区代号和用户号码一次拨完,中间不要停顿(停顿时间不要超过10秒),以免造成呼叫中断。
- Useful Expressions:
  常用词汇:

switchboard 电话总机	operator 话务员
telephone directory 电话指南	telephone number 电话号码
public telephone 公用电话	area code 区号
extension number 分机号码	incoming/outgoing calls 打进/打出电话

Exercises

Ⅰ. Topics for discussion:

1. What information should the operator get when he is taking message for the guest?
2. What kinds of the wake-up service can the guest use in the hotel? And which one

would you think is more convenient?

3. If you are an operator, what would you say to the caller when the guest isn't in?

II. Write out the questions according to the answers.

1. _____

   I'm flying to the United States tomorrow morning. Will you please give me a wake-up call in the morning?

2. _____

   At around 7:15 a.m.

3. _____

   By phone, please. I don't want to disturb my neighbors.

4. _____

   It's Calwell in Room 1025.

5. _____

   So much. Thank you.

III. Translate the following passage into Chinese.

When answering the call, you should immediately identify yourself and greet callers in a courteous and friendly manner, even if you are having a busy day. Don't put callers on hold for long periods of time. If it is necessary to hunt for information or to take another call, offer to call back. It's also a bad manner to engage in long phone conversation while you have a visitor in your office. If the call can't be handled quickly, say you will call back later. Then remember to do so.

Chapter Six　Housekeeping Service
客房服务

Unit Twelve　Chamber Service
单元 12　客房服务

Unit Thirteen　Room Service
单元 13　客房送餐服务

Unit Fourteen　Maintenance Service
单元 14　维修服务

Service Position 服务岗位

The Housekeeping Department(客房部)is one of the main operational departments of a hotel. Its main duty is to see to the cleanliness and good order of all the rooms and public areas in the hotel, provide all kinds of facilities and services so as to create a convenient, comfortable, tidy and secure living environment for the guests. It also provides supports for other departments and coordinates the work closely with other departments.

Housekeeping is the heart of the hotel industry, though it doesn't generate sales directly, while the Food & Beverage Department and the Sales Department do. The entire hotel depends on the smooth, efficient management of the Housekeeping Department.

Skills and Attainments 服务技能与素养

The clerks of the Housekeeping Department have to complete the following main services in English:

Introducing the facilities in the room, the services and the service facilities of the hotel to the guests; cleaning the room, providing turn-down service, extending a bed, handling the laundry service, providing the room service and the maintenance service; dealing with the complaints and meeting the guest's special need. Sometimes the clerks need to show the guests how to use the electric facilities and how to use the safety deposit box in the room.

It is the basic demand for the clerks of the Housekeeping to have the ability of communication in English, because they need to communicate with the foreign guests and make sure of what they want to get, and then provide all kinds of services and help for them. In order to work well, they must also have the special skills and the serious and careful working attitude.

Key Words and Expressions

the Housekeeping Department	客房部/房务部
the Food & Beverage Department	餐饮部
the Sales Department	销售部
turn-down service	晚床服务
extend a bed	加床
laundry service	洗衣服务
room service	客房送餐服务

Notes

1. It doesn't generate sales directly.　它不能直接对客人销售。
2. the smooth, efficient management　有序、高效的管理

Unit Twelve Chamber Service

单元 12 客房服务

Procedure of Service 服务流程

- Knock at the door gently three times.
- Say: "Housekeeping."
- Ask the guest whether you can go into the room.
- Greet the guest.

Cleaning the room

- Ask the guest whether you can clean the room now.
- Clean the room:
  Open the window—Dispose the rubbish—Make the bed—Clean the bathroom—Replenish the supplies—Vacuum the floor—Self-check.
- Express your wishes to the guest.

Turning down the bed

- Ask the guest if he wants turn-down service now.
- Turn down the bed:
  Turn down the bed—Drop the curtain together—Turn on some lights—Clean the bathroom—Bring in the fresh towels—Have a look around to be sure everything is done.
- Express your wishes to the guest.

Points of Service Language 服务语言要点

1. **Polite expressions**　礼貌用语

   I'm sorry to disturb you, but may I clean the room now?
   很抱歉打扰您了,现在可以打扫房间吗?

Good evening. Housekeeping. May I come in?

晚上好。客房部。我可以进来吗?

Good evening, sir. May I do the turn-down service now?

晚上好,先生。我现在可以做晚床吗?

You're welcome. I hope you have a very pleasant evening.

不用谢。祝您度过一个美好的夜晚。

It's my pleasure. I hope you'll enjoy yourselves.

不用谢。玩得愉快!

With pleasure. Good night, sir. Have a nice dream.

为您服务很荣幸。晚安,先生。祝您做个好梦。

2. **Asking what time will be convenient   询问什么时间方便**

When would you like me to clean your room, Mr. Smith?

我何时可以回来打扫房间,Smith 先生?

What time would be better for you?

您什么时候合适?

What time would/will be convenient for you?

请问您什么时间方便?

Shall I come back later, sir?

先生,要我等会儿再来吗?

Service Conversation 23

May I Do the Room Now

12-23 May I Do the Room Now. mp3

: Housekeeper

: Guest

H: Housekeeping. May I come in?

G: Come in, please.

H: Good morning, ma'am. Sorry to disturb you. May I do the room now?

G: OK. Can you clean the bathroom first?

H: Certainly. I've finished cleaning the room. Anything else I can do for you, ma'am?

G: Oh, yes. I've just taken a bath, and my hair is wet. But your hair-dryer doesn't work.

H: I'm sorry to hear that. I'll send one up right away. What else do you want? I can bring them together.

G: Several envelopes and postcards.

H: I'll come back soon.

H: Here you are.

G: Thank you, you've been very helpful.

H: You're welcome. I hope you have a good day.

> **Practice** Answer the questions according to the service conversation.

1. What does "do the room" mean?
2. Why does the guest want a hair-dryer?
3. What does the housemaid do when he heard the guest's complaint?

Service Conversation 24

What Time Would You Like Me to Come Back

Ⓗ: Housekeeper

Ⓖ: Guest

H: Good evening. Housekeeping. May I come in?

G: Come in, please.

H: Good evening, sir. May I do the turn-down service for you now?

G: Oh, I'm expecting some friends.

H: What time would you like me to come back?

12-24 What Time Would You Like Me to Come Back. mp3

G: Please come back for the turn-down service at 10:30. Could you clean the bathroom for me now? The bathroom is in disarray. My friends will be here shortly.

H: It will only take me five minutes to clean the bathroom.

G: Could I have an extra bed? One of my friends will stay here with me for a night.

H: Of course. But please call the Front Desk first. With the permission of the Front Office, I'll get you one when I come back to turn down your bed.

G: OK, I'll call them then.

H: The bathroom is clean now.

G: Thank you very much.

H: You're welcome. I hope you have a very pleasant evening.

Practice Answer the questions according to the service conversation.

1. Why does the guest want to put an extra bed?
2. How can the guest get the extra bed?
3. When will the housemaid come back to turn down the bed?

Key Words and Expressions

chamber service	客房服务
Housekeeping	客房部；客房部工作人员
disposal the rubbish	倒垃圾
make the bed	做床
replenish the supplies	补充客房物品
vacuum the floor	吸尘
turn down the bed	做晚床
do the room	打扫房间，做房
with the permission of …	经过……的许可

Points of Service Performance 服务演练要点

- Before entering a guest's room, knock at the door three times slightly, and then announce: "Housekeeping. May I come in?"
  在进客人房间前，轻敲门三下，然后通报："客房部服务员。我能进来吗？"

- Entering the room, greet the guest with a warm and natural voice: "Good morning. May I clean the room now?" or "Good evening, sir. May I turn down the bed now?"
  进入房间后，热情而自然地问候客人："上午好。我现在可以打扫房间吗？"或者"晚上好。我现在可以做晚床吗？"

- If the guest doesn't want to clean the room or turn down the bed now, ask what time is convenient and come back to the room for cleaning at the convenient time.
  如果客人不想马上打扫房间或做晚床，要询问何时方便，然后在客人认为方便的时间再回房间打扫。

Performance for Service 模拟演练

Task A

Perform cleaning the room in pairs according to the following two cards.

Guest Card	Don't want to clean the room now. The housemaid can come to clean the room at 11:00 a.m.

Chapter Six Housekeeping Service
客房服务

| **Housemaid Card** | Greet the guest.
Ask the guest whether the room can be cleaned now.
Ask what time will be better to clean the room. |

Task B

The housemaid Wang Fang is going to turn down the bed for Mr. White now. Mr. White agrees her to do now. He asks Wang Fang to put an extra bed for him, for one of his former students will come to see him and stay here for a night. The rate of the extra bed is 34 US dollars.

Position Knowledge 岗位知识

- The room attendant can know the name of the guest by the following:
  客房服务员可以通过以下途径了解客人的姓名:
  luggage tags　行李标签
  arrival list　来客单
  registration　入住登记
  restaurant reservation　餐厅预订
  convention or meeting name tags　会议用姓名标牌
  asking the guest　询问客人
- 做晚床就是将床罩拿走,将靠电话那一边的被子角掀起,折成三角形,放好枕头。接着放下窗帘,打开一些灯。最后收拾好浴室,放上一些干净的毛巾并准备好热水。
- 在客房部,客人常常会向客房部工作人员提出加床要求,但是客房部工作人员没有权力直接给客人加床。这时,要求客人打电话到前台以获得许可,或者要求客人直接到前台办理加床手续。只有在获得前台许可之后,服务员才能给客人加床。

Exercises

Ⅰ. Topics for discussion.

1. Introduce simply the procedure of turn-down service.
2. How does the guest get the extra bed?
3. How can we know the name of the guest?

Ⅱ. Write out the English equivalents of the following.

1. 枕头　　　2. 被子　　　3. 毯子　　　4. 备用毯
5. 床单　　　6. 床罩　　　7. 窗帘　　　8. 地毯

9. 电水壶　　10. 烟灰缸　　11. 针线包　　12. 台灯
13. 洗衣袋　　14. 衣架　　　15. 洗衣单　　16. 衣刷

Ⅲ. Translate the following sentences into English.

1. 早上好，White 先生。我现在可以清扫房间吗？
2. 我何时可以回来打扫房间，Smith 先生？
3. 愿意随时为您服务。
4. 客房的收入大约占酒店总收入的 50% 或更多。
5. 请问什么时间方便？
6. 晚上好，我现在可以做晚床吗？
7. 如果您需要帮助，请拨 9 到客房中心。
8. 房间已经租出去了。

Ⅳ. Translate the following sentences into Chinese.

1. For the turn-down service, take away bed cover, take a quilt corner by the telephone side and fold into a triangle. Place pillow properly. Then drop the curtain together and turn on some lights. Finally tidy up the bathroom, bring in the fresh towels and the just-boiled water as well.
2. In the Housekeeping, some guests always ask the house attendants to put an extra bed for them. But the house attendants have no right to put extra beds for the guests directly. At that time, you should ask the guest to call the Front Office for permission or ask him to handle the formality of extending the bed. Only with the permission, can you put an extra bed for the guest. Certainly you can introduce the rate of an extending bed to the guest.

 Room Service

单元 ⑬ 客房送餐服务

Procedure of Service 服务流程

Booking the Room Service

- Greet the guest.
- Get the information from the guest:
  What the guest wants.
  The special demands for cooking.
  The guest's name and his room number.
- Confirm what the guest books.
- Tell the guest the order will be ready soon.

Delivering the food to the guest's room

- Deliver the food at the gate of the guest room.
- Knock at the door gently.
- Announce: "Room service. May I come in?"
- Speak out the order and give the bill to the guest.
- Ask the guest to sign the name and room number.
- Express your wishes.

Points of Service Language 服务语言要点

1. **Explaining the Room Service　客房送餐服务说明**

   We can provide very good room service.
   我们能提供很好的客房送餐服务。
   Room service is available 24 hours a day.
   客房送餐服务一天 24 小时都提供。
   There is an extra service charge of 10% for the room service.

客房送餐服务要另加10％的服务费。

We add a 10％ service charge.

我们要另加10％的服务费。

We offer three types of breakfast: American, Continental and Chinese. Which one would you prefer?

我们提供美式、欧式和中式早餐。您要订哪一种？

We'll add the cost to your room bill. Please sign your name and room number here on the bill.

我们会把费用加在您房间的账单上。请在账单上签上您的姓名和房间号。

2. Getting the information from the guest 了解客人需求

Which breakfast would you prefer, American or Continental?

您要订哪一种早餐,美式还是欧式？

How would you like your eggs/steak?

您点的蛋/牛扒要怎样做？

Which kind of juice would you like/prefer, grapefruit or orange?

您喜欢哪种果汁,西柚汁还是橘子汁？

Would you like ham or bacon with your eggs?

您喜欢火腿还是咸肉夹蛋？

3. Payment 付款

Mr. Black, here is your bill. Please check it.

Black 先生,这是您的账单,请核对。

4. Polite expressions 礼貌用语

Good morning, Room Service. May I help you?

早上好。这里是送餐中心,有什么吩咐？

Your order will arrive in 15 minutes, see you.

您的餐点15分钟送到,再见。

Thank you for using room service. Enjoy yourself, goodbye.

谢谢您使用送餐服务。请慢用,再见。

Service Conversation 25

Your Order Will Arrive in 15 Minutes

13-25 Your Order Will Arrive in 15 Minutes. mp3

W: Room Service Waiter

H: Mrs. Hibbard(guest)

W: Good morning, room service. What can I do for you?

Chapter Six Housekeeping Service
客房服务

H: I'd like to book your room service for breakfast.

W: We offer three types of breakfast: American, Continental and Chinese. Which one would you prefer?

H: What does a Continental breakfast have?

W: Orange juice, toast with butter, coffee or tea.

H: I'll take it.

W: Coffee or tea?

H: Coffee. I'd like to book a Chinese breakfast for my husband. What does it contain?

W: Rice noodles, meat pie, millet gruel, sweet dumpling, soybean milk and boiled egg. You can choose from them.

H: Rice noodles, meat pie and soybean milk. And I'd like two boiled eggs as well.

W: How would you like your eggs?

H: Soft boiled.

W: May I have your name and room number, please?

H: Mrs. Hibbard in Room 1926.

W: Let me confirm your order. Mrs. Hibbard in Room 1926 has booked a Continental breakfast: rice noodles, meat pie, soybean milk and two soft boiled eggs. Is that right?

H: Exactly. Is there an extra charge for room service?

W: We add a 10% service charge.

H: OK. Please send them as soon as possible.

W: Your order will arrive in 15 minutes. See you.

Practice Answer the questions according to the service conversation.

1. How many kinds of breakfasts does the hotel provide for the guests? What are they?
2. What does the Chinese breakfast have?

Service Conversation 26
Here Is Your Chinese Breakfast

13-26 Here Is Your Chinese Breakfast.mp3

W: Room Service Waiter

H: Mrs. Hibbard (guest)

W: (*Knocking at the door*) It's room service. May I come in?

H: Come in, please.

W: Thank you, Mrs. Hibbard. Where would you like me to put them?

H: Please put them on the table over there.

W: All right. Here is your Continental breakfast: orange juice, toast with butter, coffee. Here is your Chinese breakfast: rice noodles, meat pie, soybean milk and two boiled eggs as well.

H: Thanks a lot.

W: Mrs. Hibbard, here is your bill. Please check it.

H: It's OK. How can I pay the bill?

W: We'll add the cost to your room bill. Please sign your name and room number here on the bill. Thank you for using room service. Enjoy yourself. Goodbye.

H: Goodbye.

Practice Answer the questions according to the service conversation.

1. Speak out the English names of the foods in the two dialogues.
2. What does the Continental breakfast have?
3. Where is the order put?
4. How is the guest required to pay?

Key Words and Expressions

Room Service	客房送餐服务；送餐中心
orange juice	橙汁
toast with butter	黄油吐司
meat pie	馅饼
millet gruel	小米粥
sweet dumpling	汤圆
rice noodles	米粉
soybean milk	豆浆
soft boiled eggs	煮得很嫩的鸡蛋

Notes

We offer three types of breakfast: American, Continental and Chinese. Which one would you prefer?

我们提供美式、欧式和中式早餐，您要订哪一种？

Points of Service Performance 服务演练要点

- Ask the guest about the demands for cooking when the guest orders by telephone.
  电话订餐时，要询问客人对点餐的要求。

- If there is minimum charge or service charge, you have to explain it clearly in advance.
  如果有最低消费或服务费,应事先说明。

Performance for Service 模拟演练

Performance in Room Service in pairs according to the following two cards.

Guest Card		
	Booking:	chilled orange juice, sweet dumpling soybean milk
	Guest name:	Mr. White
	Room number:	Room 2586

Room Service Waiter Card
Greet the guest
Explain
Ask what the guest wants
Ask how to do
A 10% service charge
Deliver
Payment

Position Knowledge 岗位知识

- Hotel keeping is known as the "hospitality industry" or "courtesy industry" or "service industry". Our aim is to create a "home away from home" for all the guests.
  酒店业是一个被称为"殷勤待客行业",或"礼貌行业",又称"服务行业"。我们的宗旨在于为所有宾客创造一种"宾至如归"的气氛。
- The guest can get the room service by telephone or by doorknob menu.
  客人可以通过电话或者填写门把菜单(挂在门把上的送餐菜单)来获得客房送餐服务。
- Some Chinese noodles:
  中式面条:
  noodles with soup 汤面
  beef noodles 牛肉面
  stretched noodles 拉面
  noodles with soybean paste 炸酱面
  Sichuan style noodles with peppery sauce 担担面
  rice noodles 米粉
- Some Chinese dumpling:
  中式馅食:
  dumpling 饺子

sweet dumpling 汤圆
wonton/dumpling 馄饨

Exercises

Ⅰ. Topics for discussion.

1. How many names of Chinese food for breakfast do you know?
2. Talk about the procedure of room service.
3. How can we create a home far away from home in the hotel for the guests?

Ⅱ. Translate the following sentences into English.

1. 您要订哪一种早餐,美式还是欧式?
2. 您喜欢哪一种果汁,西柚汁还是橘子汁?
3. 您喜欢火腿还是咸肉夹蛋?
4. 客房送餐服务要另加10%的服务费。
5. 您的餐点15分钟送到,再见。
6. 我们提供美式、欧式和中式早餐,您要订哪一种?
7. 我们会把费用加在您房间的账单上。请在账单上签上您的姓名和房间号。
8. 谢谢您使用送餐服务。请慢用,再见。

Ⅲ. Read the following passage and answer the questions and then translate it into Chinese.

The operation aim of the hotel is to create a home away from home for all the traveling guests who need a rest, food and drink. How can we create a home in the hotel? Firstly, we should regard our guests as our family members and try our best to meet the demands that the guests have put to us. Secondly, we should be good at finding out or predicting the demands that the guests don't put to us and satisfy them. If we can provide our guests with the most sincere service to make their stay here convenient, comfortable and enjoyable, they'll have the feeling of staying at their homes.

Questions:

1. What is the operation aim of the hotel?
2. How can we create a home in the hotel?
3. How can we make our guests having the feeling of staying at their homes?

Unit Fourteen Maintenance Service

单元 14 维修服务

Procedure of Service 服务流程

For the housekeeper

- Greet the guest.
- Patiently and carefully listen to what the guest says.
- Say "sorry" or "apologize" to the guest.
- Get the room number from the guest.
- Tell the guest what will be done at once.
- Inform the repairman to repair at once.
- Check what has been made by the repairman.

For the repairman

- Knock at the door, saying: " Maintenance. May I come in?"
- Say "sorry" to the guest and ask the guest about the problem in details.
- Check and repair.
- Tell the guest that everything is all right.
- Extend the wishes to the guest.
- Report the Front Desk.

Points of Service Language 服务语言要点

1. **Polite expressions   礼貌用语**

   Thank you for what you've said.
   谢谢您告诉我这一切。

   Thank you for bringing the problems to our attention.
   感谢您提出问题让我们注意。

Not at all. I wish you a good night.
不用谢。祝您度过一个美好的夜晚。

2. **Asking what's wrong 询问什么坏了**

What's the trouble, sir?

What's the matter, sir?

May I know what's wrong, sir?

有什么问题吗,先生?

Any other problems?

还有别的问题吗?

3. **Telling the facilities are wrong 告知设施坏了**

There's something wrong with the shower head and washbasin faucet.

淋浴头及水盆上的水龙头都坏了。

The color TV doesn't give clear picture.

房间的电视图像不清楚。

The shower head is clogged. The toilet can't flush. The washbasin faucet can't be turned off.

花洒堵住了,马桶不冲水,拧不动水盆上的水龙头。

The faucet keeps dripping.

水龙头不停地滴水。

The drain of the bathtub is clogged as well.

浴缸的排水孔堵住了。

There's something wrong with the air-conditioner.

空调坏了。

4. **Repairing 修理**

An electrician from the Maintenance Department will come to your room to repair the TV at 9:30 tomorrow morning.

明天上午9:30,我们维修部的电工会来您房间修理电视机。

I'll inform the Maintenance Department to repair right now. Would you please tell me your room number?

我马上通知维修部前来修理。能告诉我您的房间号吗?

The repairman will come to your room in five minutes.

维修人员5分钟内到达您的房间。

I've come to repair the facilities in the bathroom. Can you please tell me what the trouble is in detail?

我是来维修卫生间设施的,请您详细地告诉我什么坏了,好吗?

Everything is all right, sir. You can use the bathroom now, sir.

修好了,先生。您现在可以用卫生间了。

Service Conversation 27

The Repairman Will Come to Your Room Soon

H: Housekeeper

G: Guest

H: Good evening. Housekeeping. May I help you?
G: Yes. There is something wrong with some of the facilities in the bathroom.
H: I'm sorry to hear that. What exactly is the matter, ma'am?
G: The toilet doesn't flush, the shower head and washbasin faucet keep dripping, and the bathtub drain is clogged as well.
H: I do apologize for the inconvenience. I'll have the Maintenance Department fix these right now. Would you please tell me your room number?
G: 6756.
H: Room 6756. Thank you for bringing the problems to our attention. And I apologize for the inconvenience as well. The repairman will come to your room soon.
G: OK. I see.
H: I'll call you in about 25 minutes.

14-27 The Repairman Will Come to Your Room Soon. mp3

Service Conversation 28

Repairing the Facilities in the Bathroom

R: Repairman

G: Guest

R: (*Knocking at the door*) Housekeeping. May I come in?
G: Come in, please.
R: Good evening, ma'am. I've come to repair the bathroom facilities. Can you please tell me what the trouble is in detail?
G: The toilet doesn't flush, the shower head and washbasin

14-28 Repairing the Facilities in the Bathroom. mp3

faucet keep dripping, and the bathtub drain is clogged as well.

R: Thank you. I'll take a look at the facilities.

G: How long will I have to wait?

R: Fifteen minutes or so.

R: Everything is all right, ma'am. You can use the bathroom now, ma'am.

G: OK. Thank you very much.

R: Not at all. I wish you a good night.

Key Words and Expressions

inform (vt.)	告诉,报告,通知
faucet/tap	水龙头
shower head	淋浴头/花洒
bathtub (n.)	澡盆,浴缸
the Maintenance Department	维修部

Notes

The toilet can not flush, but the shower head and washbasin faucet keep dripping, and the bathtub drain is clogged as well.

马桶不能冲水,淋浴头及水盆上的水龙头不停地滴水,浴缸的排水孔堵住了。

Points of Service Performance 服务演练要点

- For the housekeeper

  客房服务员

  When the guest finishes the complaint, say sorry to him and tell him that the repairman will come to the room to fix/repair at once/as soon as possible/within five minutes.

  当客人投诉完毕,道歉并告诉客人检修人员会尽快/5分钟内到达房间检修。

- For the repairman

  检修员

  After checking, if you think the problem can't be solved in a short period of time, you have to inform the Housekeeping Department (or the Front Desk) to adopt other measures.

  检查完毕,如果你认为问题不能在短时间内解决,要通知客房部(或前台)采取其他措施。

Performance for Service 模拟演练

Task A

Perform a complaint on the telephone in pairs according to the following two cards.

Chapter Six　Housekeeping Service
客房服务

Guest Card	Room number：	Room 2935
	Problem：	I can't turn off the faucet. The bathroom will become a small lake.

Housekeeper Card	Say sorry to the guest. Tell him that a repairman will go to his room immediately.

Task B

Perform repairing the facilities in the guest's room in pairs according to the following information: the guest in Room 3241 calls the Housekeeping, because there is something wrong with the air-conditioner and the TV set. The housekeeper tells him that the repairman will go to his room in 15 minutes. The repairman repairs the air-conditioner and the TV set.

Position Knowledge　岗位知识

- 酒店经营的目的是为在外旅行需要休息、需要餐饮的客人创造一个"家外之家"。怎样在酒店创造一个"家外之家"呢？首先，我们要把客人当成家庭成员来看待，尽我们的能力满足客人所提出的要求。其次，我们要善于发现和预见客人没有向我们提出的要求，满足他们。如果我们能够给客人提供最真诚的服务，使他们住店方便、舒适、舒心，他们就会有家的感觉。

- Some abbreviations：
  缩写词：
  D. N. A. (Do Not Arrive)　　　　　客人未到
  F. I. T. (Free Individual Tourist)　　散客
  ARR(arrival)　　　　　　　　　　抵店
  C/I(Check-in)　　　　　　　　　　入住
  C/O(Check Out)　　　　　　　　　退房
  O. N. O. (One Night Only)　　　　只住一晚

Exercises

Ⅰ. Topics for discussion.

1. If a guest tells you by telephone " I can't use the toilet now", what will you do?
2. If you think the problem can't be solved in a short period of time, what will you do?

Ⅱ. **Translate the following sentences into English.**

1. 感谢您提出问题让我们注意，同时我也为给您带来的不便向您道歉。维修人员5分钟内到达您的房间。
2. 我是来维修卫生间的设施的，请您详细地告诉我什么坏了，好吗？
3. 一般来说，中国酒店没有直饮水，因此我们可以提醒外宾喝煮开的水或瓶装水。
4. 谢谢您告诉我这一切。
5. 如果客人不会使用房间电器设备，给客人演示或解释。
6. 不用客气，我愿意随时为您服务。
7. 我想把一些文件和贵重物品存放在我房间的保险箱里，但我不知道怎样使用它。

Ⅲ. **Choose one topic to write a composition.**

1. My opinion about creating a home away from home.
2. How to create a home away from home in the hotel?
3. My experience of serving a guest.

Chapter Seven　Restaurant Service
餐厅服务

Unit Fifteen　Table Reservation
单元 15　餐厅预订

Unit Sixteen　Greeting the Guests
单元 16　餐厅迎客服务

Unit Seventeen　Taking Orders
单元 17　点菜服务

Unit Eighteen　Service During the Meal
单元 18　上菜服务与席间服务

Unit Nineteen　Setting Accounts
单元 19　结账

Service Position 服务岗位

Restaurant is responsible for all the food and beverage that are prepared and served in the hotel. It operates, manages, and controls any food and beverage outlets in the hotel, as well as maintains safe handling, storing, preparation, and serving of food and beverage.

Restaurant is one of the most characteristic departments in the hotel. Its working efficiency and service standard reflect the overall management of the hotel. Its service quality makes great effect on the hotel's reputation.

 Skills and Attainments 服务技能与素养

At the reservation desk, the clerks should receive calls, give information about the restaurant, confirm reservations and make a list of reservation according to the guest's arrival date and time.

The restaurant receptionist mostly stands near the door of the restaurant. He is often responsible for providing seats for the guest and directing him to the seat. In some cases, the receptionist also deals with disputes before and after the meal and greets the guest when he leaves.

During the meal, the waiter is responsible for serving the guest, such as taking the order from the guest, introducing food and beverages, handling disputes during the meal, and accepting the guest's payment.

On one hand, the clerks of the restaurant should know everything about the features of their own restaurant; on the other hand, they must behave politely when serving the guest. Therefore, everyone of the restaurant must learn some etiquette and culture of different countries, especially restaurant etiquette and culture, to avoid offending the guest from all over the world.

Key Words and Expressions

beverage (*n.*)	饮料
reservation clerk	预订员
restaurant receptionist	迎宾员
waiter, waitress	服务员,侍应生
take the order	点菜
dispute (*n.*)	争论
payment (*n.*)	支付
feature (*n.*)	特色,特点
etiquette (*n.*)	礼仪

Unit Fifteen Table Reservation

单元 15 餐厅预订

Procedure of Service 服务流程

- Answer the phone from the guest.
- Check whether reservation is accepted.
- Ask for the guest's individual information.
- Confirm reservation.
- Greet the guest.

Points of Service Language 服务语言要点

1. **Checking whether reservation is accepted** 查看是否可以接受预订

    Just a moment, please. I'll check the availability for you. /Let me check if we have any vacancy.

    请稍候,我来为您查查是否有空位。

    I'm afraid we're fully booked for that time.

    恐怕那个时间的餐位都已经订满了。

    It's the busy time/hot time/peak time, you know.

    您知道,那是在高峰期。

    We hope we'll have another opportunity to serve you.

    我们期待下次能为您效劳。

2. **Individual reservation** 个人预订

    At what time can we expect you?

    您几点光临呢?

    Would you like a table in the hall or in a private room?

    您是喜欢大厅的餐台还是包间呢?

    We can only keep your table/room till …(certain cut-off time)

    我们只能保留您的餐位/包间到……(某个截止时间)

A deposit of 20 US dollars is required to secure your booking.

为了确保您的预订,您需要交 20 美元押金。

3. **Party reservation** 宴会预订

How many tables shall we arrange?

请问我们应该安排多少张桌子呢?

How much would you like to spend for each table?

请问每张桌子的费用标准是多少?

What kinds of fruit/desert/drinks would you like?

您想要什么水果/甜品/酒水呢?

How would you like us to arrange the tables?

您想要怎样摆放桌子呢?

We'll get everything ready in advance.

我们会准备好一切。

Reserving a Table on Valentine's Day

C:Reservation Clerk

G:Guest

15-29 Reserving a Table on Valentine's Day. mp3

C:Good afternoon, Swan Restaurant. May I help you?

G:I'd like to reserve a table for dinner on Valentine's Day, please.

C:Certainly, sir. For how many people, please?

G:Two, my wife and me.

C:At what time can we expect you, sir?

G:Around 8:00 p.m.

C:I see. Would you like a table in the main restaurant or in a private room, sir?

G:A private room, please.

C:Certainly, sir. We'll have Rose Hall reserved for you, will that be all right? May I have your name and telephone number, please?

G:Sure, it's Stevens, and my cellphone number is 139****5167.

C:Mr. Stevens, 139****5167. Thank you. By the way, we can only keep your room till 9:00 p.m., since it's the peak season now.

G: OK, I see.

C: I'd like to confirm your reservation: Rose Hall for Mr. Stevens on Valentine's Day; arrival time, around 8:00 p.m.; cell phone number, 139****5167. Is that correct?

G: Exactly, thank you.

C: We look forward to serving you, Mr. Stevens. Thanks for calling.

Practice Answer the questions according to the service conversation.

1. When will the guest come to the restaurant?
2. What kind of table does the guest reserve?
3. What should the clerk do after receiving the guest's information?

Book a Table by the Window

: Reservation Clerk

: Mike (guest)

15-30 Book a Table by the Window. mp3

C: This is the Oriental Chinese Restaurant. Good afternoon!

M: Hello, I'd like to reserve a table for two.

C: Yes, sir. When would you like to have the table?

M: Let me see…at about 7:00, no, perhaps around 7:30 p.m.

C: Where do you want the table, on the first or the second floor?

M: Can we have a table on the second floor?

C: Yes, sir. You would like to reserve a table for two at about 7:30 p.m. on the second floor, is that all right, sir?

M: Yes, that's right.

C: May I have your name, please?

M: Jones, Mike Jones.

C: Thank you, Mr. Jones.

M: Oh, by the way, is there any chance of a table by the window? My wife loves it.

C: I understand that, sir, but, as you know, we have already received many bookings, so I'll have to check first. I cannot guarantee anything, but please be assured that we'll try our best.

M: I would appreciate it if it could be arranged.

C: I'll do my best. We're looking forward to having you with us tonight, Mr. Jones. Thank you for calling us.

M: Thank you. By the way, how late does your restaurant stay open?

C: We normally close at 11:00 p.m., but usually we will wait until the last guest leaves.

M: Fine, thanks.

C: You're welcome.

Practice Answer the questions according to the service conversation.

1. How many people will go to the restaurant?
2. What special demand does the guest have?
3. Does the clerk guarantee the guest's special demand? Why?

Key Words and Expressions

Valentine's Day	情人节
private room	包间
peak time	高峰期

Points of Service Performance 服务演练要点

- When the guest makes a reservation, we should ask for the guest's basic information, such as name, room number, expected number of persons, dinner time and telephone number, etc.

  客人预订座位时,应详细询问客人的姓名、房号、预订人数、用餐时间以及电话号码等基本信息。

- When the guest makes a party reservation, we should ask for the banquet menu, budget, seating request, special demand and terms of payment besides the guest's basic information.

  客人进行宴会预订时,除了询问客人的基本信息之外,还应详细询问客人预订的菜式、预算、座位安排要求和特别要求,以及客人的付款方式。

Performance for Service 模拟演练

Task A

Perform a conversation about restaurant reservation according to the following cards.

Chapter Seven Restaurant Service
餐厅服务

Guest Card	Guest name:	Tommy Jones
	Arrival date:	August 15
	Table type required:	table of 4 people
	Persons:	a couple and their child
	Way of reservation:	telephone
	Special request:	a birthday cake for the child
	Telephone number:	159****9026

Reservation Clerk Card	Guest name
	Arrival date
	Table type required
	Persons
	Way of reservation
	Special request
	Telephone number
	Express the wishes

Task B

Mr. Williams of ABC Company wants to book twenty tables, totally 200 persons at Rainbow Restaurant on Friday, June 1 from 7 to 10 p.m. His company will hold an evening party at that time. Discuss with partners about the details of the reservation and try to fill in the form below according to the above information.

BANQUET RESERVATION RECORD

BANQUET NAME: _____
GUEST NAME: _____   TELEPHONE NO. _____
COMPANY NAME: _____
BANQUET DATE: _____
TIME: FROM _____ TO _____
BANQUET BUDGET: RMB _____ /TABLE
NUMBER OF PERSONS: _____   NUMBER OF TABLES: _____
SEATING REQUEST: _____
TERMS OF PAYMENT: _____ (CREDIT CARD, CASH, CHECK)
BANQUET MENU: _____
_____
_____

续表

```
DRINKS: _____
DESERT: _____
FRUIT: _____
SPECIAL DEMAND: _____
             _____
DEPOSIT: RMB _____  CLERK SIGNATURE: _____
RESERVATION DATE: _____ (YYYY) _____ (MM) _____ (DD)
```

Position Knowledge 岗位知识

- If the restaurant has extra requirements, such as the room charge or minimum charge, you should make it clear in advance to the guest who makes the reservation of a private room or a banquet.
  如果餐厅有像包间费和最低消费限制这样的额外要求,要事先给预订包间或宴会的客人解释清楚。

- Four different ways of reserving table:
  四种不同的订餐方式:
  Face-to-face Reservation　面对面预订　　Telephone Reservation　电话预订
  Fax Reservation　传真预订　　　　　　　Internet Reservation　网上预订

- No matter in which kind of way the reservation is made by the guest, you should make clear the following information: the name of the guest who makes the reservation, his phone number, the time of arrival and the number of the guests.
  无论客人使用哪一种预订,都要弄清楚下列信息:预订人姓名、电话号码、客人抵达餐厅的时间和用餐人数。

- Some useful expressions in a restaurant:
  餐厅常用术语:
  host　男领位员　　　　　　　　　　hostess　女领位员
  waiter　男侍应生　　　　　　　　　waitress　女侍应生

Exercises

I. Topics for discussion.

1. What information is necessary when reserving a table in restaurant?
2. What should a reservation clerk do when the guest's special demand can not be satisfied?

Chapter Seven Restaurant Service
餐厅服务

Ⅱ. Read the following passage and answer the questions.

C: Clerk of Reservation Department of the Triumph Restaurant

G: Guest

Part 1 Making a banquet reservation

C: Triumph Restaurant reservations. What can I do for you?

G: I'm calling from Lenovo Company. I'm calling to enquire about holding a charity party in your hotel.

C: I'm glad to help you. For how many people, sir?

G: A party of 300. And there will be 50 attendees (与会者) coming from overseas. We need suites as well as a big conference hall.

15-30-x1 Making a banquet reservation. mp3

C: When will the event be held?

G: November 18th.

C: Let me check, please...Sorry to have kept you waiting, sir. We do have available suites and a conference hall at that time.

G: That's good. Our attendees are all famous people. Is it possible that they each can have a suite?

C: Don't worry, sir. Since ours is an all-suite convention center, every attendee is offered a suite and therefore receives VIP treatment.

G: I like that very much. Then what is the rate?

C: We offer rates competitive with standard hotel rooms, 1,230 RMB per person per day, an equivalent to 180 US dollars. Besides, we also offer complimentary "perks (额外补贴)", including breakfast and coffee hours. The conference hall is 10,000 RMB per night.

G: Great. It sounds reasonable.

C: Exactly, sir. If you are really interested in our hotel, I'll send you a reservation form and a prospectus about our meeting facilities.

G: That's very kind of you. Can you send them by fax?

C: Yes, sir. May I have your name and your fax number?

G: Ding Yi. D-I-N-G, Y-I. My fax number is 01086****52.

C: Mr. Ding, your fax number is 01086****52. Yes, I'll make it right away, Mr. Ding.

G: Thank you very much. Goodbye.

C: Goodbye, Mr. Ding. Thanks for calling.

Questions:

1. What does Lenovo Company want to reserve at the Triumph Restaurant?
2. What are perks at the Triumph Restaurant?
3. What is the rate of conference hall?

113

Part 2　Discussing details of the banquet

G: I've already informed you that we'd like to use conference hall tomorrow evening, but I'd like to check the details.

C: Well, your banquet dinner starts at 7:00 p.m. Could I get your menu choice to start with?

G: We'd like the routine entree（主菜）and chef's choice for the banquet.

15-30-x2　Discussing details of the banquet. mp3

C: How would you want the banquet to be served?

G: French service. Do you offer electronic pour（自动计量斟酒）?

C: Sorry, but we don't have enough electronic pours to go around for 100 guests. What about free pour（无计量斟酒）? In fact, that will make the banquet more lively.

G: Fine. Can your crew set up the banquet furniture before 6:30?

C: Sure. Our workmen（会议服务勤杂工）will take care of it.

G: What is the minimum you charge for each attendee?

C: 400 RMB per person, premium brands（名牌饮品）excluded.

G: How are call brands（指定品牌饮品）charged?

C: Usually by the bottle（按瓶计价）, but we can also charge by the drink if you like.

G: I prefer the latter. Is there any service charge for it?

C: Yes. There will also be other charges, such as corkage（开瓶费）if drinks are brought from outside.

G: Well, in that case, house brands would be fine.

C: I think that can be arranged, sir. Now we haven't discussed table decorations yet.

G: I think it would be appropriate to have the flags of the participating countries on the table and some flowers.

C: What kind of flowers will there be?

G: Perhaps pink carnations（康乃馨）would be a neutral color.

C: Will you be requiring any background music at all?

G: I guess not. Tastes are different, you know.

C: I understand. Well, we've covered all the points, haven't we?

G: Yes. By the way, put the charges on the master account.

Questions:

1. What is Lenovo Company's menu choice?
2. What kind of service does Lenovo Company want the banquet to be served?
3. What is the minimum charge for each attendee?
4. Does Lenovo Company require background music? Why?

Unit Sixteen Greeting the Guests
单元 16 餐厅迎客服务

Procedure of Service 服务流程

- Welcome the guest.
- Ask whether there is a reservation.
- If there is a reservation, direct the guest to the table.
- If there is no reservation, ask for the number of the guests and then direct them to a table.
- If there is no vacant table, apologize to the guest and tell him that he has to wait a moment.

Points of Service Language 服务语言要点

1. **Welcoming the guest who has no reservation**　迎接没有预约的客人

    How many persons, please?
    总共几位?
    Where would you prefer to sit?
    您喜欢坐在哪里?
    I'll show you to your table.
    我来为您领位。
    Is this table fine?/How about this table?
    这张桌子怎么样?/可以吗?
    A waiter/waitress will come soon to take your order.
    服务员很快就会来为您写菜单。
    Do you have a meal voucher/breakfast voucher?
    您有餐券/早餐券吗?

2. **Welcoming the guest who has the reservation**　迎接有预约的客人

    Do you have a reservation?
    请问您有预约吗?
    We were expecting you.

我们正在恭候您的光临。

I'm afraid the table you reserved is not ready yet.

恐怕您预订的餐桌还没有准备好。

I'm afraid that we let another guest sit at your table since you did not arrive at the reserved time.

因为您没有按照预订的时间来，所以我们将座位安排给另一位客人了。

Would you mind waiting until it is free or would you prefer another table?

您介意等一会儿吗？或者您去另一张桌子，好吗？

3. Keeping the guest waiting for a while 请客人稍候

We can seat you very soon.

我们很快就安排您入座。

Could you wait in line until a table is free, please?

请您排队等候空位，好吗？

I'm afraid this table is reserved for 7:00 p.m.

恐怕这张桌子已经有人预订7点了。

4. Arranging the table for the guest 餐桌安排

I'm afraid we cannot seat you at the same table.

恐怕没办法让你们坐同一张桌子。

Would you mind sitting separately?

你们介意分开坐吗？

Would you like a high chair for your child?

要不要给您的孩子拿一把高椅呢？

Would you mind sharing a table?

您介意拼桌/和他人同桌吗？

Some other guests wish to join this table.

别的客人想跟您共享这张桌子。

Another guest wishes to sit at the counter. Could you move down one seat, please?

另一位客人想坐在柜台边。您可以挪过去一点吗？

Service Conversation 31

Arranging One Table for the Non-reserved Guest

16-31 Arranging One Table for the Non-reserved Guest. mp3

H: Hostess

G: Guest

H: Good evening, sir. Welcome to Sunshine Restaurant. How many people, please?

G: A table for two, please.

H: Certainly, sir. How about that table by the window? You may enjoy the beautiful setting sun view out of the window.

G: Fine. Thanks.

H: This way, please.

> Practice Answer the questions according to the service conversation.

1. What kind of the table does the guest require?
2. What should we do when the guest has no reservation?

Service Conversation 32

Arranging One Table for the Reserved Guest

H: Hostess

M: Mike Jones

H: Good evening. Welcome to our restaurant.

M: Good evening. My name is Mike Jones. We've reserved a table for two this evening.

H: Please wait a moment, sir. (*Two minutes later*) We have your reservation, Mr. Jones. This way, please. (*Leading them to a table by the window*)

16-32 Arranging One Table for the Reserved Guest. mp3

> Practice Answer the questions according to the service conversation.

1. What is the name of the guest?
2. What should we do when the guest has a reservation?

Points of Service Performance 服务演练要点

- When directing the guest, the receptionist should ask the guest whether there is reservation and the number of persons firstly.

  为客人引座时，迎宾员应先询问客人数量及是否有预订座位等。

- When there is no vacancy, we should ask the guest in English: "Would you mind

sharing a table with others?"
若餐厅客满,不得不让客人共用餐桌时,应询问客人:"您介意与别人共用桌子吗?"
- When there is no vacancy and we have to keep the guest waiting, we can say:"I'm afraid all our tables are taken." or "Would you mind waiting?"
若因客满而不得不让客人等待时,可以说:"恐怕我们已客满。"或者是"你介意等一会儿吗?"

Performance for Service 模拟演练

Task A

Performance in pairs about greeting the guest according to the following two cards.

Guest Card	Guest name:	Mike Lee
	Persons:	2 (One will come later)
	Reservation:	no
	Table request:	a table by the window facing the sun-set
	Special demand:	playing the violin during the dinner

Restaurant Clerk Card	Greet the guest and ask whether there is a reservation
	Name of the guest
	Number of persons
	Ask whether there is special table request
	Show the way to the table
	Ask whether there is any other special demand

Task B

Mr. Johnson comes to Beijing Snacks Restaurant in the evening. But there is no vacancy at that time. A hostess advises him to share a table with others. Perform a conversation in pairs according to the above information.

Position Knowledge 岗位知识

When the guest comes into the restaurant, the waiter should greet the guest, pull the chair out for the guest, unfold napkins and put them on the guest's laps.
客人来到餐厅时,侍应生应问候客人,为客人拉椅、让座,打开餐巾放在客人膝盖上。

Topics for discussion.

1. How to serve the guest who has reserved a table?
2. How should we deal with it when there is no vacancy in the restaurant?

 Taking Orders

Procedure of Service 服务流程

- Show the menu to the guest (*a few minutes later*).
- Take the guest's order.
- Introduce food and beverage.
- Confirm the order.

Points of Service Language 服务语言要点

1. Introducing food to the guest 介绍菜式

Would you like to have table d'hote or a la carte?
您是选择套餐还是单点呢?
We have both buffet-style and a la carte dishes, which would you prefer?
我们有自助餐和点菜式,您喜欢哪一种呢?
What is today's special?
今天的特价菜是什么?
We serve Cantonese, Sichuan, Shanghai and Beijing cuisine, which cuisine would you prefer?
我们有粤菜、川菜、沪菜和京菜,您喜欢哪一种呢?
Generally speaking, Cantonese cuisine is light and clear; Sichuan cuisine is strong and hot; Shanghai cuisine is oily and Beijing cuisine is spicy and a bit salty.
一般来说,粤菜比较清淡,川菜浓烈而辛辣,沪菜比较油,而京菜香而且有点咸。
It's crisp/tasty/tender/clear/strong/spicy/aromatic.
它很酥脆/可口/鲜嫩/清淡/浓烈/辛辣/香味扑鼻。
Which brand of milk/beer/cigarettes/wine/…would you prefer?
您喜欢什么牌子的牛奶/啤酒/香烟/葡萄酒……
I'm afraid …is not on our menu.

恐怕我们的菜单上没有……这道菜。

2. Confirming the details of the order   确认细节

Would you like to put it on your hotel bill?

是不是把费用记到您酒店的账上？

How would you like your egg/coffee/steak?

您要我们怎样做您点的鸡蛋/咖啡/牛排？

Would you like your fried eggs sunny-side up?

您点的煎蛋是不是只煎一面，蛋黄朝上？

Would you like your beer draught or bottled?

您喜欢扎啤还是瓶啤？

With ice or without ice, sir?

先生，请问加冰还是不加冰？

Service Conversation 33

Can You Recommend Some Chinese Food

W: Waitress

G: Guest

17 - 33　Can You Recommend Some Chinese Food. mp3

W: May I take your order now, sir?

G: Ur...I don't know much about Chinese food, can you recommend something?

W: Certainly. How about Cabbage in Oyster Sauce? It's tender and tasty.

G: Good, I'll take it. What's the Corn Soup with Minced Chicken like?

W: It's soup with corn and minced chicken. It's sweet and delicious.

G: Well, I'll take this, too.

W: Anything else, sir?

G: No, thanks. That's all.

W: Shall I bring you a knife and fork?

G: No, thanks. The chopsticks will do.

Practice　Answer the questions according to the service conversation.

1. What does the waitress recommend to the guest?

2. How does the Cabbage in Oyster Sauce taste like?

3. Does the guest want a knife and fork?

Service Conversation 34

The Chinese Cuisine Is Divided into Eight Styles

W: Waiter

M: Mike Jones

L: Linda Jones

17-34 The Chinese Cuisine Is Divided into Eight Styles. mp3

W: (*Bringing a menu to them*) Here is the menu. (*A few minutes later*) Excuse me, Mr. and Mrs. Jones, are you ready to order?

M: Yes, we are. But there are so many things on the menu and they all look good. You know, it's our first time in China, and we know so little about Chinese food, could you recommend something?

W: My pleasure, Mr. Jones. Let me introduce Chinese food in general. Chinese food is divided into eight styles of cuisine. They are Cantonese style, Shandong style, Sichuan style, etc. Their flavors are different. Some are light, like Cantonese style; some are spicy and hot, like Sichuan style.

M: Then what hot food would you like to recommend?

W: I think Kongpao chicken is quite special. Oh, yes, our chef recommends broccoli with crabmeat sauce for today, but it may not be as hot as you expect. The broccoli is a local vegetable, very delicious and a little bit different from yours. It's worth a try, I think.

M: All right, we'll try it then.

W: Would you like some drinks?

L: We want to try some Chinese beer. Have you got Tsingtao beer here?

W: Yes, we have. Would you like the beer to be served first or with the meal?

M: With the meal, please.

W: All right, Mr. Jones. You've ordered Kongpao chicken, broccoli with crabmeat sauce, and beer served with the meal.

M: Yes, exactly.

W: Your order will be ready in five minutes.

Chapter Seven Restaurant Service
餐厅服务

Practice Answer the questions according to the service conversation.

1. What does the waitress introduce to the guest about the Chinese food?
2. Which cuisine tastes spicy and hot?
3. Would the guest like the beer to be served first or with the dishes?

cuisine (*n.*)	烹饪方法；菜系
Cantonese (*adj.*)	广东的
light (*adj.*)	清淡的
spicy and hot (*adj.*)	辛辣的

Notes

1. Cabbage in Oyster Sauce　蚝油生菜
2. Corn Soup with Minced Chicken　鸡茸玉米汤
3. Kongpao Chicken　宫保鸡丁
4. Broccoli with Crabmeat Sauce　蟹粉椰菜

Points of Service Performance 服务演练要点

- Table d'hote is used in the western restaurant to indicate a menu where multi-course meals with limited choices are charged at a fixed price.
  套餐常见于西餐厅，指的是餐厅以固定的价格在一定的范围内搭配的菜式，一般客人只能选择主菜肉类。
- A la carte may refer to a menu of items priced and ordered separately rather than selected from a list of preset multi-course meals at fixed prices.
  零点餐指的是独立设置的菜式和价格，客人可以任意选择搭配的点菜方式。

Performance for Service 模拟演练

Task A

Mr. Hoover and his family want to try Chinese hot-pot. A waitress introduces three kinds of hot-pot to them. Perform in pairs about taking the order according to the following two cards.

Guest Card	Want to know the Chinese hot-pot Choose Sichuan-style hot-pot Drinks：　　　cold beer Special demand：not too spicy and hot

Waiter Card

Introduce three styles of hot-pot:

  Mutton-style: tastes mild, the main ingredients are prime mutton, bean curd（豆腐）, sesame pancakes（芝麻烧饼）and Chinese cabbages

  Sichuan-style: tastes very spicy and hot; the main ingredients include chicken breast（鸡胸）, beef tripe（牛肚）, goose intestines（鹅肠）and mushrooms（蘑菇）

  Cantonese-style: tastes sweeter and features the seafood ingredients, such as fresh shrimps（虾）, scallops（扇贝）, crab meat（蟹肉）and squid（鱿鱼）

Ask which one to choose

Drinks

The guest's special demand

Task B

Mr. Tom Smith and his girl friend Mary are sitting in a Chinese restaurant. They want to try some Chinese breakfast but they don't know how to choose. The waiter Zhang Ming introduces some Beijing specialties to them and recommends eight treasure porridge（八宝粥）and spring pancake（春饼）. The guests agree with him and order salted or pickled vegetables（榨菜）with the porridge.

Position Knowledge 岗位知识

- The waiter should introduce the House Specialty and Today's Special to the guest.
  点菜时餐厅侍者应给客人介绍一些招牌菜或者当日有特价的菜式。
- The different time for cooking steak:
  牛排的成熟度：
  well-done　全熟　　　medium-well　七成熟
  medium　五成熟　　　rare　三成熟
- The order of serving west food:
  西餐的上菜顺序：
  appetizer(开胃菜)—soup(汤)—salad(沙拉)—main course(主菜)—dessert(甜点)
- The order of serving Chinese food:
  中餐的上菜顺序：
  cold dishes(冷盘)—beverage and wine(饮料和酒)—hot dishes(热菜)—soup(汤)—rice or noodles(主食)—fruits and dessert(水果和甜品)
- The eight cuisines in Chinese food:
  中国菜的八大菜系：

Sichuan Cuisine	四川菜,简称川菜	Shandong Cuisine	山东菜,简称鲁菜
Cantonese Cuisine	广东菜,简称粤菜	Jiangsu Cuisine	江苏菜,简称苏菜
Fujian Cuisine	福建菜,简称闽菜	Hu'nan Cuisine	湖南菜,简称湘菜
Anhui Cuisine	安徽菜,简称徽菜	Zhejiang Cuisine	浙江菜,简称浙菜

Exercises

Ⅰ. Fill in the blanks.

W: Waiter

G: Guest

W: _____1_____ ?

G: For an appetizer, Smoked Salmon.

W: _____2_____ ?

G: Two T-bone steak and a Rump Steak.

W: _____3_____ ?

G: Medium-rare. And we'd like three large Salad and three Hamburgers.

W: Would you like some vegetables?

G: The curry vegetables.

W: _____4_____ ?

G: Fish soup, French Style.

W: Anything for dessert?

G: Vanilla ice cream for all.

W: _____5_____ ?

G: No, I'm afraid that's all.

Ⅱ. Translate the following sentences into Chinese.

1. Which flavor would you prefer, sweet or chili?
2. Generally speaking, Cantonese cuisine is light and clear; Sichuan cuisine is strong and hot; Shanghai cuisine is oily and Beijing cuisine is spicy and a bit salty.
3. It looks good, smells good and tastes good.

Unit Eighteen Service During the Meal

单元 18 上菜服务与席间服务

Procedure of Service 服务流程

- Serve the dishes and drinks one by one.
- Take empty plates away.
- Change the plates for the guests.
- Serve the fruits and dessert.

Points of Service Language   服务语言要点

Serve the guests during the meal   客人用餐服务

The Chinese way is to serve the food first and then the soup; if you like, we'll bring you the soup first.
按中国的方式,是先上菜再上汤;如果您喜欢,我们可以先上汤再上菜。

Shall I change this plate with a smaller one?
我把这个换成小一点的盘子,好吗?

I'm afraid we don't accept tips. It's against our regulations. Thank you all the same.
我们不收小费。收小费是违反规定的。但还是一样谢谢您。

It's complimentary. / That would be on the house.
这是免费奉送的。

Service Conversation 35

Serving the Guest During the Meal

W: Waitress
G: Guest

W: Your steak, salad and red wine, sir. Please enjoy.

W: Excuse me, may I take your plate?

G: Sure, go ahead.

W: May I show you the dessert menu?

G: OK.

W: Here you are.

G: I'd like to have a chocolate pudding.

W: Your chocolate pudding, sir. Shall I bring your coffee now, or later?

G: Later, thank you.

G: May I have the bill? And the coffee, please.

W: Certainly, sir. (*After a while*) Here is your coffee. How is everything?

G: Fine, thank you.

18-35 Serving the Guest During the Meal. mp3

Points of Service Performance 服务演练要点

If making mistakes when serving the dinner, we should make an apology to the guest immediately and find practicable solutions.

服务中如发生错误,要立即向客人道歉并寻找可行的解决办法。

Performance for Service 模拟演练

Task

Perform a conversation in pairs according to the following information. Mike and Carol are having dinner at a restaurant. A waitress Lily is serving them. After the dinner, Mike wants to give Lily some money as tips, but Lily refuses it and explains that there is the regulation not to accept tips of the guest.

Exercises

Translate the following sentences into English.

1. 我现在可以上菜了吗?
2. 我可以把这个盘子移到一边去吗?
3. 我可以撤掉这个碟子了吗?
4. 对不起,先生,我好像上错了一道菜。

127

Unit Nineteen Setting Accounts

单元⑲ 结账

Procedure of Service 服务流程

- Ask the guest whether there is anything else to need.
- Give the guest the bill.
- Answer questions or explain uncertainty about the bill.
- Ask the guest the way of payment.
- Give the guest the receipt and meal voucher if possible.
- Thank the guest for coming.

Points of Service Language 服务语言要点

1. **Paying the bill** 结账

   Can I pay here?
   可以在这儿付账吗?
   One bill, or separate bills?
   是合单还是分开付账?
   I think there is a mistake in the bill.
   账单有一处错误。
   Can I pay with this credit card?
   可以用这张信用卡付账吗?
   May I have the receipt, please?
   能给我收据吗?

2. **Thanking the guest** 对客人表示感谢

   Hope to see you again soon!
   希望不久再见到您!
   Please don't leave anything behind.
   请不要遗忘您的东西。

Mind (or watch) your step!
请走好!
Thank you for coming.
谢谢您的光临。
Glad to be of service.
很高兴为您服务。
At your service.
乐意为您效劳。

Service Conversation 36

I Forgot to Bring My Wallet with Me

19-36 I Forgot to Bring My Wallet with Me.mp3

G: Guest
W: Waitress

G: I did enjoy the dinner today. Now, will you please give me the bill?
W: Sure, sir. Will you pay by credit card or in cash?
G: I'd like to pay with Master Card.
W: One moment, please.
   (*Serves a new cup of tea*)
W: Have some hot tea. I'll go to the cashier and bring you the bill.
   (*3 minutes later*)
W: Sorry to keep you waiting. Here's the bill, sir.
G: How much?
W: Your bill totals 220 yuan. Please check it.
   (*The guest goes over the bill carefully.*)
G: All in Chinese. I can't understand it at all. What is the 20 yuan for?
W: It's a 10% service charge. You see, the 170 yuan is for the meal, and the 30 is for the beverage.
G: I see. How much is the total in US dollars?
W: Let me count …It comes to about 32 dollars and 40 cents at today's exchange rate.
G: OK. Ouch, I forgot to bring my wallet with me. What should I do?
W: Are you staying in our hotel?
G: Yes, I'm in Room 513.
W: In that case, did you bring the room card with you?

G: Yes. Here you are.

W: That's all right. You only need to sign your name at the bottom of the bill and settle it when you check out.

G: So nice. Thank you very much.

W: Not at all. Have a nice day.

Practice Answer the questions according to the service conversation.

1. How does the guest pay the bill?
2. What is the 20 yuan for in the bill?
3. How many ways can be used as payment for the guest?
4. What does the waitress serve when the guest is waiting for his bill?

Service Conversation 37 — Do You Accept Credit Cards

19-37 Do You Accept Credit Cards. mp3

W: Waiter
L: Linda Jones

W: How is everything?

L: It's very delicious. Thank you.

W: Would you like something else?

L: Yes, you see the dumplings the girl is eating over there? Would you please pack half a kilo for us?

W: Yes, of course. Anything else?

L: That's all, thank you. Just the bill, please.

W: (*Having brought the bill*) Here is your bill, ma'am. It totals 268 yuan.

L: How much is that in US dollars?

W: One moment, please. Let me calculate it for you. It's about 39 dollars and 40 cents according to today's exchange rate.

L: (*After seeing the bill*) I am afraid I don't have enough cash with me. Do you accept credit cards?

W: Yes, ma'am.

L: Here's my Visa Card.

W: Could I take a print of your card?

Chapter Seven Restaurant Service
餐厅服务

L: Sure.

W: Thanks.

(*A few minutes later, the waiter comes back with the card.*)

W: I'm sorry to have kept you waiting, ma'am. Here is your card. Could you please sign your name on this print?

L: Sure. (*Linda signs her name and returns the print.*)

W: Thank you. I hope you two have a wonderful evening.

Practice Answer the questions according to the service conversation.

1. What does Linda order before she pays the bill?
2. How much is the bill in RMB and US dollars?
3. What should the waiter do when the guest wants to pay the bill with credit card?

Key Words and Expressions

credit card	信用卡
cash (*n.*)	现金
Master Card	万事达卡(信用卡的一种)
cashier (*n.*)	付款台
service charge	服务费
dumpling (*n.*)	饺子
pack (*v.*)	打包
kilo (*n.*)	千克
Visa Card	维萨信用卡(信用卡的一种)
print (*n.*)	信用卡对账单

Points of Service Performance 服务演练要点

- When checking the bill, the waiter should ask the guest the way of paying bill, for example, "One bill, or separate bills"?
  付账时,侍者应询问客人付账的方式,如"是分单还是合单结账"?

- After the guest pays the bill, the waiter should thank the guest's coming and give him the best wishes.
  客人付账后,侍者应对客人的光临表示感谢并祝福客人。

Performance for Service 模拟演练

Task A

Performance in pairs about paying the dinner according to the following two cards.

Guest Card	Call the waiter Ask the waiter for packing the dishes left over Require to pay the bill Check the bill Pay the bill in cash
Waiter Card	Ask whether there are any other orders Pack the dishes left over with suitable containers Show the bill to the guest Ask the way of payment Give the invoice to the guest Express the wishes

Task B

Jerry and Lily are having dinner at restaurant. They almost finish the meal. But they don't know how to pay the bill by visa and they are not familiar with exchange rate between RMB and US dollars. Besides, they have questions about charge of private room. They are asking about these questions with a waitress. The waitress answers their questions one by one. Make a conversation with your partners according to the above information.

 Position Knowledge 岗位知识

- The waiter in restaurant should be familiar with the exchange rate between different currencies and also know how to pay the bill in different ways.
  餐厅侍者应熟悉各种货币之间的兑换率,以及如何以不同的方式付账。
- The waiter should give the guest invoices voluntarily after the guest pays the bill.
  餐厅侍者应在客人付账后自觉向客人提供发票。

Ⅰ. Fill in the blanks.

A: Waiter.

B: Yes. What can I do for you, sir?

A: I'm afraid _____1_____, but you gave me the ice cream.

B: I'm sorry, sir. _____2_____. I do apologize for that.

A: That's all right. Would you please bring me the cheesecake?

B: _____3_____. We have no offer of any cakes today.

A: No cakes? _____4_____?

B: Because our baker slipped from a ladder and has broken his arms.

A: I'm sorry to hear that. Hope he will be better soon.

B: _____5_____?

A: Just bring me a cup of coffee and the bill, please.

II. Translate the following sentences into English.

1. 可以在这儿付账吗?
2. 感谢您的光临。
3. 账单有一些错误。
4. 可以用这张信用卡付账吗?
5. 请给我收据。

III. Translate the following sentences into Chinese.

1. Is there any chance of a table by the garden?
2. —Would you like the Champagne to be served first or with the main course?
   —First, please.
3. I do apologize for bringing a wrong dish.
4. It totals 220 yuan, including 10% service charge.
5. One bill, or separate bills?

Chapter Eight　Bar Service
酒吧服务

Unit Twenty　General Service
单元 20　常规服务

Unit Twenty-one　Dealing with Complaints and a Drunken Guest
单元 21　处理投诉和醉酒客人

Service Position 服务岗位

The Bar is a cozy place in the hotel which is mainly responsible for selling alcohols or drinks while providing quality service. In addition to the provision of drinks and snacks, music and art performance are also common factors in the bar. Based on different functions, a bar can be designed as the main bar, the lounge, the service bar or the banquet bar.

Excellent service in the bar not only represents its image, but also shows the level of management of the hotel. It can even become a source of attraction for the potential guests.

Skills and Attainments 服务技能与素养

A bar tender needs to complete the following main services in English: greeting the guests, taking orders and serving wines, asking for the guests' opinion, dealing with complaints, communicating with the guests, bringing the bill and saying goodbye to the guests.

A bar tender should cater to every guest with his smile and excellent service. To achieve that, one must equip himself with knowledge of the food and drinks provided by the bar, and always be ready to answer the guests' questions about them. In case of settling complaints, the bar tender must show his willingness and sincerity in helping the guests.

Key Words and Expressions

bar (*n.*)	酒吧
main bar	主酒吧
lounge (*n.*)	酒廊
service bar	服务酒吧
banquet bar	宴会吧
complaint (*n.*)	投诉
willingness (*n.*)	乐意
sincerity (*n.*)	真诚
cater to	向……提供

Unit Twenty General Service
单元 20 常规服务

Procedure of Service 服务流程

- Greet the guest and show the way.
- Take orders.
- Serve wine.
- Communicate with the guest.
- Ask for the guest's opinion.
- Bring the bill to the guest.
- Say goodbye to the guest.

Points of Service Language 服务语言要点

1. **Polite expressions 礼貌用语**

   Would you like a table for how many people?
   请问您需要几人桌？

   Just a moment please, I will arrange another table for you.
   请稍等，我会给您安排另外一个位置。

   I'm afraid there are no other places free at the moment. Would you mind waiting a while?
   现在恐怕没有空位，您介意稍等一下吗？

   Would you care to have a drink in the lounge while waiting?
   等待时您想在大厅先喝点饮料吗？

   Your order will be coming up immediately.

   They'll be ready in a minute.

   I'll be right back.
   请稍等，马上就来。

2. **Assisting the guest to take orders** 协助客人点单

What would you like, ladies and gentlemen?

Would you care for something to drink?

May I take your order?

Good evening, what is your pleasure, sir?

请问您想要点什么?

I would recommend …

我向您推荐……

3. **Confirm** 确认

You have ordered a sweet Martini cocktail and crisps, is that all?

您点了马蒂尼甜鸡尾酒和薯片,还需要其他的吗?

4. **Apologizing for mistakes** 为错误道歉

I'm deeply sorry, sir. There might be some mistakes. I'll have it changed at once.

非常抱歉,可能有一些错误,我马上换掉这张单子。

I'm really sorry for the mistakes. Would you mind looking at it again?

非常抱歉出这个错误。您介意再看一下吗?

Service Conversation 38

Serving Drinks

20-38 Serving Drinks. mp3

B: Bar tender

G: Guest A and Guest B

B: Good evening, sir, welcome to our bar!

G: Good evening.

B: Do you have a reservation?

G: Yes.

B: May I have your name?

G: Jordan White.

B: How many people are there in your party?

G: Two.

B: Would you prefer a smoking area or non-smoking?

G: A non-smoking area, please.

B: This way please. Mind your step.

Would you like to sit near the window or by the bar counter?

G: Near the window, I think.

B: Is this seat all right?

G: Sure, thank you very much!

B: My pleasure.

G: Could you recommend something to drink?

B: We have soft drinks, fresh juice, mineral water and alcohol. What kind would you like?

G: What kind of spirits do you have?

B: We have all kinds, from aperitifs to brandy.

G: Well, Irish whiskey I think.

B: Do you like it on the rocks or straight up?

G: Are there any other choices?

B: Some guests prefer to mix it with cola.

G: That sounds good. I'll try one like that.

B: Would you like a particular brand of cola?

G: Well, I think so. What about Pepsi?

B: That's fine. So an Irish whiskey with Pepsi?

G: Of course, thank you.

B: And you, sir?

G: I like to drink fresh juice, what kinds do you have?

B: We have orange, pineapple, grapefruit, mango, peach and tomato juice.

G: Give me a mango juice.

B: Yes, one moment, please.

G: Thank you.

B: Sorry to have kept you waiting. Here is your whiskey and mango juice. Would you like anything else?

G: No, thanks.

B: You're welcome. Enjoy your drink!

G: By the way, I am from Melbourne. This is my first time in Beijing. Could you tell me some places to have fun?

B: Certainly. I suggest you first visit some historic sites like the Forbidden City, the Summer Palace and the Temple of Heaven. They all represent the history of the city. If you're interested in seeing the modern side of the city, you could have a look at the central business district and do some pleasant shopping.

G: Fantastic. I think I really need to plan my trips in this large city. There are so many places to go. Thank you very much.

B: My pleasure.

G: The bill, please.

B: Yes, please wait a moment. Here's your bill, sir. It is 100 yuan.

B: How would you like to pay? We accept cash and credit card.

G: I'm staying here. Can I put it on my hotel bill?

B: Sure. May I have your room number?

G: Room 1012.

B: Room 1012. Could you sign your name here, please?

G: Sure.

B: Thank you. Have a good night.

Practice Answer the questions according to the service conversation.

1. What do the two guests order respectively?
2. What does one of the guests want to know from the bar tender?
3. How does the bar tender answer his inquiry?

Key Words and Expressions

non-smoking area	无烟区
mineral water	矿泉水
aperitif (*n.*)	开胃酒
brandy (*n.*)	白兰地
on the rock	加冰
straight up	不加冰
peculiar (*adj.*)	某一个

Points of Service Performance 服务演练要点

- When providing the bar service, use the polite language.
  对客服务中注意使用礼貌服务用语。
- After getting all the order information, be sure to confirm.
  在获取所有点单信息之后，一定要确认。
- When disagreement about the bill arises, the guest may ask you for the bill details. Be sure to clarify each item politely and patiently.
  当客人对账单有疑问时，会询问具体花费。一定要礼貌耐心地指明每项花费。
- Some guests prefer to pay cash while others may use credit card. There are also guests who hope to add the amount to the final room bill. If the bill will be paid together with the room bill, ask the guests to sign the bill and write down the room number.
  有些客人选择现金支付，有些选择使用信用卡。还有一些客人希望把账单加在房费中。如果客人选择最后与房费一起支付，让其在账单上签字并写下房间号。

Chapter Eight Bar Service
酒吧服务

Performance for Service 模拟演练

Task A

Practice in pairs according to the following two cards.

Guest Card		
	Seat type required:	non-smoking area by the bar counter
	Persons:	a couple
	Order:	drinks: whisky and soda (no ice); ginger ale snacks: peanuts and crisps
	Payment:	by credit card

Bar Tender Card	
	Greet the guest and show the way
	Take orders
	Serve wine
	Bring the bill to the guest
	Say goodbye to the guest

Task B

Mr. Green is sitting at the bar counter alone and Chen Lin develops a free conversation with him while serving him the wine. They talk about Beijing, and their hobbies. Chen Lin learns that the guest is on vacation here and recommends some famous tourism spots to the guest. Please form a dialogue with your partner according to the given information.

Position Knowledge 岗位知识

- Etiquette 礼仪
  - Etiquette in serving the wines:
    服务员为客人送酒时,应注意以下礼仪:
    The drinks should be served from the right side of the guest.
    服务员应将调制好的饮品用托盘从客人的右侧送上。
    Pay close attention to the designated service area, clean away the empty glasses and bottles on the table and empty the ashtray at appropriate time.
    服务员要巡视自己负责的服务区域,及时撤走桌上的空杯、空瓶,并按规定要求撤换烟灰缸。
    Introduce to the guest the promotions or special offers in the bar.
    适时地向客人介绍优惠和特价产品,以提高酒吧的营业收入。
    Handle all the devices gently. Keep the hands off the brims of any containers for sanitary reason.

在送酒服务过程中，服务员应注意轻拿轻放，手指不要触及杯口，处处显示礼貌卫生习惯。

◆ Etiquette in settling the bill：

服务员为客人结账时，应注意以下礼仪：

On settling the bill, the bar tender should double check the number of the table and the name/quantity/price of the drinks to confirm its correctness. On informing the guest of the bill, the bar tender should use polite language, for example："Your bill totals 200 yuan. Here is the change, thank you and look forward to serving you the next time."

为客人结账时，服务员要认真核对台号、酒水的品种、数量及金额是否准确。服务员要使用礼貌用语，如："一共是 200 元，这是找您的钱，谢谢您的惠顾，希望下次再为您服务。"

● Bar styles 星级饭店酒吧服务形式

In a five-star hotel, all the bars are in the charge of the Beverage Department, which is a division of the Food and Beverage Department. Based on their different styles, a bar can be called the Lobby Bar, the Lobby Lounge, Main Bar, Tea House/Lounge, Soda Bar, Banquet Bar or the Beer Garden in the open air in summer.

在星级饭店尤其是高星级饭店，一般都设有饮料部，它隶属于餐饮部，分管饭店内所有酒吧。这些酒吧风格形式不同，常见的类型有大堂吧、大堂酒廊、主酒吧、茶室或茶廊、餐厅酒吧（又称水吧）、宴会酒吧等。盛夏时节许多饭店会应时设立环境非常宽敞的露天酒吧，称为啤酒花园。

Exercises

Ⅰ. **Please speak out the English counterparts of the following words.**

1. 加冰块　　　　　糖水　　　　　　冰水　　　　　　软饮料
   餐后甜酒　　　　酒精　　　　　　汤力水　　　　　基酒
   开胃酒　　　　　甜食酒　　　　　利口酒　　　　　金酒
   伏特加　　　　　特基拉　　　　　朗姆酒　　　　　威士忌
   白兰地　　　　　啤酒　　　　　　比特苦酒　　　　鸡尾酒
   苏打水　　　　　姜啤酒

2. 瓶起子　　　　　香槟桶　　　　　酒钻　　　　　　吸管
   削冰器　　　　　调酒杯　　　　　制冰机　　　　　啤酒杯
   香槟杯　　　　　平底无脚酒杯　　葡萄酒杯　　　　高脚杯
   白兰地杯　　　　圆锥形酒杯

3. 樱桃　　　　草莓　　　　柠檬　　　　橄榄
   丁香　　　　薄荷　　　　菠萝　　　　西柚
   葡萄

Ⅱ. Translate the following sentences into English.

1. 您想坐在窗边还是挨着吧台？
2. 您想要瓶装啤酒还是扎啤？
3. 很乐意为您效劳。中国最畅销的是燕京啤酒，您想尝试一下吗？
4. 有鲜橙、菠萝、葡萄、芒果、桃和番茄口味的。
5. 请给我一杯冰镇啤酒。
6. 我们有从开胃酒到白兰地的所有品种。

Ⅲ. Read the following passage and answer the questions.

Bars are sometimes exempt from smoking bans that restaurants are subject to, even if those restaurants have liquor licenses. The distinction between a restaurant that serves liquor and a bar is usually made by the percentage of revenue（收入）earned from selling liquor. Historically, the western United States featured saloons. Many saloons survive in the western United States, though their services and features have changed with the times. Newer bars have been built in the saloon style to duplicate the feeling of the older saloons. In the UK bars are either areas that serve alcoholic drinks in the hotels, restaurants, universities, or are a particular type of place which serves alcoholic drinks such as wine bars, "style bars", private membership only bars. Some bars are similar to nightclubs in that they feature loud music, subdued（柔和的）lightening, or operate a dress code and admission policy.

Questions：

1. What's the distinction between a restaurant and a bar?
2. What's the origin of Saloon in the hotel?
3. What is "private membership only bar"?
4. What are the features of a bar similar to a nightclub?

Unit Twenty-one Dealing with Complaints and a Drunken Guest

单元 21 处理投诉和醉酒客人

Procedure of Service 服务流程

Dealing with complaints

- Listen to the guest patiently and show your sympathy towards his incident.
- Apologize for any inconvenience or delay caused by the hotel party.
- Search for the effective way to solve the problem.

Dealing with a drunken guest

- Interfere with the drunken guest at appropriate time.
- Provide the drunken guest with drinks that can relieve the alcoholic effect.
- Suggest resting back in the room or having a walk in the open air.

Points of Service Language 服务语言要点

1. **Expressing your willingness to solve the problem 表达积极解决问题的意愿**

    Thank you for telling us about it, sir. I'll look into the matter at once.
    感谢您为我们提供这些情况，我立即去了解。
    I'll speak to the person in charge and ask him to take care of the problem.
    我会对负责人员讲，让他来处理这件事。
    Please calm down, sir, I'll try to help you.
    先生请您冷静，我会尽力帮助您。
    Please relax, madam. I will take care of it according to your request.
    请放心，夫人。我将按您的要求办。

2. **Apologizing for mistakes 为错误致歉**

    Sorry, sir, I will solve the problem for you as soon as possible.
    对不起，先生，我会尽快为您解决这个问题。

I'm awfully sorry for my carelessness.
对于我的粗心我非常抱歉。

I Am Not Happy with the Steak

21 - 39 I Am Not Happy with the Steak. mp3

W：Waiter

G：Guest

W：Good evening, sir. What can I do for you?

G：I am not at all happy.

W：Perhaps you could tell me what the problem is.

G：It's the steak.

W：What's wrong with it, sir?

G：What I want is a medium-rare one, but this one is over-cooked. I think I told the waiter very clearly when I ordered.

W：I'm extremely sorry about it, sir. I'm sure the waiter didn't mean to make the mistake. Perhaps he didn't understand you correctly. I do apologize for it. I'll have the steak changed right away.

G：OK.

W：This is the medium-rare steak and a free salad. Enjoy your meal!

G：Thank you.

Practice Answer the questions according to the service conversation.

1. What does the guest complain about in the conversation?
2. How does the waiter deal with the complaint?

A Drunken Guest

21 - 40 A Drunken Guest. mp3

B：Bar tender

G：Guest

B: Good evening, ladies and gentlemen. Will this table do?

G: We want one far away from the band, the music is too loud.

B: Just a moment, please. I'll arrange another table for you.

G: This is much better.

B: May I take your order now?

G: Let's have a bottle of whisky.

(*One hour later, one of the guests gets drunk and begins to shout and sing.*)

B: Here is a cup of tea. I think the gentleman may need it. It's very stuffy here. Would you mind taking your friend out for some fresh air, ladies and gentlemen?

G: We're sorry for disturbing others. He's too excited today.

B: It's all right, sir. Good night and have a good rest.

Practice | Answer the questions according to the service conversation.

1. Should the bar tender interfere with a drunken guest? Why?
2. What can a bar tender do when faced with a drunken guest?

Key Words and Expressions

complaint (*n.*)	投诉
medium-rare (*adj.*)	半熟的
extremely (*adv.*)	非常地
apologize (*v.*)	道歉
stuffy (*adj.*)	空气不流通的
disturb (*v.*)	打扰
interfere with	干预

Points of Service Performance 服务演练要点

- When handling the guest's complaints, use the polite language.
  在处理投诉中,注意使用礼貌服务用语。
- Remember to apologize sincerely and tell the guest what effort will be made to solve his problem in a case of complaint.
  在处理投诉中,一定要真诚道歉,并告知客人为解决问题你将做哪些努力。

Performance for Service 模拟演练

Task A

Performance in pairs according to the following two cards.

Guest Card

Order: an ice-cold beer
Complaint: not happy with the beer with ice cubes in it

Chapter Eight Bar Service
酒吧服务

Waiter Card	Serve the guest with a beer with ice cubes inside Apologize for the mistake Get the beer changed right away

Task B

Wang Li is working in the bar one night while a guest enters and orders a bottle of vodka. After a while, the guest gets drunk. Wang Li will serve him a cup of tea and suggest taking some rest back in his room.

> **Position Knowledge 岗位知识**

In answer to the complaints from the guest, it is very important to keep the following four things in your mind: listening, commiserating, apologizing, and telling the guests what will be done to solve their problems.

在应对客人投诉时，要牢记四点：倾听、同情、道歉、告诉客人你们将做哪些努力。

Exercises

Ⅰ. Topics for discussion.

1. In what way should a bar tender deal with a guest's complaint about the bar service?
2. What four points should you keep in mind when handling a complaint from the guest?

Ⅱ. Fill in the blanks.

1. What I want is a _____（半生的牛排）, but this one is almost over cooked.
2. We want one _____（离乐队远一些的）, the music is too loud.
3. I _____（确实要道歉）for it.
4. I'll _____（马上把薯条换掉）.
5. _____（您介意）taking your friend out for some fresh air?

Ⅲ. Translate the following sentences into English.

1. 感谢您为我们提供这些情况，我立即去了解。
2. 我会对负责人员讲，让他来处理这件事。
3. 请放心，夫人。我将按您的要求办。
4. 对不起，先生。我会尽快为您解决这个问题。
5. 对于我的粗心我非常抱歉。

Ⅳ. **Translate the following sentences into Chinese.**

1. An aperitif or some white wine?
2. How about our special cocktail?
3. And how would you like your scotch, straight or on the rock?
4. Here is 45 yuan, and you can keep the change.
5. That's very kind of you. But there is no tipping in our bar.

Chapter Nine Business Center Service (Ⅰ)
商务中心服务（一）

Unit Twenty-two   Secretarial Service
单元 22   文秘服务

Unit Twenty-three   Computer Renting and Internet Services
单元 23   计算机租赁和网络服务

Service Position 服务岗位

The Business Center of a hotel is a section which provides the comfort and convenient service for all the guests of the hotel, and also caters to the specific needs of business and conference guests staying at the hotel. The modern hotels equip their Business Center and its conference rooms or halls with all kinds of up-to-date electronic devices and facilities to streamline these guests' work and working surroundings.

Today's Business Center is not an office but a 24-hour locale with comfortable seating with secure online access, computers and a number of other office services such as copying and wireless printing. The small multi-purpose meeting rooms or halls with docking stations and free Wifi, laptops, tablets, electronic device chargers, projectors, scanners are available for short-term rental.

Skills and Attainments 服务技能与素养

The work of the Business Center staff is multifarious, including secretarial services, translation service, business event and conference services, courier service, ticket reservation assistance and tour service. Employees at this section are required to have outstanding communication with business guests and the related hotel sections. They should be proficient in English language to make their service and assistance effective and satisfying. They also need to be familiar with the latest soft-wares, apps and websites for booking tickets and couriering, be skillful at operating facilities like wireless printer, scanner, projector, having the ability to undertake the business event and conference and to use the conference facilities. Like staff working at other sections of the hotel, employees of Business Center should have the following essential competencies as well: positive attitude, efficient problem solving, good collaboration and diligence.

Key Words and Expressions

the Business Center	商务中心
secretarial service	文秘服务
cater to	迎合；满足
up-to-date	最新的；现代的
streamline	使现代化；使集成化
multi-purpose	多功能
docking station	扩充口；扩展器
multifarious	多方面的；多样性的
courier	快递；速递
business event	商务活动
translation service	翻译服务

Unit Twenty-two Secretarial Service

单元 22 文秘服务

Procedure of Service 服务流程

- Greet the guest.
- Ask for the demands of the guest.
- Reply the guest's questions and explain the relevant items.
- Record the guest's demands accurately and make confirmation.
- Explain the service charge and ways of payment.
- Confirm the guest's name and the room number in the computer.
- Keep tight contact with the guest.
- Fill in the relevant forms and put them in a file.

Points of Service Language 服务语言要点

1. Polite language   礼貌用语

Welcome to the Business Center!
欢迎光临商务中心!

Is there anything I can do for you?
我能为您做点什么吗?

Could you wait for a moment, please?
请您稍等片刻。

It's my pleasure.
乐意为您效劳。

You are welcome.
不客气。

Don't mention it.
不用谢。

2. Asking for the demands of the guest　询问客人需求

What size would you like for the copies?
您想使用多大的纸张？
What color would you like? Colored ones or black and white?
请问是用复印彩色还是黑白的？
Would you like me to copy these on one side of the paper or both?
您是想双面复印还是单面复印？
How would you like to staple them, on the left side or on the top?
您是想装订在左侧还是上方？
What font and size do you like?
您要什么字体，多大字号？

3. Explaining the service charge and procedure of dealing　解释服务价格和办理过程

Two yuan for each page photocopied, five yuan for each page printed. It's 90 yuan in total
复印每页两元，打印每页 5 元，总计 90 元。
How would you like to pay, in cash or with your room rate?
您想如何支付，用现金还是计入房费？
The charge for an interpreter is 400 yuan per hour.
口译员每小时 400 元。

Service Conversation 41

Printing and Photocopying the Documents

E：Employee

G：Guest

E：Good afternoon. Welcome to the Business Center! Is there anything I can do for you?

G：Good afternoon. I'm David Green from Room 312. I'd like to have this document photocopied.

E：No problem, Mr. Green. How many copies would you like?

G：20 copies.

E：What size do you want?

G：A4 will do.

E：Would you like to photocopy the document on one side of the paper or both?

G：Just one side.

E：Do you want colored one or black and white?

Chapter Nine Business Center Service(Ⅰ)
商务中心服务（一）

G: Black and white.

E: I got it.

G: By the way, There is another document I'd like to print on A4, one side and colored, 10 copies.

E: I see. Please wait a moment. The two documents will be done in 5 minutes. Here you are!

G: Thank you! How do you charge?

E: Two yuan for each page photocopied, five yuan for each page printed. It's 90 yuan in total. How would you like to pay, in cash or with your room rate?

G: With my room rate.

E: Could you show me your room card, please? Thank you. Give you your card.

G: Thank you.

E: It's my pleasure.

> **Practice** Answer the questions according to the service conversation.

1. What does Mr. Green want to do with the documents?
2. What' the total charge?
3. How would Mr. Green like to pay?

Service Conversation 42

I Need an Interpreter and a Translator Tomorrow

E: Employee

G: Guest

E: Good afternoon! Welcome to the Business Center! What can I do for you?

G: Good afternoon! I'm going out for a city tour tomorrow and need an interpreter. Could you hire one for me?

E: Yes, certainly. What language service do you need?

G: English, please.

E: Do you need a male interpreter or a female one?

G: Female one is better.

E: I see. You need a female interpreter tomorrow, for the whole day, right?

G: Yes, from 9:00 am to 5:00 pm.

153

E: Approximately 8 hours. The service charge for the interpreter is 1350 yuan per day.

G: That' great. I also need a translator to put the Chinese in this contract into English. Please keep in mind: The content of the contract must be kept confidential.

E: Absolutely. The charge for Chinese-English translation is 360 yuan per 1000 Chinese characters. I'll contact the translation company for you at once, and inform you as soon as possible after the interpreter and translator have been chosen.

G: You have been of great help to me.

E: Glad to serve you. May I have your name and room card, please?

G: I'm Alice Smith from Room 612.

E: Ms. Smith. I will call you if I get everything done and you need to sign a contract here.

G: OK! Thanks.

E: You are welcome.

Practice   Answer the questions based on the service conversation.

1. What service does the guest need?
2. What is the charge for interpreting and translation service respectively?
3. What special requests does the guest demand?

Key Words and Expressions

photocopy (v.)	复印
print (v.)	打印
in total	总计
interpreter (n.)	口译(员)
translation (n.)	翻译
font (n.)	字体
size (n.)	字号
character (n.)	字符

Points of Service Performance 服务演练要点

- When printing and photocopying the documents, the staff must take into consideration of the pages to be printed and photocopied, font, size and color of the paper to make sure everything meets the needs of the guests.

  工作人员在打印和复印文件时必须了解打印和复印的页数,以及文件字体、纸张的颜色、大小以确保符合顾客的需要。

- When providing interpreting and translation services, the staff must inform the guest of the service charge and contact the translation company as soon as possible

Chapter Nine　Business Center Service(Ⅰ)
商务中心服务(一)

to get everything ready.
当工作人员提供翻译服务时,必须告知服务的费用,及时联系翻译公司做好准备。
- The information about the documents which are printed, photocopied and translated must be kept confidential. The staff can't feel free to talk about the content.
工作人员对于给顾客打印、复印及翻译的信息必须保密,不能随意提及其中的内容。

Performance for Service 模拟演练

Task A

Act in pairs according to the following two cue cards.

Guest Card	Guest name:	Fiona Swift
	Room number:	2018
	Requirement:	Copying a document
	Charge:	2 yuan per page
	Ways of payment:	in cash

Employee Card	Know the name of the guest
	Know the number of the room
	Meet any special request

Task B

A hotel guest comes to the Business Center to inquire about the interpreting service. Now he is talking to an employee at the Business Center. The employee asks questions to know about the guest's requirement for the interpreter.

Position Knowledge 岗位知识

The key elements of the secretarial services at the Business Center:
商务中心文秘服务工作的要点:
- The secretarial service of the Business Center is mainly made of the following services: copying, photocopying, typing, and translation.
商务中心的文秘服务服务主要有打印、复印、打字和翻译。
- When providing printing and photocopying services to a guest, the staff should count the pages and make sure what kind of paper will be used at first, then copy a model for the guest for checking the effect. Only through the guest's confirmation can you print the whole pages out. Bind the pages in a volume and give it to the guest after

checking the copied pages with the guest.

提供打印和复印服务时,工作人员应该清点页数,确认使用的纸张。接着复印一份交客人审查,经确认后,再进行所有的复印工作。当复印完毕后,将总页数与客人确认,装订后交予客人。

- When you type the document for the guest, first of all, you should know well about the demands of him, glance over the document, inform the charge and the time that you need, then you begin typing. Only after the guest conform, can you print the drafter. When finishing typing, you should exam the draft very carefully from the beginning to the end, then you give it to the guest for his examination. Make a copy of the file for the guest if he needs after printing.

  打印文档时,首先要清楚地了解客人的要求,快速浏览文件,告知客人收费标准以及打印所需要的时间,再开始打印文档。只有经客人确认无误后,才可打印。打印完毕后,从头至尾仔细检查,然后交付给客人复查。询问客人是否需要保存文件,如果需要,则将这份文件复制给客人。

- When providing translation service, you should ask what language service and what kind of dragoman the guest needs. If an interpreter is needed, you should also make sure to get the length of time the interpreting service is needed and inform him of the service charge of per day or per hour. If a translator is needed, tell him the charge of per thousand words.

  做翻译服务,要询问客人需要哪类语言服务,是口译还是笔译。如果是口译员,还可以问是需要男性译员还是女性译员,还要确认服务的时长,告知客人每天或每小时服务的费用。如果是笔译员,要告知每千字的翻译收费。

Exercises

Ⅰ. Topics for discussion.

1. How do you provide a photo copying service to a guest?
2. How many ways can the guests settle the payment? What are they?
3. Introduce the service procedures of secretarial services.

Ⅱ. Translate the following sentences into Chinese.

Take care of all your professional needs in a convenient location at the entrance to the convention facility. Our Business Service Center is equipped with Internet, office services and supplies, communication rentals, shipping and receiving, and rental of private mini-suites.

Chapter Nine Business Center Service(Ⅰ)
商务中心服务(一)

Ⅲ. Read the following service conversation and answer the questions.

E：Employee

G：Guest

E：Good afternoon, Madam. MayI help you?

G：Yes, I would love to print some documents in my thumb drive.

E：Sure. Please give me the drive and let me see the documents.

G：Here you are. Please print document 3. Could you help me make some changes of the format?

E：Certainly. How do you want to make the change?

G：Please help me resize the chart so as to make it in one page.

E：Ok, I see. Any thing else?

G：Oh, I forgot to insert the page number. Please help me add that.

E：Sure. Is itright ?

G：Let me check. It is fine. You can get it printed.

E：There is a colored picture in the document. Do you need colored printing or black and white one?

G：The black and white will do.

E：How many copies do you want?

G：Five copies.

E：Here you are. Don't forget your thumb drive.

G：Thanks a lot. How much should I pay?

E：2 yuan for each page. It totals 120 yuan. How would you like to pay, in cash or with your room charge?

G：In cash. Here you are.

E：Please keep the receipt and change.

G：Thank you very much.

E：You're more than welcome.

Questions：

1. What does the guest want the employee to do for him?

2. What changes does the employee make before printing the document?

3. What's the charge?

4. How does the guest pay for the service?

Unit Twenty-three Providing Computer Renting and Internet Services

单元 23 计算机租赁和网络服务

Procedure of Service 服务流程

- Greet the guest.
- Confirm the demands of the guest.
- Check the condition of the computer and the network.
- State the relevant policies concerning the service.
- Explain the service charge and ways of payment.
- Confirm the guest's name and the room number in the computer.
- Fill in the relevant forms and record the service.

Points of Service Language 服务语言要点

1. **Inquire about the demands of the guest**　询问客人的需求

   We have four brands of computer for renting in our hotel.
   我们酒店有四种品牌的计算机可供租用。
   Which brand would you prefer?
   您需要哪种品牌的计算机?

2. **Inform the guest of thedeposit for renting a computer and service charge as well as ways of payment**　告知客人租用计算机的押金、服务费用及付款方式

   The deposit for the laptop is the 4000 yuan in case of damage and loss.
   手提电脑的押金是 4000 元以防损害或者遗失。
   It's 20 yuan per hour for renting a computer.
   租用计算机的费用是每小时 20 元。
   For the deposit, you can pay in cash, by credit card or with We Chat or Alipay.
   您可以用现金、信用卡、微信或者是支付宝来支付押金。

3. **Make sure the guest checks the information and signs on the renting agreement**　确保顾客在租用计算机之前核对协议信息并签订租用协议

   Would you like to check the information in this renting agreement and sign your name and the date here?

请您核对一下租用协议的信息并签署您的名字和日期。

I Wonder If I Can Rent a Computer from You

E: Employee

G: Guest

E: Good morning, sir. Welcome to the Business Center. May I help you?

G: Yes. There is something wrong with my laptop. It simply can' get started. I wonder if I can rent one from you.

E: Certainly. We have four brands here. Apple Mac, Surface, Think Pad and Huawei. They are all portable. Which one would you prefer?

G: I'd like to have one Surface. Thank you.

E: No problem. The deposit for the laptop is the 4000 yuan in case of damage and loss.

G: How much do you charge? I may just rent the computer for several hours.

E: If you'd like to rent the computer by hours, it's 20 yuan per hour. By the way, it's 200 per day.

G: I see. I just need the laptop to process some documents. Several hours will suit my needs

E: Great. For confirmation, what's your name and room number?

G: I am Harold Finch from Room 1808. This is my room card.

E: Would you like to check the information in this renting agreement and sign your name and the date here?

G: Sure.

E: Mr. Finch, for the deposit, you can pay in cash, by credit card or with WeChat or Alipay. As for the rent, you can go with your room rate as well as the above-mentioned ways of payment.

G: I'll do by Alipay.

E: Please wait here for a minute. I'll go for the laptop and check if it works.

G: No problem.

E: The computer runs normally. Here you are. You can check it.

G: Everything is OK. Thank you very much.

E: Anytime.

Practice Answer the questions according to the service conversation.

1. What brands of computer does the hotel offer?
2. How much is the deposit for renting the computer?
3. How would the guest like to pay?

We Have Free Wi-Fi Service

E: Employee

G: Guest

E: Nice to see you, Madam. Is there anything I can do for you?

G: Yes. Does the hotel provide internet service?

E: Certainly. We have free Wi-Fi service. The user's name is Crown999 and the password is*** 258.

G: Great. My mobile phone can log into the internet right now. But I need a computer to surf the internet and do some paper work.

E: We have a private section here in the Business Center for the guests to access internet. Two desktops are offered. Would you like go there?

G: That's good. How much do you charge for the service?

E: The desktop is free to use. The internet service is free of charge for the first 20 minutes and then 20 yuan per hour. The internet access there is more efficient and the signal is much stronger than free Wi-Fi.

G: Sounds wonderful.

E: What's your name and room number, madam?

G: Grace Shaw from Room 606.

E: How would you like to pay, in cash or by credit card, WeChat or Alipay? You can go with you room rate as well.

G: I'd like to go with my room rate.

E: No problem. Ms. Shaw, this way, please.

G: Thank you for your assistance.

E: Don't mention it. Please let me know if you need any help.

Chapter Nine Business Center Service(Ⅰ)
商务中心服务(一)

Key Words and Expressions

renting agreement　　　　　　　　　　　租赁合同
process the document　　　　　　　　　文档处理
log into the internet/surf the internet　　上网
laptop(n.)　　　　　　　　　　　　　　笔记本电脑
desktop(n.)　　　　　　　　　　　　　　台式电脑
assistance(n.)　　　　　　　　　　　　　帮助，援助

Points of Service Performance 服务演练要点

- Confirm the brand of the computer the guest wants to rent.
  确认客人租用计算机的品牌。
- Inform the guest the deposit and renting charge of the computer.
  告知客人押金和租用的费用。
- Tell the guest to check the information in the renting agreement and sign the name.
  告知客人核对租用协议里的信息，并且签名。
- Check if the computer can run normally.
  检查计算机是否能正常运作。

Performance for Service 模拟演练

Task A

Act in pairs according to the following two cue cards.

Guest Card		
	Guest name：	John Ashley
	Room number：	2809
	Requirement：	Renting a computer
	Brand：	Apple Mac
	Charge：	20 yuan per hour
	Ways of payment：	by Wechat

Employee Card	
	Greet the guest
	Know the name of the guest
	Know the number of the room
	Check the condition of the computer

161

Task B

Mrs. Bush needs to do word processing work. Unfortunately, her computer breaks down. So she goes to the Business Center for help. Thomas works there and helps Mrs. Bush to rent a laptop.

Position Knowledge 岗位知识

When providing computer renting and internet service, the staff should inform the guest of the brands of the computer that a hotel offers and introduce the charge.

当工作人员向客人提供计算机租赁和网络服务时,应该询问客人需要酒店提供计算机的品牌并介绍收费。

The staff need to remind the guest to sign an agreement when he or she is renting a computer from a hotel and charge the deposit in advance.

当客人从酒店租用计算机时,工作人员需要提醒客人签署租用协议,并且预收押金。

Exercises

Ⅰ. Topic for discussion.

1. How can you help the guest to rent a computer? Explain the main points.
2. What information should be filled in the renting agreement?
3. What are the advantages of accessing the internet in the Business Center compared with using free Wi-Fi in the hotel?

Ⅱ. Translate the following sentences into English.

In this era the internet usage has increased, internet settled into our homes and everywhere via our mobile devices and accessing the information has become easier. Thus, the use of internet has become an obligation in the hotel business which provides abstract product.

Ⅲ. Translate the following sentences into Chinese.

1. 无论你是公务旅行还是休闲度假,都需要可靠的网络服务。
2. 旅行时要记住的一件事是,并非所有地方都有很好的无线网络接入。
3. 酒店可以用更高效的移动计算机取代他们的前台计算机,并且可以为员工提供个人平板电脑以协助他们完成工作。

Chapter Ten Business Center Service (Ⅱ)
商务中心服务(二)

Unit Twenty-four Ticket and Tour Assistance
单元 24 票务和旅游预订协办

Unit Twenty-five Business Event and Courier Services
单元 25 商务活动承办和快递服务

Unit Twenty-four Ticket and Tour Assistance

Procedure of Service 服务流程

- Greet the guest.
- Make sure the kind of transport the guest wants.
- Get the following reservation information from the guest:
  The name of the guest and his mobile phone number.
  The departure place, the destination and the time of departure.
  The number of the tickets the guest needs.
- Check on the booking app or website to search for the ticket available.
- Ask the guest to show his proof of identification or tell his identification number.
- Confirm the following information:
  The ID number or passport number.
  The mobile phone number and email address.
- Inquire about the method of payment.
- Tell the guest the ways of fetching the ticket.
- Extend best wishes to the guest.

Points of Service Language 服务语言要点

1. **Ask the types of transport the guest wants to travel by** 询问客人预订交通工具信息用语

   Which day's tickets would you like?
   您要哪一天的票?
   How many tickets would you like to book?
   您需要订几张票?
   Bullet trains run very frequently between Beijing and Shanghai everyday. What time would you like to take the train?

Chapter Ten Business Center Service(Ⅱ)
商务中心服务(二)

北京到上海的高铁车次频繁,您需要搭乘哪个时段的列车?
Which seat would you like, business-class seat, first-class seat or second-class seat?
您是要商务座、一等座还是二等座?
The tickets of that train are sold out.
那趟火车票已经售完了。
There are nine flights on that day including connecting and direct flights. Which one do you prefer?
包括中转和直飞,这天一共有九个航班,您是要中转还是直飞的?
Air China has a flight leaving at 9:20 a.m. Is that OK?
国航有一个上午 9:20 起飞的航班,您看可以吗?
Now there are only first-class tickets and business-class tickets available. Would you like to buy?
目前只有一等座和商务座票,您还需要吗?
Which one do you want, economy class, business class or first class?
您是要经济舱、商务舱还是头等舱?
Would you like a window seat or an aisle seat?
您是要靠近窗户的座位还是靠近通道的座位?

2. **Inquire the guest of the method of contact and the way of payment**　要求客人留下联系方式并询问付款方式

Could you please show me your identification card in order to make a reservation?
请您出示身份证,我帮您预订?
Can I have your mobile phone number?
请您留下手机联系方式?
That's 553 yuan. How would you like to pay, by credit card, with WeChat or Alipay?
票款是 553 元。请问您怎么支付,信用卡、微信还是支付宝?
Please scan this QR code here.
请您扫这边的二维码。

3. **Tell the guest the way of fetching the ticket**　告诉客人取票方式

The tickets are booked. You can pick up your tickets on the self-service machine at the railway station or pass through the gate with your ID card。
票为您订好了,您可以到火车站自助机取票或者不取票直接用身份证过闸机乘车。
Your receipt and ticket confirmation have been emailed to you. Please save the email confirmation in a save folder. Your mobile will also receive a text message.
您的收据和机票确认信息已通过电子邮件发送给您。请将邮件保存在一个安全的文件夹中。您的手机也会收到一条短信。
You can check in at the self-serve kiosk or the check-in counter of Air China at the airport with your booking reference and passport.
您可以携带您的预订凭证和护照到机场国航值机自助机或值机柜台办理登机手续。

Booking a Train Ticket

E: Employee

G: Guest

E: Good morning, madam. Can I help you?

G: Good morning. I want to book a train ticket from Beijing to Shanghai on May 2nd. I don't know how to use this app.

E: Don't worry. Let me check, Madam. Bullet trains run very frequently between Beijing and Shanghai everyday. What time would you like to take the train?

G: The early the better, I think. What is the train number?

E: The earliest train number is G112 leaving at 6:37 am. I'm afraid it's not very easy to book the ticket, because now the traffic is very heavy for the holiday. The tickets are in great demand. Anyway, let me check whether there are still tickets available. Just wait a moment, please.

G: That would be fine.

E: Madam, all second-class seats are sold out. Now there are only first-class seats and business class seats available. Would you like to book?

G: What about the trains from 7:00 to 8:00?

E: OK. One moment, please. There are five trains in this hour, 7:00, 7:13, 7:27, 7:38 and 8:00. There are plenty second-class seats left at 7:13. That's G104.

G: Great! I'd like to book it.

E: May I know your name, your ID number and your telephone number?

G: Certainly! I have written them down on the paper. Here you are!

E: Thank you! That's 553 yuan. How would you like to pay, by credit card, with WeChat or Alipay?

G: With Alipay.

E: Please scan this QR code here.

G: Sure.

E: Done. The ticket is booked. You can pick it up on the self-service machine at the railway station or pass through the gate with your identity card.

G: Thank you very much!

E: You're welcome. Good bye, Ms. Jane! Have a pleasant stay at our hotel.

Chapter Ten Business Center Service(Ⅱ)

商务中心服务(二)

Practice Answer the questions according to the service conversation.

1. What kind of train ticket does the guest want to book?

2. How many kinds of seats are mentioned there? What are they?

3. In the end, which train and what kind of train ticket has the guest booked?

4. How does the guest pay for the ticket?

Service Conversation 46

Booking a Transfer Air Ticket

E: Employee

G: Guest

E: Good morning, Sir! Can I help you?

G: I'd like to book an air ticket from Beijing to Singapore on February 10th.

E: One moment, please. Let me check on my computer. Air China has flights every hour on the day. Six in the morning and afternoon respectively, three in the evening. When is suitable, morning, afternoon or evening?

G: I would like a direct flight around 8:00 in the morning.

E: There is a flight leaving at 8:30 a.m. But it is not a direct flight. You need to transfer at Hangzhou Xiaoshan International Airport. Is that all right?

G: That would be fine. I would like to book an economy class ticket.

E: Okay. Which one do you prefer, a window seat, an aisle seat or a middle seat?

G: An aisle seat, please.

E: Could I have your passport to make the reservation?

G: Sure. Here you are.

E: May I know your mobile number and email address, please?

E: Here is my business card.

G: Thank you. You want an air-ticket from Beijing to Singapore on February 10th, is that right?

G: Yes! That's right.

E: Booked. You need to pay within 15 minutes. WeChat, Alipay or credit card payment are all acceptable.

G: How much is that?

E: The charge is 5,200 yuan altogether. How would you like to pay for it?

G: By credit card.

E: Thank you. Your receipt and ticket confirmation have been emailed to you. Please save the email confirmation in a save folder. Your mobile will also receive a text message. You can check in at the self-serve kiosk or the check-in counter of Air China at the airport with your booking reference and passport.

G: Good. Thank you!

E: Not at all! Have a pleasant day!

Practice   Answer the questions according to the service conversation.

1. What kind of ticket does the guest want to book?
2. Where is he going to fly?
3. Where will the guest take his connecting flight?
4. How much is the flight?

Air China	中国国际航空公司
HangzhouXiaoshan International Airport	杭州萧山国际机场
check-in counter	值机柜台
self-serve kiosk	值机自助机
economic class	普通舱
business class	商务舱
bullet train	高铁
WeChat	微信
QR code	二维码
Ali-pay	支付宝
train number	车次
first-class seat	一等座
second-class seat	二等座
business-class seat	商务座
soft berth	软卧
hard berth	硬卧

Points of Service Performance 服务演练要点

- The staff in the Business Center should be familiar with the latest booking softwares, apps and websites suchCtrip, 12306 China Railway and Air China.
  商务中心工作人员要熟悉各种订票软件和订票平台，比如携程、铁路12306和中国航空。

Chapter Ten　Business Center Service(Ⅱ)
商务中心服务(二)

- When a guest comes to the Business Centre for help to book a ticket, first listen to the guest carefully to keep the destination and the type of transport in mind. Then ask the guest when he or she wants to take the transport.
  客人来到商务中心订票,先要听清客人要前往的目的地和希望搭乘的交通工具。然后询问客人要搭乘的具体列车次或航班次。
- Quickly check whether there is a ticket available. If the required ticket is fully booked, ask the guest if he or she has other options。
  快速查询余票。如果客人要的车次或航班已被订满,询问客人是否可以搭乘其他车次或航班。
- Ask the guest to show their proof of identification. Before clicking the confirm button, confirm the information with the guest.
  让客人出示身份证明。在单击确认键前,和客人确认信息。
- Remind the guest of paying time limit, confirm way of payment.
  提醒客人付款时限,确认付款方式。

Performance for Service 模拟演练

Task A

Performance in pairs according to the following two cards.

Guest Card	Guest name：	John Smith
	Room number：	Room 508
	Purpose：	book two bullet train tickets
	Destination：	Harbin
	Special request：	ask the assistance to rent a wheelchair
	Date：	Tuesday, February 22, 2022

Employee Card	Name of the guest
	Room number
	Where to go
	When to go
	How many tickets
	Any special request
	Suggestions：confirm early

Task B

Wang Fang is going on a trip to Brisbane in her winter holiday. She comes to the booking office in the Business Center to book an air ticket. She explains her demands. And at the same time, she hopes the staff can help her get some detailed information about the flight because it is the first time for her to take such a long journey. Now she is talking to the employee in the Business Center. IF you are the employee, what will you say?

Position Knowledge 岗位知识

Ticket booking was originally the service provided by the Business Center of hotels to facilitate guests' travel, entertainment and tour, mainly including reserving tickets of aircrafts, trains, ships, coaches, cars, as well as shows, performance and sight-seeing. However, the soaring popularity of portable electronic devices ranging from laptops, ipads to smartphones and the rapid development of network technology have greatly changed the traditional way of buying and selling tickets. Therefore, it's very essential for the staff in the Business Center to be familiar with both the traditional booking methods and the latest booking softwares, apps and websites and be competent to make efficient booking on them to meet the needs of different guests. Employees at this section should also be proficient in English language in this respect to make their assistance and services successful and effective.

票务预订原本是酒店商务中心为满足客人的出行便利等需求而提供的一个服务项目，主要包括飞机、火车、轮船、汽车等交通工具，还有娱乐旅游活动等的票务预订。但是随着手提电脑、平板、智能手机等便携式电子产品的极大普及和网络技术的飞速发展，票务的买售方式都发生了很大变化。这对员工的要求就更高了，既要掌握传统的订票方式，还要熟悉各种票务软件和订票平台，并熟练掌握为有需要的旅客在计算机和手机上帮助他们订票的技能；此外商务中心的员工还要熟练掌握相关的英语表达，才能有效地开展各项票务预定协办服务。

Ⅰ. Topics for discussion.

1. What is the guest destination?
2. What kind of information should the clerk provide for the guest?
3. What sort of booking software, app or website do you prefer to use?

Ⅱ. Write out the questions according to the answers.

1. _____

   Just a minute. I'll check on my computer to see if there are flights on that day.

2. _____

   The earlier the better.

3. _____

The train number is G102.

4. _____

With We Chat. Shall I scan the QR code here?

Ⅲ. Translate the following sentences into English.

1. 上海到杭州的高铁运行频繁。
2. 您要二等座、一等座还是商务座?
3. 对不起,直飞的航班都订满了。您看在香港转机的可以吗?
4. 您要哪儿的座位,靠窗的还是靠通道的?

Ⅳ. Translate the following paragraph into Chinese.

If you want me to plan the trip for you, I would suggest an Air China direct flight from Beijing to Sydney and another Virgin Australia flight from Sydney to Brisbane. You can stay one or two days in Sydney to have a rest and do sightseeing, such as climbing the SydneyHarbour Bridge, watching a great show at Sydney Opera House, encountering koalas and cuddling up to them at the Taronga Zoo, meeting the only pair of dugongs on display in the world at Aquarium Wharf of Darling Harbour. And don't forget to have a seafood lunch off Watson's Bay before you fly to Brisbane.

Unit Twenty-five Business Event and Courier Services

单元 25 商务活动承办与快递服务

Procedure of Service 服务流程

Business Event Service

- Greet the guest.
- Get the following reservation information from the guest:
  The name of the guest.
  The name of the company.
  The date of the event.
  The number of participants.
  The type of conference room requested.
- Get information of other requests during the event.
- Provide recommendation for banquets and tours.
- Ask the guest for mobile phone number and email address.
- Confirm all the information.
- Inform the meeting director of contacting the guest.

Courier Service

- Greet the guest.
- Get the following reservation information from the guest:
  The items to be couriered.
  The name of the consignor (if the consignor is not the guest).
  The destination.
  The weight and volume of the parcel.
- Offer different Couriers for the guest to select.
- Log on to the Courier's website and ask the guest to fill in detailed information of the consignor and receiver on the computer provided.
- Double check the following information with the guest:

Special request.

Payment.

Pickup time.

- Offer the anticipated price to the guest.
- Notify the courier to pick up the parcel.

Points of Service Language 服务语言要点

1. **Find out what service the guest requests　了解客人需要的服务**

    May I ask how many people will be in the promotion?

    请问有多少人参加这次推广活动?

    Do you need room reservation for the participants?

    请问您要为与会者安排住房吗?

    When would you like to host your event, Miss Carl?

    卡尔小姐,请问您公司哪天举办活动?

    Do you prefer a western style luncheon or a traditional Chinese one ?

    您希望午宴是西式的还是中式的?

    What do you want to courier?

    请问您要快递什么?

    What is inside your parcel?

    请问您包裹里的快递是什么?

    Does your parcel have any fragile items?

    您的包裹里有易碎物品吗?

    When would you like the courier to pick up the parcel?

    请问您希望快递员什么时候来取件?

2. **Introduce the business events and Courier services　向客人介绍商务活动和快递服务信息**

    The conference room can accommodate 120 people with freeWiFi, plasma screens and interactive whiteboards. Our experienced meeting director will take care of the more detailed decoration and arrangement of the conference room.

    这间会议室可以容纳120人,有免费WiFi、等离子屏幕和交互式白板。我们经验丰富的会议主管将和您接洽具体的活动厅装饰和布置事宜。

    How about this package tour: visit the Mausoleum of the First Qin Emperor and the Terracotta Warriors in the afternoon after check-in, enjoy delicious Chinese cuisine and Tang dynasty songs and dances atTangyue Gong in the evening? .

    下午参观秦始皇陵和兵马俑,晚上前往唐乐宫,边享用传统中国美食边欣赏地道大唐歌舞。您看这个安排如何?

    We offer DHL, FEDEX, EMS and SF Express. Which one do you prefer?

    我们可以联络敦豪、联邦快递、中国邮政速递和顺丰快递。您喜欢哪种方式?

    The head weight of a standard express is 18 yuan per kg and the excess weight is 9 yuan per kg. The head weight of a speedy express is 23 yuan per kg and the excess weight is 13 yuan per kg.

标快首千克是 18 元,续重是每千克 9 元。特快专递的首千克是 23 元,续重是每千克 13 元。

What payment would you like? Cash on shipment or Cash on delivery?

请问您是寄付现结还是到付?

3. **State the price about the services** 告知客人代办服务的价格

The anticipated price is 72 yuan. The courier will collect the charge when he picks up the parcel.

预估费用是 72 元。快递员收包裹时会收取具体费用。

I will inform our meeting director immediately. He'll talk to you in detail about the budget.

我会立刻通知我们的会议主管,他会跟您详细谈会议室的租金与预算。您看这样可以吗?

Reserving a Business Event and a Tour Package

E: Employee

G: Guest

25 – 47　Renting Equipment. mp3

E: Good afternoon, Grand Park Xi'an. What can I do for you?

G: I'm Richeal Carl, secretary of the HT Electric co. , Ltd. Our company would like to conduct a new product promotion at your hotel.

E: May I ask how many people will be in the promotion?

G: 99.

E: Do you need room reservation for the participants?

E: Just our staff members. Five twin beds rooms and three executive suites.

G: Get it. When would you like to hold your event, Madam?

G: On the 9th of October from 9:00 a. m. to 2:00p. m. .

E: Classroom style or banquet style, which one do you prefer?

G: New product introduction accounts for a big part of the promotion. Classroom style is better.

E: The conference room can accommodate 120 people with free WiFi, plasma screens and interactive whiteboards. Our experienced meeting director will take care of the

Chapter Ten Business Center Service(Ⅱ)
商务中心服务(二)

more detailed decoration and arrangement of the conference room. He will contact you after the reservation.

G: We would also like the hotels to arrange for a luncheon.

E: Do you prefer a western style luncheon or a traditional Chinese one?

G: Traditional Chinese, please. Our three foreign managers are big fans of Chinese cuisine. They also want to visit one or two of the most interesting tourist attractions in the city after the business event.

E: How about this package tour: visit the Mausoleum of the First Qin Emperor and the Terracotta Warriors in the afternoon, enjoy delicious Chinese cuisine and Tang Dynasty songs and dances at Tangyue Gong in the evening? .

G: Excellent! What about the charge?

E: I will inform our meeting director immediately. He'll talk to you in detail about the budget.

G: OK!

E: Could I have your phone number and email address, madam?

G: Sure. My mobile phone number is 1865*** 560, and email me at RichealCarl@HT Electric. com.

E: Thank you, Ms Carl! You have ordered a business event in our hotel, including a conference room, a luncheon, five twin beds rooms and three executive suites for one night. Additionally, a package tour is booked after the business event. Your mobile phone number is 1865*** 560, and your email address is RichealCarl@HT Electric. com.

G: Correct.

E: I'm Wang Hua. Our meeting director will contact you soon. And the confirmation letter will send to you at the given email address.

G: Thank you. Bye.

E: Bye, Ms Carl. Have a nice day!

> **Practice** Answer the questions according to the service conversation.

1. What event is the company going to host at the hotel?
2. How many people will the company invite to the event?
3. What kind of conference room has the guest chosen?
4. What food will be served at the luncheon?
5. How many entertainments has the employee recommended to the guest, what are they?

Service Conversation 48

Delivering a Parcel

25-48 Postal Expressing. mp3

E: Employee

G: Guest

E: Good morning, Sir. Is there anything I can do for you?

G: G: I need to send this parcel to Shanghai. Can you call a courier for me?

E: Certainly, sir. What is inside your parcel?

G: Samples of clothing for exhibition.

E: Does your parcel have any fragile items?

G: No.

E: Let's see how much it weighs. It weighs 7 kilos. We offer DHL, FEDEX, EMS and SF Express. Which one do you prefer?

G: SF Express, please. What is the charge?

E: There are two options: standard express and speedy express. The standard express is cheaper. The head weight of a standard express is 18 yuan per kg and the excess weight is 9 yuan per kg. The head weight of a speedy express is 23 yuan per kg and the excess weight is 13 yuan per kg.

G: I'll take standard express.

E: Would you please fill in the detailed information of the consignor's and the receiver's on this computer?

G: All right.

E: Thank you, Sir. When would you like the courier to pick up the parcel?

G: Now.

E: OK. Pickup time is between 15:00 and 16:00. Article name is Clothing and the weight is 7 kilos. Is that right?

E: Would you like a return proof of delivery, Sir?

G: No, thanks.

E: What payment would you like? Cash on shipment or Cash on delivery?

G: Cash on shipment.

E: Fine. The anticipated price is 72 yuan from. The courier will collect the charge when he picks up the parcel.

E: What's your room number, Mr Green?

G: Room 712.

E: Thank you. I'll call you when the courier comes to pick up the parcel.

G: Thank you.

E: You're welcome. Have a pleasant stay.

Practice Answer the questions according to the service conversation.

1. What Courier does the guest prefer?
2. What are the options of delivery?
3. Cash on shipment or Cash on delivery, which one has the guest chosen? .
4. What is the anticipated price of the delivery?

Key Words and Expressions

luncheon	午宴
Chinese cuisine	中国美食
the Mausoleum of the First Qin Emperor and the Terracotta Warriors	秦始皇陵和兵马俑
plasma screen	等离子显示屏
classroom style	讲厅型
banquet style	宴会型
meeting director	会议主管
Courier service	快递服务
DHL	敦豪
FEDEX	联邦快递
standard express	标快
speedy express	特快
cash on shipment	寄付现结
cash on delivery	到付
a return proof of delivery	签单返还

Points of Service Performance 服务演练要点

- When a guest calls for a reservation of a conference room, first ask the guest the type of the business event, the date and the number of the participants. Then quickly check whether there is a vacancy. If the conference room meets the needs of the guest, introduce it and then find out more specific requests before, during and after the event.
客人打电话来询问举办会议事宜,先要询问客人要举办什么商务活动,与会日期与人数。然后快速查询空余活动厅。介绍符合客人需求的活动厅,然后进一步询问客人会前，会中，会后对活动的具体要求。
- Kindly ask the guest if the accommodation is needed. Make sure the number and the types of rooms if room reservation is needed.
  友善地询问是否要为与会人安排食宿。如果需要，就确认房间数和房型。
- Be sure to politely introduce thebanquets，tours and entertainment arrangements.
  要礼貌地向客人介绍宴会、旅游和其他娱乐安排。
- Ask the guest for mobile phone number and email address.
  要求客人留下手机号码和电子邮箱。

Performance for Service 模拟演练

Task A

Act out a dialogue of hosting a training session in pair according to the following two cards.

Guest Card		
	Guest name：	Margaret Ramona
	Guest's company：	Beijing Branch of Hallstatt Wine Co. LTD
	Purpose：	to book a versatile conference room for a training session
	Room type：	banquet style
	Room size：	to accommodate 150 people
	Special request：	arrange for breakfast and lunch
	Guest's mobile phone number：	186＊＊＊8765

Employee Card	
	Name of the guest
	Guest's company
	Purpose of the guest
	Room type
	Room size
	Special request
	Way of contact

Task B

Mr. Raymond, a hotel guest who wants to deliver a box of fresh grape, comes to the hotel Business Center. He doesn't know what Couriers operating around. He wants to deliver grapes bought from Turpan, the Xinjiang Uygur Autonomous Region, to Xining,

Chapter Ten Business Center Service(Ⅱ)
商务中心服务(二)

Qinghai Province. He missed the post office in Putaogou. The employee at the Business Centre offers two Couriers, EMS and SF Express to him. Now he is inquiring about the cost of speedy delivery by the two Couriers.

Position Knowledge 岗位知识

Courier services provide a safe and quick way of transporting important documents and other shipments from one place to another. However, it is not convenient for a hotel guest to hire a local courier service, especially if he is not a member of certain courier. To facilitate guests' delivery process, the Business Centre in a hotel keeps close contact with the couriers, such as DHL, UPS, FEDEX, EMS and SF Express. The employees at the Business Centre need to have a clear idea of all the services that are available for the guest to use and their pricing structures. It is thoughtful to offer the best pricing for the different types of shipments .

快递服务提供了一种安全快捷的方式,将重要文件和其他货物从一个地方运送到另一个地方。然而,对于酒店客人来说,直接联系当地的快递服务多有不便,特别是当客人不是某个快递公司的会员时。酒店商务中心与德国敦豪、美国联合包裹、联邦快递、中国邮政快递、顺丰等快递公司保持紧密联系,方便客人发送快递。商务中心的员工需要清楚地了解客人可以使用的所有快递服务以及它们的定价结构。提供给客人不同类型快递的最优价格是非常体贴的服务。

Ⅰ. Topics for discussion.

1. What information must you obtain from the guest for delivering a parcel?

2. To inform the guest of the anticipated price, what do you need to know about the parcel?

3. To facilitate the guestdecision-making, what you need to have a clear idea of?

4. How to complete the service procedures of a standard express delivery?

Ⅱ. Write out the questions according to the answers.

1. _____

   Samples of clothes for exhibition.

2. _____

   SF Express, please.

3. _____

   Cash on shipment.

4. _____
Between 15:00 and 16:00.

Ⅲ. **Translate the following sentences into English.**

1. 先生,您的包裹里有易碎物品吗?
2. 午宴可以提供中式传统菜肴和民乐演奏。
3. 顺丰有特快和标快两种方式。
4. 免费的高速无线网络覆盖所有会议区域。
5. 经验丰富的商务活动团队为您提供包括出行、住宿、餐饮、旅游以及通信技术支持。

Ⅳ. **Translate the following sentences into Chinese.**

1. Provide your guest an estimate with the approximate size and weight of his package.

2. Collect information about the type of deliveries demanded, the weight and size of the items to be shipped, and the distance from the shipment's point of origin to the destination.

3. You should notify the courier to pick up parcel at once after the charge has been confirmed.

4. The high ceilinged 1,220-square-meter Regency Ballroom is ideal for large meetings and events.

Chapter Eleven
Health & Recreation Center Service
康体中心服务

Unit Twenty-six　Body Care Service
单元 26　康体服务

Unit Twenty-seven　Bathing Service
单元 27　洗浴服务

Unit Twenty-eight　Entertaining Service
单元 28　娱乐服务

Service Position 服务岗位

The Health and Recreation Center is a section which provides some kinds of recreational services for the guests in the hotel. It is one of the sections which can entertain the guests. It mainly includes the health center (body care center) and the recreation services center. The recreation center includes night club, karaoke room and chess & card room; the health center includes the barber's, beauty parlor, sauna room, massage room and health club, as well as swimming pool, golf course, bowling room, tennis court and billiards room, etc. Different department carries different procedures. In general, the work of the health & recreation center service can be summed up as follows: preparations for the job, greeting the coming guests and seeing off the guests. Different hotels provide different items according to their own conditions.

Skills and Attainments 服务技能与素养

The clerks of the Health and Recreation Center need to complete the following main services in English:

In the body care center the clerks carry out a series of service items which can meet the demands of the guests on keep-fit exercising and health-caring. This service mainly includes basketball, volleyball, badminton, tennis, golf, shuffle board, table tennis, billiards/snooker, bowling, gym, arrow shooting, gymnastics, etc.

In the beauty salon & health center the staff should learn to meet the demands of the guests on looks-improving and body-improving. It includes cosmetology, body-caring, physical therapy, medical examinations, etc.

The bathing service includes bathing, sauna, SPA, fragrant herbal bath, swim, rub-down, massage, etc.

In the entertaining services center the staff should learn to meet the demands of the guests on recreation and amusement. It mainly includes singing & dancing, KTV, disco, video games, net bar, cards & chess, imitation ball match, emulation shooting, etc.

The Health and Recreation Center is the department which can make the guests of the hotel feel happy. It can supply all kinds of entertainment to them. If a guest feels uncomfortable or feels tired, he can go to the health center to make his body relax. So the staff of the Health and Recreation Center should be all patient and skillful at the service. They must also have the higher ability of English for services in the hotel.

Key Words and Expressions

the Health and Recreation Center	康体中心
beauty salon	美容院
karaoke (*n.*)	卡拉OK

Chapter Eleven　Health & Recreation Center Service
康体中心服务

barber's	理发店
sauna room	桑拿室
massage room	按摩室
bowling (*n.*)	保龄球
billiards room	台球室
shuffle board	沙狐球
billiards/snooker	台球/斯诺克
arrow shooting	射箭
gymnastics (*n.*)	体操,健美操
fragrant herbal bath	香薰浴疗
rubdown (*n.*)	按摩
massage (*n.*)	推拿,按摩
amusement (*n.*)	娱乐,消遣
disco (*n.*)	迪斯科
video games	电视游戏
emulation shooting	射击竞赛

Unit Twenty-six Body Care Service

Procedure of Service 服务流程

Accept the guest at the Body Care Center

- Greet the arriving guest.
- Introduce main service items and facilities to the guest, and reply his inquires if needed.
- State the charge of the item and know the way of payment.
- Examine the room cards of the guest and confirm the records on the computer.
- Go through the relevant procedures and make records clearly.
- Lead the guest to the place where the service facility is provided.
- Introduce the method of using facilities and remind the guest the points for attention.
- Provide excellent services to the guest according to Hotel Operational Procedures.
- Set account for the guest according to procedures.
- See the guest off, inviting him to come again and showing good wishes to him.

Points of Service Language 服务语言要点

1. **Introducing the main service items and facilities to the guests** 介绍服务项目及设施设备情况

   Bowling is one kind of sports which has a long history and many people are keen on it.
   保龄球是一项具有悠久历史的体育项目,深受人们喜爱。
   We offer all kinds of exercise equipments, such as exercise bicycles, Nautilus machines, Stairmasters and so on.
   我们提供各种各样的运动器材,比如,运动脚踏车、全身型健身器和楼梯机等。
   There are such classes as martial arts, yoga, and Pilates.
   我们有武术、瑜伽和普拉提课程。

Chapter Eleven Health & Recreation Center Service
康体中心服务

2. Reminding the guests the points for attention   为客人提供运动指导及注意事项

You'd better warm up at first.
您最好先做一下热身运动。

I'd like to tell you a good way to work your muscles.
我想告诉您一个训练肌肉的好方法。

Would you like to play bowling?
您是否愿意打保龄球?

Please wipe off the machines after you finish using them.
请您在使用完健身器后擦拭干净。

We have a night club, a gym, a bowling room and a swimming pool.
我们有夜总会、体育馆、保龄球馆和游泳池。

Please put on sneakers before entering the court. If you didn't bring shoes yourself, you can rent at the service counter.
请你们换上球鞋。如果自己没有带,我们这里有备用鞋可以出租。

Would you like to switch on the marking board?
需要帮您开启记分牌吗?

You'd better warm up before the exercises in order to avoid ankle sprain, muscle injury or knee hurt.
运动之前,请先做好热身运动,以免发生脚踝扭伤、肌肉拉伤、膝盖损伤等意外事故。

How many lanes would you like to have, one or two?
是开一个球道还是两个球道?

Please don't strike the pin deck and throw the bowling too high.
注意不要击打球瓶区,抛球也不要过高。

3. Clearing the charge of item and knowing the way of payment   介绍收费标准并了解付款方式

The charge is one basket for 30 minutes (include less than it) for one unit. Please go through your procedures at the service counter when you leave.
半场的租用时间以每30分钟为1个计算单位,不足30分钟的按30分钟计算。请在活动结束后到服务台办理结账手续。

The charge is counted according to the number of lanes. You have two choices: 300 yuan per hour or 50 yuan for a round.
我们是按球道收费的。有两种方式:如按时间计算,则每小时的费用为300元人民币;如按局数计算,则每局按50元人民币收费。

Service Conversation 49 — Serving Basketball

26-49 Serving Basketball. mp3

E: Employee
G: Guest

E: Good afternoon! Welcome to the basketball court. I'm a staff member here. And it's my pleasure to provide services to all of you.

G: Good afternoon! This court looks very spacious and bright. And everything looks lovely.

E: Thank you for your kind words. It has just been redecorated. Is basketball your favorite sport?

G: Yes! I love basketball.

E: So do I. How many people are going to play?

G: There are six altogether.

E: OK. Do you want, one basket or two?

G: One is enough for us I think. How do you charge?

E: The charge is one basket for 30 minutes for 800 yuan. Please go through your procedures at the service counter when you leave.

G: I see.

E: Please put on sneakers before entering the court. If you didn't bring shoes yourselves, you can rent them at the service counter.

G: We've brought our own shoes.

E: Would you like some drinks?

G: Mineral water is OK.

E: OK! What else would you like to have?

G: Can you prepare some towels for us?

E: No problem. Would you like to use the scoreboard?

G: We just play for fun.

E: What else can I do for you?

G: Nothing. Thank you!

E: In order to avoid muscle or knee injury you'd better warm up first.

G: Thank you for your reminding us.

E: You're welcome. Hope all of you have a pleasant game. If you have any problems, please let me know at once.

Chapter Eleven　Health & Recreation Center Service
康体中心服务

> **Practice**　Answer the questions according to the service conversation.

1. How many people are going to play at the basketball court?
2. According to the employee, what should the guests do before they start playing?
3. What about the charge?

Service Conversation 50

Serving Bowling

26–50　Serving Bowling. mp3

E: Employee

G: Guest

E: Good afternoon! Welcome to the bowling center. I'm very pleased to provide services to you all.

G: Good afternoon! This alley looks very new. It's very nice to play in this pleasant environment.

E: Thank you! Many people are keen on bowling; and it has a long history. How many people are there altogether?

G: There are five.

E: How many lanes would you like to have, one or two?

G: Two lanes, I think. By the way, can you tell me what the bowling alley's hours are and what the charge is?

E: The bowling alley is open from 10:00 a.m. to 12:00 midnight. The charge is counted according to the number of lanes. You have two choices:300 yuan per hour or 50 yuan for a round.

G: Oh, I see. We'd like to pay by the round.

E: That's fine. May I know your way of payment?

G: We'll pay in cash.

E: Thank you.

G: Do you have any special rules?

E: Yes, sir. First, you have to wear special bowling shoes which are available in the bowling alley. Second, no smoking is allowed in the run-up area. And last, please don't throw the bowling ball too high.

G: Thank you. We'll remember.

E: I'll turn on your lane. What about the sizes of your shoes?

G: They're about 40 or 41.

E: You'd better warm up before bowling in order to avoid any sort of injury.

G: I see. Can you bring us some drinks?

E: What kind of drinks would you like?

G: Tea is OK.

E: All right! I'll get them at once. By the way, the towels are here.

G: Thank you!

E: The lane is ready. Have a nice time and have fun.

Practice Answer the questions according to the service conversation.

1. How many people are going to play in the bowling room?
2. How many lanes does the guest like to have, one or two?
3. According to the employee, what are the service hours of the bowling room?

Key Words and Expressions

basketball court	篮球场
hoop/ring (n.)	篮圈
marking board	记分牌
bowling (n.)	保龄球
go bowling/rolling	打保龄球
bowling alley/room	保龄球馆
pin (n.)	保龄球瓶
pin deck	球瓶区
gutter channel	沟槽
pit (n.)	落瓶窖
lane (n.)	球道
strike (n.)	大满贯
hook shot	弧旋球
turkey (n.)	连续三次大满贯
foul (n. & v.)	犯规
indoor/outdoor tennis court	室内(室外)网球场
gym/gymnasium (n.)	健身房,体操馆
warm-up	热身运动,准备活动

Points of Service Performance 服务演练要点

- Familiar with the rules and skills of playing each game, and accompanying the guests on playing if needed.

Chapter Eleven Health & Recreation Center Service
康体中心服务

熟悉各类项目的规则和技能，如需要可提供陪练服务。
- Knowing the methods of operating the equipments and facilities and the ways of fixing a simple breakdown.
  熟悉设施设备的使用方法，并掌握简单故障的处理办法。
- Familiar with the points for attention, knowing how to deal with ordinary accidents happened on the spot.
  熟知各项运动的注意事项，并熟悉客人常见事故的处理方法。
- Knowing well about the charge of each item and the way of payment for the guest.
  了解各种服务项目的计费方法和收费标准。

Performance for Service 模拟演练

Task A

Performance in pairs according to the following two cards.

Guest Card		
	Guest name:	John Smith
	Room number:	Room 1231
	Purpose:	rent a bowling alley
	Charge:	280 yuan per hour or 40 yuan for a round
	Service hour:	10:00 a.m. to 11:00 p.m.
	Number of persons:	10
	Special requests:	two of the guests will leave before the ending hour; the staff should remind them at that time

Employee Card	
	Name of the guest
	Telephone number of the guest
	What kind of service
	Opening hour
	Any special request
	Express the wishes

Task B

A hotel guest, Mr. Bush, and his friends are in the basketball court of the hotel. They want to play basketball. An employee in the basketball court receives them warmly and provides services for them after going through the procedures. It is the first time for most of the guests to come here, so they ask the staff many related questions about the play. At the same time, the staff explains the rules and attentions in detail.

Position Knowledge 岗位知识

The Points for Attention for Body Care Guests:
康体活动宾客注意事项:

- Please put on sneakers before entering the court.
  进入场馆时,请穿着运动鞋。
- No smoking. No spitting. Please throw the wastes into the dustbin.
  场馆内严禁吸烟,禁止出现随地吐痰、吐口香糖等不良行为。
- No admittance for the guest who is as drunk as a lord.
  谢绝饮酒过量者入内。
- Those guests who have hypertension, heart disease or are unsuitable for violent exercises must use the facilities cautiously.
  凡患有心脏病、高血压等不适合剧烈运动者,请慎用场馆设施。
- For children's entering into the court, they must be kept watching by their parents.
  凡未成年儿童,请在家长陪同下进入场内活动。
- Please use the facilities under the direction of our staff. Any damages caused by wrong uses must be compensated according to the regulation.
  请自觉爱护场馆的设备设施。凡因使用不当造成损坏的,须按照酒店规定予以赔偿。

Exercises

Ⅰ. Topics for discussion.

1. If you work in the bowling room, what kinds of special knowledge are you required to master?
2. Suppose your hotel has a newly-built bowling center. How do you introduce the bowling service to the guests?
3. Introduce one of the main service items and facilities to the guests.

Ⅱ. Write out the questions according to the answers.

1. _____
   We like two lanes.
2. _____
   Yes, please switch on the marking board.
3. _____
   We offer all kinds of exercise equipments, such as exercise bicycles, Nautilus

machines, Stairmasters and so on.

4. _____

Yes, sir. You have to wear special bowling shoes which are available in the bowling room. No smoking is allowed in the run-up area.

Ⅲ. Translate the following sentences into English.

1. 请您在使用完健身器后擦拭干净。
2. 我们有武术、瑜伽和普拉提课程。
3. 这项运动对您的四肢有好处。
4. 请你们换上球鞋。如果自己没有带,我们这里有备用鞋可以出租。
5. 半场的租用时间以每 30 分钟为 1 个计算单位,不足 30 分钟的按 30 分钟计算。
6. 运动之前,请先做好热身运动,以免发生脚踝扭伤、肌肉拉伤、膝盖损伤等意外事故。

Ⅳ. Answer the questions according to the passage.

Bowling started in Germany and Holland. Before A. D. 4th century, bowling was only a religion ceremony. It was said that pillars representing evils were usually erected in hall or passages, the ball representing judgment was kicked to the pillars by believers of religion to get the luck. Until 16th century, the Holland immigrants brought this nine-pillar game to America, because of its entertainment contention and interest; it was quickly accepted and changed from outdoor to indoor. In mid-19th century, this game became a ten-pillar game which was first named "bowling". It became an elegant entertainment item from then on.

Questions:

1. Where did bowling begin?
2. According to the passage, what was bowling before A. D. 4th century?
3. In 16th century, who brought this game to America?
4. When was this game first named "bowling"?
5. Can you use your own words to state the origin of the bowling?

Unit Twenty-seven Bathing Service

Procedure of Service 服务流程

- Stand at your post to welcome the arriving guest.
- Introduce main service items and facilities to the guest and reply his inquires if needed.
- Clear the charge of items and know the way of payment.
- Examine the room card and confirm the record on the computer.
- Go through the relevant procedures and make records clearly.
- Lead the guest to the place where the service facility is provided.
- Introduce the method of using facilities, remind the guest the points for attention, pay much attention to guest's safety such as his valuables laid in the change-room cabinet.
- Provide excellent services to the guest according to Hotel Operational Procedures.
- Answer inquiries related to specialties and provide suitable ways of treatment to the guest.
- Settle account for the guest according to the procedures.
- See the guest off and show good wishes to him.

Points of Service Language 服务语言要点

1. **Introducing main services to the guests and replying their inquires if needed**　介绍服务项目情况并回答客人问询

   The swimming pool is free of charge for hotel guests.
   我们酒店的客人可以免费使用游泳池。
   We have a well-equipped indoor swimming pool and the bathing center.
   我们有设备良好的室内游泳池以及洗浴中心。
   We supply the free bath towel, bath foam, and shampoo.
   我们提供免费的浴巾、沐浴液以及洗发液。

Chapter Eleven　Health & Recreation Center Service
康体中心服务

Our swimming center opens from 10:00 a.m. to 11:00 p.m.

我们游泳中心从上午10点营业到晚上11点。

Sir, excuse me, the bathing center is to be closed in ten minutes.

对不起,先生,洗浴中心只有十分钟就要结束营业了。

You can practice in the shallow area of the pool at first, and the life guard nearby is getting ready to help you whenever you need.

您可以先在浅水区练习,我们的救生员随时在旁边做好帮助您的准备。

2. **Clearing the charge of items and knowing the way of payment　介绍收费标准并了解付款方式**

The charge is 78 yuan per time (no longer than 3 hours) for one person only.

每人每次78元,最长时间为3小时。

You can sign instead of paying cash.

你可以签单,而不付现金。

The bathing suit is 90 yuan for one and the bathing trunks are 70 yuan.

这种泳衣是90元一件,泳裤是70元一条。

The charge is 58 yuan per person.

费用是每人58元。

3. **Reminding the guests the points for attention　提醒客人注意事项**

Here is the key to your locker.

这是您更衣室的钥匙。

If you feel uncomfortable, you'd better relax with soft drinks and some cakes at the rest room beside the sauna room.

如果您感觉不舒服,您最好到桑拿房旁边的休息室内休息一下,那里提供饮料和点心。

Please don't stay in the sauna room too long. If you feel uncomfortable, please let us know as soon as possible.

请您不要蒸太长时间。如果感觉不舒服,请立即停止并通知我们。

This is the key to the cabinet. Please keep it well. Change-room is over there. Ladies' is in the left and gentlemen's in the right.

这是您更衣室的钥匙,请保管好,更衣室在那里。女更衣室在左边,男更衣室在右边。

This is the key to your change-room cabinet. Please return it to the service counter when you leave.

这是您的更衣柜钥匙,在您离开时,请将钥匙交回服务台。

4. **Answering inquiries related to specialties, providing suitable ways of treatment to guests　为客人提供服务项目的专业咨询和技术指导**

Please take on your slippers and take a shower first. Go this way to the showers, please.

请您换好拖鞋,先去淋浴。让我带您去淋浴间吧。

Our saunas include damp, dry, salt and ice treatment.

我们有湿蒸浴、干蒸浴、盐浴和冰蒸浴几种。

They say that if you have such diseases as hypertension or heart diseases, or if you drink too much or feel uncomfortable, please do not use the sauna facilities.

凡患有高血压、心脏病或饮酒过量及感觉身体不适者,请慎用桑拿设施,以免发生危险。

The temperature of the sauna room is heated up, you can go in now.

桑拿房的温度已调节好了,您可以进去了。

Please take a shower at first, then put on the bathing suit and swimming cap. Dip your feet in the disinfect pool before going to the swimming pool.

请您在进入游泳池前,先进行淋浴,然后换好游泳衣、戴上泳帽,将脚放在消毒池里浸泡一下。

You'd better do some warm-up exercises before swimming in order to avoid muscle cramps.

您在下水游泳前,最好做些热身运动,以防出现肌肉痉挛现象。

Service Conversation 51

Serving Sauna

27-51 Serving Sauna.mp3

R: Receptionist at the Bathing Center

G: Guest

E: Employee in the Sauna Room

R: Welcome to our bathing center, sir! Is there anything I can do for you?

G: I'd like to use the sauna.

R: Are you a hotel guest?

G: Yes, I am.

R: Which room are you in?

G: I'm in Room 1298.

R: Thank you.

G: Oh, by the way, how much does it cost?

R: The charge is 58 yuan per person. And how would you like to pay?

G: I'll pay cash.

R: OK. Please sign this form.

G: All right.

R: All set. This is the key to your locker. Please return it to the service counter when you leave.

Chapter Eleven Health & Recreation Center Service
康体中心服务

(Later the guest has arrived in the Sauna Room.)

E: Good evening, sir! Welcome to the change room. Let me see your key tablet. Oh, here's your locker.

G: OK. Thank you.

E: Please put on your slippers and take a shower first. Go this way to the showers, please.

G: How many kinds of sauna do you offer?

E: Our saunas include damp, dry, salt and ice treatments. What do you prefer, sir?

G: I think I prefer to take a damp treatment.

E: All right. Please take a look at the hotel regulations. They say that if you have such diseases as hypertension or heart disease, or if you drink too much or feel uncomfortable, please do not use the sauna facilities.

G: Oh, I see.

E: Please don't stay in the sauna room too long. If you feel uncomfortable, please let us know as soon as possible.

G: Yes.

E: Would you like something to drink?

G: Just give me a bottle of mineral water.

E: The sauna is heated up. You can go in now.

G: Thanks a lot!

E: Enjoy your sauna.

G: Thank you!

Practice Answer the questions according to the service conversation.

1. Which room does the guest live in the hotel?
2. How much does it cost for the guest to take a sauna?
3. How many kinds of sauna bath services does the hotel supply?

Service Conversation 52

Serving Swimming

R: Receptionist at the Bathing Center
G: Guest
E: Employee in the Change Room

27-52 Serving Swimming.mp3

R: Welcome to our bathing center, sir! What can I do for you?

G: I want to go swimming.

R: OK. Are you a hotel guest?

G: Yes, I am.

R: In that case, the swimming pool is free. Could you please show me your room card and registration card? I have to fill in this form.

G: OK! By the way, I didn't bring bathing trunks with me. Do you have any to sell?

R: Sure, we have. The bathing trunks are 70 yuan. Do you want a pair?

G: Yes, I want to select one. The black one is OK.

R: That's fine. All set. Please sign here. This is the key to your locker. Please return it to the service counter before you leave.

(Later the guest has arrived in the Change Room.)

E: Good afternoon, sir! Welcome to the locker room. Let me see your key tablet. Oh, here is your locker.

G: Thank you. What's the temperature of the water?

E: 27℃.

G: What's the depth of the pool?

E: The depth of the swimming pool varies from shallow to deep. The deepest place is about 2.3 meters, while the shallowest is 1.6 meters.

G: I like swimming, though I'm not good at it.

E: Don't worry about it. You can practice in the shallow end of the pool at first; and the life guard nearby is ready to help you whenever you need.

G: That's very kind of you!

E: My pleasure. Swimming has brought on a new trend of healthy culture. It is one of the best sports to alleviate fatigue.

G: You're right. Swimming can improve the blood circulation. So people who swim regularly are less likely to fall ill. I've made up my mind to keep on swimming.

E: For sure. Hope you have good health forever. Please take a shower at first, then put on the bathing suit and swimming cap. Dip your feet in the disinfect pool before going to the swimming pool.

G: All right.

E: We supply a bath towel, shampoo, and bath foam for free. Help yourself! You'd better do some warm-up exercises before swimming in order to avoid muscle cramps.

G: OK.

E: Please don't dive. The water is so shallow that your head will be hurt.

G: I got it. When will the swimming pool close?

E: Don't worry, sir! It will be open until midnight.

G: Thanks a lot.

Chapter Eleven　Health & Recreation Center Service
康体中心服务

E: You're welcome! Hope you have a wonderful time here!

Practice　Answer the questions according to the service conversation.

1. What is the temperature of the water?
2. How does the hotel charge the hotel guest when he goes swimming at the swimming pool?
3. What does the employee ask the guest to do before swimming in order to avoid muscle cramp?

Key Words and Expressions

sauna (n.)	桑拿浴
change-room cabinet	更衣柜
damp treatment	湿蒸(桑拿)
dry treatment	干蒸(桑拿)
salt treatment	盐浴
ice treatment	冰蒸浴
uncomfortable (adj.)	不舒服
natatorium (n.)	游泳馆
open-air/indoor pool	室外(内)游泳池
gentleman's/lady's changing room	男(女)更衣室
bathing trunks	游泳裤
rubber float	游泳圈
underwater swimming	潜泳
dip (v.)	浸,泡
shower (n.)	淋浴
shampoo (n.)	香波,洗发液
bath foam	沐浴液
disinfect (n. & v.)	灭菌,消毒;给……消毒
alleviate (n.)	缓解,减轻

Points of Service Performance 服务演练要点

- The staff should be skilful at swimming; and provide help for the guests who are new to swim.
  工作人员应熟练掌握常用游泳技巧,以便为生手客人提供技术指导。
- The staff should be familiar with the knowledge of normal emergency treatment; and give the first-aid to the guests who are in an accident.
  工作人员应熟练掌握常用急救知识,以便为客人提供紧急救护。

- The staff should know the main effect of different kinds of sauna; and recommend suitable ways of treatment to the guest according to their personal conditions.
  工作人员应了解各种桑拿浴的功效,以便有针对性地向客人进行推介。

Performance for Service 模拟演练

Task A

Performance in pairs according to the following two cards.

Guest Card		
	Guest name:	John Porter
	Persons:	John and his family
	Room number:	Room 1907
	Purpose:	go swimming and play in the water
	Special request:	John's children want to play in the water, but one of those is too young to play with others. John is afraid that he cannot take care of all the children, so he asks the staff to help him.

Employee Card	
	Name of the guest
	Introduce the facilities of the Swimming Center
	Any special request
	Express the wishes

Task B

Mr. George Brown is walking to the Bathing Center. He will reserve in the sauna room because half an hour later his boss and the staff of the company will come here to take sauna treatment. Now he comes first to make sure the service of the sauna, such as the kinds of sauna treatment, the way of payment, and the service hours. The employee in the Bathing Center receives him and explains the items in detail.

Position Knowledge 岗位知识

- Notices for guests who go swimming   游泳宾客须知
  - Take care of your personal belongings and leave your valuables with the service counter.
    请妥善保管随身物品或将贵重物品寄存在服务台。
  - No admittance for the guests who have infectious and skin diseases or drink too much.

凡患有皮肤病和传染病以及饮酒过量者请勿入内。
- For children's entering into the water, they must be kept watching by their parents.

  凡儿童游泳，必须在家长的带领下方可入内。
- No smoking. No spitting. Please throw the wastes into the dustbin.

  泳池区域禁止吸烟。严禁随地吐痰和乱丢废弃物。

• Notices for Guests who Take a Sauna   桑拿宾客须知
- Take care of your personal valuable belongings and cash.

  请妥善保管好随身携带物品及现金等贵重物品。
- In order to stop steam evaporation, please close the door as soon as you open it.

  为减少热气蒸发，请在进出桑拿室时随手关门。
- No admittance for the guests who have infectious and skin diseases.

  凡患有皮肤病和传染病者请勿入内。
- Please don't smoke. Keep quiet.

  室内严禁吸烟。严禁大声喧哗。

Exercises

Ⅰ. Topics for discussion.

1. If you work in the bowling room, what kinds of special knowledge are you required to master?
2. What is sauna? What kinds of sauna treatment can you remember? What kind do you prefer?
3. How do you think a staff in the Swimming Center can become a good staff? In other words, what kinds of abilities should a staff own?

Ⅱ. Translate the following sentences into Chinese.

The bathing services are a general term of a series of service items in a hotel which meet the demands of the guests on detoxifying and relaxing. It mainly includes bathing, sauna, SPA, fragrant herbal bath, swim, rubdown, massage, etc. Different hotels provide different items according to their own conditions.

Ⅲ. Read the following passage and answer the questions.

Sauna Bath, also named as Steam Bath, is one kind of health care bathing. It has an effect of eliminating tiredness and enhancing quality of body. It is also helpful to treat some diseases.

Dry Sauna Bath, also called Turkish bath, started in Eastern Europe. People sit in round in a wooden room bathing the steam from the mineral stones which are sprinkled by cold water after burnt in red. It has an effect of sweating weight off, accelerating blood circulation and metabolism. It is suitable for people whose skins are oily.

Damp Sauna Bath, also named as Finland Bath, is that people stay in a very hot room to let the human body absorb steam. It has an effect on helping to dilate blood capillary and smooth the skin. It is suitable for people whose skins are damp.

Salt Sauna Bath, is that people stay in a room whose four sides are coated with salt to let the body absorb the molecule which gives out from the salt by high temperature. It has an effect on helping to smooth skin and kill virus.

Ice Sauna Bath, is a comparative cold place where people can stay for a while between the dry or wet sauna. It has an effect on helping to adjust body temperature and soothe the nerves.

Rubdown which is popular among the people in China is a simple health care treatment. The technician gives the guest a rubdown with a damp towel to massage his back and other places of the body after he takes a shower. Through the network of passages vital energy circulates. It has an effect on helping to prevent illness and prolong life.

Questions:

1. How many kinds of sauna bath are mentioned in the passage? And what are they?
2. What is Dry Sauna Bath according to the passage?
3. How do you understand Damp Sauna Bath?
4. What is Salt Sauna Bath?
5. Can you introduce Ice Sauna Bath?
6. What is Rubdown? And how does the technician do to the guest?

Unit Twenty-eight Entertaining Service

单元 28 娱乐服务

Procedure of Service 服务流程

- Greet the guest.
- Introduce main service items and facilities to the guest.
- Explain the charge of items and know the way of payment.
- Examine the room card of the guest and confirm the record on the computer.
- Lead the guest to the place where the service facility is provided.
- Introduce the method of using facilities and remind the guest the points for attention.
- Provide excellent service to guest according to hotel operational procedures.
- Settle account for the guests according to procedures.
- See the guest off.

Points of Service Language 服务语言要点

1. **Polite expressions 礼貌用语**

   It's my pleasure. We look forward to your arrival.
   很高兴为您服务。我们恭候您的光临。

2. **Introducing main service items and facilities to the guests 介绍服务项目及设施设备情况**

   I'll switch on the power; you can use the net by pressing this key.
   我帮您接通电源,开启计算机,您只要单击这个键,便可直接上网。

   Well, it's well equipped with first-class stereo and lighting systems; and the dance floor is decorated fashionably.
   我们有一流的立体声音响和照明设备,舞台的装修也很时尚。

   We have all kinds of songs, such as pop songs, folk songs, rock and roll, and so on. Besides English songs, we have also Cantonese songs, Japanese songs, Korean songs, etc.
   我们有各种类型的歌曲,如流行歌曲、民间歌曲和摇滚歌曲。除了英文歌曲外,我们还备有粤语歌曲、日本歌曲和韩国歌曲等。

As you know, the computer in our center has a wide variety of English songs which includes all kinds of European and American songs. You can choose almost any song.

正如您所知,我们的英文歌曲十分齐全,几乎涵盖了所有欧美的经典歌曲。您几乎可以从中找到每一首歌。

3. Introducing the method of using facilities and remind the guests the points for attention 介绍设施设备的使用方法并提醒客人注意事项

The technician has installed all songs into the computer, from which you can find out your favored songs.

歌厅的歌曲已全部输入计算机,您可以直接在计算机上点歌。

You can first select the codes of the songs you prefer and then press the key "input". And if you have any difficulty, please do not hesitate to ask our staff for help.

您可以选择您所喜欢的歌曲代码,然后按输入键。如果觉得操作不方便的话,可以请在场服务人员帮忙。

Please do not smoke in the KTV parlor because it is neither safe nor healthy. And the sound levels have already been adjusted well. Pleases do not twiddle with the equipment. If you have problems, please let the technician know.

请不要在房间吸烟,因为这既不安全,又影响健康。我们的音响效果是预先设置好的,请不要自己去摆弄;如果需要调整,请音响师帮忙。

Please use our network according to the rules and regulations of the Guests' Notice issued by the hotel.

您请按照酒店《宾客须知》的规定使用上网服务。

4. Giving the information about the charge 告知客人价钱

We have a KTV parlor for ten people; the charge is 480 yuan per hour. And a parlor for twenty; it is about 900 yuan per hour.

我们有一间可容纳10人的包厢,价格为每小时480元。还有一间容纳20人的,价格为每小时900元。

The charge is 10 yuan per hour.

费用为每小时10元。

Service Conversation 53

Serving Ballroom

28-53 Serving Ballroom.mp3

R: Receptionist
G: Guest

R: Good evening! It's nice to see you in the entertainment center!

Chapter Eleven Health & Recreation Center Service
康体中心服务

G: Good evening! I'd like to book a KTV parlor for singing.

R: Have you made a reservation?

G: No. I've just made the decision.

R: Are you a guest in our hotel?

G: Yes, my company held a conference in your hotel.

R: OK. How many people are in your party?

G: I think it's about 20 people altogether.

R: How do you want to settle your account, please?

G: Go with room charge, I think. And by the way, how do you charge?

R: We have a KTV parlor for ten people; the charge is 480 yuan per hour. And a parlor for twenty; it is about 900 yuan per hour.

G: I see. What is your KTV parlor like?

R: Well, it's well-equipped with first-class stereo and lighting systems; and the dance floor is decorated fashionably. When you're here it will feel like a dream.

G: That sounds nice. What kind of songs do you have?

R: We have all kinds of songs, such as pop songs, folk songs, rock and roll, and so on. Besides English songs, we have also Cantonese songs, Japanese songs, Korean songs, etc. And every evening at 7:00 p.m. we have a folk song and dance party. Are you interested in that?

G: That's good, but most of my colleagues prefer to sing in a KTV room, I think. And some of us are interested in singing English songs.

R: Oh, I see. As you know, the computer in our center has a wide variety of English songs which includes all kinds of European and American songs. You can choose almost any song.

G: Good, thank you. Would you please tell me how to use the machine when we sing?

R: You can first select the codes of the songs you prefer and then press the key "input". And if you have any difficulty, please do not hesitate to ask our staff for help.

G: That's very kind of you.

R: It's the least we can do. And for drinks, we only offer tea for free. The alcohol, snacks and fruits are extra.

G: I see!

R: Please do not smoke in the KTV parlor because it is neither safe nor healthy. And the sound levels have already been adjusted well. Please do not fiddle with the equipment. If you have problems, please let the technician know.

G: I got it.

R: We hope you enjoy yourselves and relax completely.

> **Practice** Answer the questions according to the service conversation.

1. How about the contents of the songs?

2. How can the guest find out the songs?
3. Tell us the rule in the parlor.

Service Conversation 54 — Serving Net Bar

28－54 Serving Net Bar. mp3

R: Receptionist

G: Guest

R: Good morning! Very nice to see you in the entertainment center!

G: Good morning! I'd like to use a computer in the net bar to find some material.

R: Are you a hotel guest?

G: Yes, I'm staying in Room 1008.

R: Would you please show me your room card? I have to make a record.

G: Here you are.

R: Thank you! How would you like to settle your payment?

G: Go with my room account I think. What do you charge?

R: The charge is 10 yuan per hour. As you know, the environment and equipment in our hotel are first class; and the computers are very fast. Please pay close attention to the regulations in the Guests' Notice.

G: OK!

R: This is your computer. Is it all right? I'll switch on the power; you can use the net by pressing this key.

G: That's fine.

R: For any problems please ask our staff. Please sign your name at the service desk when you leave.

G: OK.

Practice Answer the questions according to the service conversation.

1. Why does the guest want to use the computer in the hotel?
2. How does the guest settle her account?
3. What rules must the guest follow when using the computer of the hotel?

Chapter Eleven Health & Recreation Center Service
康体中心服务

discotheque (n.)	迪斯科舞厅
karaoke (n.)	卡拉OK
KTV parlor	KTV 包间
Karaoke hall	卡拉OK 厅
KTV private room	KTV 包厢
accompanying video	伴唱机
high-tech equipment	高科技设备
stereo system	立体音响
catalogue/list (n.)	歌单,目录
remote control	遥控器
volume (n.)	音量

Points of Service Performance 服务演练要点

- Knowing the operational skills of all equipments, such as the ways to adjust acoustics and run computers.
  熟练掌握各项设备的操作方法,如音效调试、计算机操作等。
- Knowing well where the classic and popular songs are stored and the way of touching on the computer.
  熟悉经典、流行和常见歌曲的存储位置及点播方法。
- Ensuring the service area's safety and civilization and be skilful at treating drunkard and fire prevention.
  确保服务场所的文明和安全,如妥善处理醉酒客人、避免发生火灾事故。

Performance for Service 模拟演练

Task A

Performance in pairs according to the following two cards.

Guest Card		
	Guest name:	David Jones
	Persons:	nine other persons
	Purpose:	David and other 9 friends come into a KTV room to celebrate the birthday.
	Special request:	To have a big KTV room and ask the staff to prepare a birthday cake for them.

Receptionist Card	Name of the guest Explain: The room for nine people is not available. The rooms are either bigger or smaller. Advise them to have a bigger room. Patiently show them how to use the machine. Express the wishes

Task B

Miss Allen and her boyfriend, as well as 10 other friends come to the recreation center. They will graduate from college in two weeks. So they decide to come here to celebrate their graduation. They want to select a big ball room. Being college students, they ask the staff to give them 80% discount. After confirmation, the staff shows them how to use the machine patiently. The staff wishes them a good time.

Position Knowledge 岗位知识

The Points for Attention for Guests in the Net Bar:
网吧宾客须知:

- Please don't use illegally copied video disc and unlicensed CD in the net bar.
  请勿上机使用非法盗版、未经许可的 CD 盘及各种软盘。
- Please don't listen, watch and copy unhealthy contents which are obscene, superstitious or reactionary. It's not allowed to do anything which has nothing to do with the service contents.
  不得在网吧收听、收看、复制淫秽、迷信、反动等不健康的内容。不得在网吧从事与服务内容无关的其他任何活动。
- It's forbidden to send ill E-mails and advertisements. Otherwise, the user have to bear legal responsibility for all the serious consequences arising therefore.
  禁止在网上发送恶意、挑衅性的邮件和商业广告,否则,由此造成的一切法律责任均由使用者本人承担。
- If you meet any problems when you are running the computer, please ask our staff for help. Don't change or delete data of the computer by yourselves.
  上网时,若遇到疑难问题,请咨询服务人员帮忙解决。不得擅自对计算机的网络功能及存储、运行、传输的数据和应用程序进行更改、增减或删除。
- Please use the equipments carefully according to the regulation. Any artificially imposed damages caused by wrong use will be compensated.
  请按照操作规范使用网吧设备,自觉维护设备安全,凡因人为使用不当所造成的损坏均须按酒店规定予以赔偿。

Chapter Eleven Health & Recreation Center Service
康体中心服务

Exercises

Ⅰ. **Topics for discussion.**

1. In what cases will you go to a ball room?
2. If you want to become a member of a fitness club, what information about the club do you want to know?
3. What kinds of sport games do you prefer? Why do you like it?

Ⅱ. **Write out the questions according to the answers.**

1. _____

   We have all kinds of songs for you to choose.

2. _____

   Yes, I'm staying in Room 1008.

3. _____

   You can first select the codes of the songs you prefer and then press the key "input".

4. _____

   In the KTV room, you will feel like a dream.

Ⅲ. **Translate the following sentences into English.**

1. 如果您有任何问题,请告知技术人员。
2. 我们有设备一流的立体声音响和照明设备。
3. 我们酒店的环境和设备是一流的,计算机的运行速度也是非常快的。
4. 您可以选择您所喜欢的歌曲代码,然后按输入键。
5. 请您按照酒店《宾客须知》的规定使用上网服务。
6. 我们的音响效果是预先设置好的,请不要自己调整。

Chapter Twelve
Convention & Exhibition Center Service
会展中心服务

Unit Twenty-nine　Convention Service
单元 29　会议服务

Unit Thirty　Exhibition Service
单元 30　展览服务

Service Position 服务岗位

The Convention and Exhibition Center(会展中心) is responsible for offering convention service or exhibition service to some organizations both from home and aboard. It provides comprehensive convention and exhibition services including the activities planning, convention and exhibition equipments leasing, simultaneous interpretation, documents translation, ballroom decoration, stage performance and so on. Some of the conventional hotels have a remarkable reserve of advanced convention and exhibition equipments, ranging from the slide projector, the full simultaneous interpretation facilities to the audio and video equipments and the office equipments.

The Convention and Exhibition Center is an auxiliary department of a hotel. It is becoming one of the leading pillars that support the hotel industry. What it does can builds up the image of the hotel, adds much to the convenience and pleasure of the guests, and at the same time makes greater financial success for the hotel.

Skills and Attainments 服务技能与素养

The excellent abilities both in communication and in harmonization, and the fair abilities both in organizing and in planning are required for the services in the convention and exhibition.

Compared with the services in the other positions of the hotel, the convention and exhibition service is a kind of comprehensive and diversified service. The clerks of the Convention and Exhibition Center offer services directly in English including: booking the meeting or the conference, planning the event, discussing the service details with the planner of the meeting or the exhibition, decorating the meeting hall, setting up the exhibition, preparing for the meeting or the exhibition, serving the meeting or the exhibition, harmonizing the related departments with the planer of the meeting or the exhibition, meeting the guest's urgent needs, and making the payment.

They are always needed to communicate and cooperate with the other departments in order to finish the service task, deal with the urgent business of the guests, and harmonize between the other departments with the guests. So the clerks of the Convention and Exhibition Center ought to have the excellent English abilities both in communication and in harmonization, and the fair abilities both in organizing and in planning in addition to being expert at one thing and good at many.

Key Words and Expressions

comprehensive (*adj.*)	全面的,完整的,包含多的,综合的
auxiliary (*adj.*)	辅助的
lease (*vt.*)	出租

simultaneous interpretation	同声传译
projector (*n.*)	幻灯机，放映机
decorate (*vt.*)	修饰，装饰，布置
harmonize (*vt.*)	使调和，使一致；使和睦，调停
urgent (*adj.*)	紧急的，迫切的
build up	加强

Notes

1. setting up the exhibition　布展
2. harmonize the related departments with the planer of the meeting or the exhibition
  协调相关部门和会议策划人或布展商
3. meeting the guests' urgent needs　满足客人急需
4. Compared with the services in the other position of the hotel, the convention and exhibition service is a kind of comprehensive and diversified service.
  与酒店的其他岗位服务相比，会展服务是一种综合性全方位的服务。
5. The excellent abilities both in communication and in harmonization, and the fair abilities both in organizing and in planning are required for the services in the convention and exhibition.
  会展服务需要较高的沟通能力、协调合作能力，以及一定的组织策划和领导能力。
6. So the clerks of the Convention and Exhibition Center ought to have the excellent English abilities both in communication and in harmonization, and the fair abilities both in organizing and in planning in addition to being expert at one thing and good at many.
  所以，会展服务工作人员除了一专多能外，还要具有较高的沟通能力、协调合作能力和一定的组织策划与领导能力。

Unit Twenty-nine Convention Service

Main Service 主要服务

- Booking the meeting.
- Discussing the service details of the meeting.
- Showing the meeting planner the facilities of the meeting and the decoration of the meeting hall.
- Registering for the conference.
- Serving during the meeting.
- Making the payment.

Procedure of Service 服务流程

Booking the meeting

- Greet the meeting planner.
- Get the following information from the meeting planner:
  What size of the conference or how many participants;
  What kind of conference or what kind of function room;
  The special demands for the meeting facilities;
  The special demands for the meeting service;
  The time of the conference;
  The number of the rooms needed.
- Introduce the facilities and services of the hotel according to the information above.
- Get the name of the meeting planner and his telephone number and the date of the discussion about the service details for the conference.
- Express your wishes.

Chapter Twelve Convention & Exhibition Center Service
会展中心服务

Discussing the service details

- Greet the meeting planner.
- Discuss and confirm the previous reservation.
- Discuss the service details.
- Establish the services.
- Express your wishes.

Points of Service Language 服务语言要点

1. **Getting the information for the reservation from the meeting planner   获得会议预订信息**

    What kind of conference will you hold and how many people will attend?
    请问会议的类型和会议的规模?
    Could you please tell me your catering requirements for arranging catering for the conference?
    请问您对会议的餐饮安排有什么要求?
    Have you finalized the number of participants?
    已经确定了与会代表的人数吗?
    What kind of function room do you need?
    请问需要什么功能的房间/会议室?
    How many participates will there be/attend the meeting?
    请问参加会议的人数?
    How many rooms would you like?
    需要多少个房间?

2. **Introducing the meeting facilities and meeting services   介绍会议设施和会议服务**

    We have a fully-equipped convention center that provides complete secretarial service.
    我们会议中心设备齐全,提供全套秘书设备。
    Our Conference Center has just been equipped with full simultaneous interpretation facilities.
    我们的会议中心配置了全套的同声传译设备。
    We have two large conference halls. One can seat 300 people; the other can be seated for 500 attendants.
    我们有两个大会议厅,一个能坐300人,另外一个可以坐500人。
    We can provide audio-visual equipment, for example, a television, VCR and multi-media projector, as well as more traditional equipment such as a flip chart and white board.
    我们可以提供视听器材,比如,电视机、录像机、多媒体投影机,此外,还有一些传统的器材,如活动挂图和白色书写板。
    The center of the multi-purpose hall is the main conference auditorium seating 500 people.

213

多功能厅主会场能容纳 500 人。

Beside the largest conference hall, there are five small meeting rooms which can hold 60 people and a small exhibition room for display purpose.

在最大的会议厅旁边有五个小的能容纳 60 人的会议室,还有一个可用于陈列展品的小展室。

We can offer some office support services such as telex, photocopying and secretarial services.

我们能提供电传、复印和秘书办公服务。

There is a discount for the conference reservations this month.

本月会议预订有折扣。

Please choose two among the three kinds of breakfasts as the breakfast of the conference.

请您从这三种早餐中挑选两种作为本次会议的早餐。

3. **Meeting special requirements　满足特殊需要**

Besides the Service Guidance and the price list of the services in our hotel, I'll send you a floor plan of the actual conference center. Now, would you please switch on your fax machine?

除了本酒店的服务指南和服务价目单以外,我还给您传一张会议中心的平面图。现在,请您打开传真机,好吗?

The suppers on the first day and the last day of the conference are banquets.

会议的第一天和最后一天的晚餐为宴会。

Our restaurant carters for various religions.

我们餐厅为各种宗教人士提供食品饮料。

We can arrange for you.

我们能为您安排。

Reserving the Conference on the Phone

29-55 Reserving the Conference on the Phone. mp3

M: Convention Service Manager

W: Martin Washington, a convention planner

M: Good morning. Beijing International Hotel Convention Center. How can I help you?

W: Good morning. This is Martin Washington speaking. We want to hold a conference in your hotel in September. May I speak to your manager?

Chapter Twelve Convention & Exhibition Center Service
会展中心服务

M: I'm the Convention Service Manager. My name is Zhong Lin. What kind of conference will you hold and how many people will attend, Mr. Washington?

W: It's an international seminar for teaching Chinese. The exact number of delegates has not been finalized. We expect that 400 participants will attend the conference. What sort of facilities can you offer?

M: We can provide audio-visual equipment, for example, a television, VCR and multimedia projector, as well as more traditional equipment such as a flip chart and white board.

W: Can you provide a simultaneous interpretation system?

M: Certainly, we can offer full simultaneous interpretation facilities.

W: How about your conference halls and small meeting rooms?

M: We have two large conference halls. One can seat 400 people; the other can accommodate up to 600 people. We also have ten small meeting rooms which can hold 40 to 60 people.

W: What's the daily charge for the larger hall with the full simultaneous interpretation facilities?

M: 15,000 US dollars.

W: We'd like to book the largest conference hall for two days and 7 small meeting rooms for a day.

M: What about the time of the conference?

W: September 5th to 8th.

M: Would you like some rooms?

W: Yes, we'd like to reserve 300 standard rooms. Can you give us detailed information about your services and their prices? That way, we can make a good plan for the conference.

M: Certainly. Besides the Service Guidance and the price list for the services, I'll send you a floor plan of the actual conference center. Now, would you please switch on your fax machine and tell me when you have received the material?

W: OK. I've received them and they're very clear. Thank you.

M: And can I contact you at the fax number, Mr. Washington?

W: Certainly.

M: Would you like to discuss this further with us?

W: I'll come to your hotel to discuss the details with you on July 15th.

M: I'd like to confirm the reservation for you, Mr. Washington.

W: Please.

M: You've booked the larger conference hall for two days and 7 small meeting rooms for one day. Your conference will be on September 5th to 8th. You need 300 standard rooms. Your telephone number is 23****89. Is that correct?

W: Yes, that's correct. Thanks a lot.

M: You're welcome. I look forward to your arrival on July 15th.

Practice Answer the questions according to the service conversation.

1. What kind of conference will be held in the hotel?
2. What does Zhong Lin send to Mr. Washington?
3. When will the planner come to discuss the service details?

Discussing the Service Details

29 – 56　Discussing the Service Details. mp3

Ⓜ: Convention Service Manager

Ⓦ: Martin Washington, a convention planner

M: Good morning, sir. Welcome to our hotel. May I help you?

W: Good morning. I'm Martin Washington. I'd like to talk with your manager.

M: Pleased to meet you, Mr. Washington. I'm Zhong Lin. I've been expecting you.

W: Pleased to meet you, too, Ms. Zhong.

M: Have you finalized the number of participants?

W: Yes, we have. 500 people will attend our International Seminar of Teaching Chinese. We'll need the larger conference hall with the simultaneous interpretation system and multi-media projector for September 5th and 8th, and 8 small meeting rooms for September 6th.

M: What about the rooms?

W: 350 standard rooms. Is there any discount for conference reservations this month?

M: No. But I went to see the General Manager yesterday, and he agreed to discount your conference. We'll give you 10% off.

W: Thank you very much.

M: It's my pleasure. Could you tell me your catering requirements for the conference?

W: The suppers on the first day and the last day of the conference are Chinese banquets. The other meals will be buffets. Besides an American breakfast, please offer some Chinese snacks as breakfast.

M: Two Chinese banquets and some Chinese snacks, good idea. What beverage would you prefer for the Chinese banquets?

W: The famous Chinese wine, Mao-tai, and Tsingtao beer.

Chapter Twelve Convention & Exhibition Center Service
会展中心服务

M: Mao-tai and Tsingtao. Is there anything else I can do for you?

W: We need 6 special clerks to register our conference attendees and to work as interpreters on September 6th and 7th.

M: Have you any special requirements for the 6 special clerks?

W: Two of them should know German, two French, two Russian.

M: By the way, when will we get your deposit check?

W: I'll see that Ms. Robinson sends a check out next week. Just one last minor detail: a few of my colleagues will arrive on September 2nd to prepare for the conference.

M: I'll make their arrangements.

W: Thanks for your help. Goodbye.

M: Goodbye. We look forward to serving you.

Practice Answer the questions according to the service conversation.

1. How many participants will there be?
2. Could you tell us the requirements of the meeting planner of arranging catering for the conference?
3. Does the meeting planner have any special demands for the 6 special clerks? What are they?

Key Words and Expressions

participant (n.)	参加者,与会代表
seminar (n.)	(专家)研讨会
delegate (n.)	代表
audio-visual equipment	视听设备
video record	录像机
multimedia projector	多媒体投影仪
the full simultaneous interpretation facilities	全套同声传译设备
plan of the actual conference center	会议中心的平面图
accommodate (vt.)	照应,招待
International Seminar of Chinese Teaching	国际汉语教学研讨会
discount (n.)	折扣,让头
register for our conference	为会议报道
check (n.)	支票
colleague (n.)	同事,同行

Notes

1. what kind of conference or what kind of function room 会议类型或所需具有何种

功能的会议室

2. the date of the discussion about the service details for the conference　商讨会议服务相关细节的日期

3. It's an International Conference of Seminar Chinese Teaching. The exact number of delegates has not been finalized.
   这是一次国际汉语教学研讨会,到会代表的人数还没有最后确定。

4. Besides the Service Guidance and the price list of the services in our hotel, I'll send you a floor plan of the actual conference center. Now, would you please switch on your fax machine?
   除了本酒店的服务指南和服务价目单以外,我还给您传一张会议中心的平面图。请您打开您的传真机,好吗?

5. I'll see that Ms. Robinson sends a check out next Friday.
   我会确保下周五让 Robinson 女士寄一张支票过来。

Points of Service Performance 服务演练要点

When discussing the service details with the meeting planner:
和会议策划人讨论会议服务细节:

- Pay attention to whether the reservation has been changed or not.
  注意预订有无变化并予以确认。
- Discuss the arrangements and demands for catering for the meeting.
  会议餐饮安排和要求。
- Pay attention to the demands in detail of the meeting services and some special requirements.
  留意对会议服务和对会议设施布置的细节要求以及一些特殊需要。

Performance for Service 模拟演练

Task A

Perform booking the conference service on the phone in pairs according to the following two cards.

Guest Card	The aim: hold a meeting to launch the new products The time: June 24 The size of the meeting room: about 200 square meters Want to know the rate

Chapter Twelve　Convention & Exhibition Center Service
会展中心服务

The Manager's Card

What kind of the meeting
What time of the meeting
What size of the meeting room
The rate is 9,000 yuan for every 100 square meters

Task B

Make up a dialogue according to the following:

The meeting planner is discussing the service details with the Conference Service Manager. The number of the participants is increased to 500. They need a multi-purpose hall with at least 500 seats. Some attendants are overseas Chinese. The meeting planner thinks it would be a good idea to serve some Chinese breakfast in addition to American breakfast.

Position Knowledge　岗位知识

- Different from the room reservation, the conference planner(exhibition planner) of the conference reservation (exhibition reservation) will have several discussions about the conference business with the Conference Service Manager before it begins.
  与客房预订不同的是,会议(还有展览)预订的会议组织者(办展商)与会议服务经理在会议开始前的一段时间还需要多次会面商谈会议的有关事宜。

- Some conference facilities:
  一些会议设备:

earphone　耳机	microphone　麦克风
loudspeaker　扩音器	flip chart　活动挂图
white board　白色书写板	laser printer　激光打印机
laptop computer　笔记本电脑	audiovisual　视听设备
projector　投影仪	slide projector　幻灯片投影仪
multimedia projector　多媒体投影机	film projector　电影放映机
television　电视	recorder　录音机
video recorder　录像机	

Exercises

I. Topics for discussion.

1. What should we pay more attention to when we do a conference reservation?
2. What should you do as a conference manager?

II. **Translate the following sentences into English.**

1. 早上好。我们想在你们酒店里举行会议,我可以和负责这项工作的人谈一谈吗?
2. 我们的会议中心配置了全套的同声传译设备。
3. 你能给我们提供你们酒店的各种服务以及服务价目表的详细信息吗? 只有这样,我们才能制订好会议计划。
4. 见到您我也很高兴。我想和您协商一下会议服务的一些细节。
5. 会议的第一天和最后一天的晚餐为宴会。

III. **Translate the following sentences into Chinese.**

1. They also need some office support services, such as the telex photocopying and secretarial services, and 20 laptop computers as well.
2. Can you send us a VIP list so that we can assign the proper rooms for them?
3. From the conference service guide, I know that you can provide advanced conference facilities. Could you offer some office support services such as the telex photocopying and secretarial services?
4. Good morning, sir. Would you like to register for the conference?
5. Mr. Robinson, you've been arranged in Room 3678. This is a deluxe suite. Here is your key card. And here is your meeting badge and meeting packet.
6. Dr. Peter Moran from Colombia University is coming to register for the conference. He has pre-registered.

Unit Thirty Exhibition Service

Main Service 主要服务

Book an exhibition.
- Discuss something about the exhibition.
- Set up the booths.
- Serve during the exhibition.
- Tear down the booths.
- Make the payment.

Procedure of Service 服务流程

Booking the exhibition

- Greet the guest.
- Get the following information from the exhibition planner:
  The size of the exhibition hall;
  The number of the participants;
  The number of the visitors;
  What kind of exhibits and special demands for the exhibition hall;
  Whether a storehouse is needed or not and what size;
  The demands for the exhibition;
  The special demands for the clerks who will take part in setting up the exhibition service;
  The time of the exhibition.
- Introduce the facilities and services of the hotel according to the information above.
- Get the name of the exhibition planner and his telephone number.

- Express your wishes.

Points of Service Language 服务语言要点

1. **Polite expressions   礼貌用语**

   Welcome to our Convention and Exhibition Center.

   欢迎您来到我们会展中心。

   We're very happy to be chosen for your exhibition. We'll try our best to make your exhibition successful.

   酒店被选为展出之地我们不胜荣幸,为成功地办好此次展览会我们将竭尽全力。

   I'm very happy to serve you. Please send your exhibits at once. We'll set up booths for you.

   为你们服务我很高兴。请把你们的展品马上送来,我们为你们布展台。

2. **Asking the guest about his demands   询问客人对服务的要求**

   What kind of exhibition will you hold?

   请问什么类型的展览?

   Do you have any special requirements for the exhibitions?

   您对展出还有什么特殊的要求?

   How can we arrange the exhibition halls?

   我们怎样安排展厅?

   How about setting up the stands?

   怎样布展台?

   Would you like some flowers and plants to decorate the booths and the halls?

   展台和大厅需要用鲜花和绿色植物来装饰吗?

   Will you provide some snakes and beverages for the visitors?

   为参观者提供小吃和饮料吗?

   Are there any other suggestions and requirements for our work?

   对我们的工作还有什么建议或要求?

3. **Introducing   介绍**

   We have an exhibition hall that will accommodate 800 at a time.

   我们有一次能容纳 800 人的展览大厅。

   Our storehouse can contain 25 containers at a time, and it is beside the West Exhibition Hall.

   我们的仓库一次能容纳 25 个集装箱,而且就在西展厅的旁边。

Chapter Twelve Convention & Exhibition Center Service
会展中心服务

Service Conversation 57

Reserving an Exhibition

30-57 Reserving an Exhibition. mp3

M: Manager of the Convention Service

H: Roger Henson, an exhibition planner

M: Good morning. Welcome to our Convention Center. What can I do for you?

H: Good morning. My name is Roger Henson. We want to hold an exhibition in your hotel.

M: Glad to meet you, Mr. Henson. My name is Zhong Lin. I'm the Convention Service Manager for our hotel. When would you like to hold the exhibition?

H: On December 24th to 26th.

M: What kind of exhibition will you hold?

H: We want to show some advanced teaching instruments and equipment. Do you have an exhibition hall that will accommodate 400 at a time?

M: Yes, we have. We have two halls. The South Hall has a capacity of 600. The North Hall can accommodate just 400 people. How many exhibitors will you have?

H: About 31. Can you describe the two halls in detail and give me some suggestions?

M: Certainly. Each hall has two rooms which can be used as offices.

H: Do you have a storehouse?

M: There is a storehouse beside the South Hall. The North Hall has a small exhibition in it. You have so many exhibitors, and maybe some containers will be sent here. I think it would be better for you to choose the larger one.

H: We have 7 containers and the actual number of the visitors may be more than the number we calculate now. OK, I'll take the South Hall.

M: Do you have any special requirements for the exhibitions? Would you like some flowers and plants to decorate the booths and the hall?

H: Certainly. And we have some special requirements for the lights as well.

M: May I have your phone number?

H: My phone number is 0044777 *** 2441.

M: Thank you, Mr. Henson. You have reserved the South Hall and its two rooms as offices and the storehouse. Your phone number is 0044777 *** 2441. The exhibition will be on the 24th to 26th of December. Is that correct?

H: Yes.

M: Could you please sign your name here?

H: OK.

M: Thank you.

H: When will you begin to set up the booths?

M: December 21st.

H: Our exhibits will arrival on December 20th.

M: Everything will be ready on the morning of December 22nd. Would you like to come to check it?

H: Certainly. Thanks.

M: We're very happy to be chosen for your exhibition. We'll try our best to make your exhibition successful.

| Practice | Answer the questions according to the service conversation. |

1. When will the exhibition be held?
2. What will be shown?
3. Could you tell us something about the exhibition halls?

We're in an Urgent Need for Your Help

M: Manager of the Convention Service

H: Roger Henson, an exhibition planner

30-58 We're in an Urgent Need for Your Help. mp3

M: Good evening, Mr. Henson. The clerks have been busy tearing down the booths for two hours. Some equipment has been loaded into the containers. Don't worry, Mr. Henson. We'll finish the work ahead of the schedule.

H: Oh, no, Miss Zhao. We really appreciate your capable preparations for the exhibits and your warmhearted service. It's with your help that the exhibition is so successful. We have signed lots of contracts with our customers and we have made lots of new friends as well.

M: We're very glad to hear that.

H: But now we have urgent need for your help.

M: What can I do for you, Mr. Henson?

H: Many visitors want us to prolong the exhibition for one more day, because they want the people involved to visit. Can you help us?

M: Certainly. Our clerks will rearrange the booths for you tonight.

H: Thank you very much. By the way, we'll add 30,000 yuan to cover tonight's extra expenses for the clerks' wages, and as a reward for your enthusiastic service.

H: Thanks a lot. Everything will be ready before 9 o'clock tomorrow morning.

Practice Answer the questions according to the service conversation.

1. How long have they been working?
2. What does the exhibition planner want to do? Why?
3. What will the clerks do?

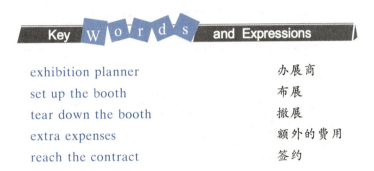

exhibition planner	办展商
set up the booth	布展
tear down the booth	撤展
extra expenses	额外的费用
reach the contract	签约

Notes

1. the number of the participants 参展商数
2. what kind of exhibits and special demands for the exhibition hall 展品的类型及展品对展厅的要求
3. Whether a storehouse is needed or not and what size? 是否需要仓库,要多大的仓库?
4. Do you have an exhibition hall that will accommodate 500 at a time?
   贵酒店有一次能容纳 500 人的展览大厅吗?
5. We want to show some advanced teaching instruments and teaching equipment. Do you have an exhibition hall with an attendance of 400 at a time?
   我们想展出一些先进的教学仪器和教学设备。贵酒店有能容纳 400 人的展览大厅吗?
6. The South Hall has a capacity of 600.
   南厅能容纳 600 人。
7. We have urgent need for your help.
   我们急需你的帮助。
8. We'll increase 30,000 yuan as tonight's extra expenses for the clerks, and a reward for your enthusiastic service.
   我们将增加 30,000 元作为今晚额外的费用和员工的加班工资,以及对你们热情周到服务的奖励。

Performance for Service 模拟演练

Task

Performance in pairs according to the following two cards.

Guest Card		
	Book:	an exhibition hall containing 400 people at a time
	Time:	March 6 to 8
	Exhibits:	all kinds of books
	Number of the participants:	40

Clerk Card	
	What size
	How many participants
	How many people at a time
	What exhibits
	Time
	Special demands

Position Knowledge 岗位知识

The staff of the hotel must follow the 5-point creed:
酒店员工必须遵循以下五点:

- Smile and offer an appropriate hospitality comment when seeing a guest.
- Speak to the guest in a friendly, enthusiastic and courteous tone and manner.
- Answer the question and request of the guest quickly and effciently, or take personal responsibility to get the answer.
- Anticipate guest needs and resolve quest problems.
- Follow up wherever and whenever necessary and possible.

Exercises

I. Topics for discussion.

1. What should you do as a qualified clerk of the Convention Center?

2. What should you do to build up the sound and friendly relationship between the clerk and the guest?

II. Please write out 15 English names of the convention facilities.

_____   _____   _____   _____   _____
_____   _____   _____   _____   _____
_____   _____   _____   _____   _____

III. How to ask the guest about the service demands in exhibition?

1. 询问展览类型。
2. 怎样安排展厅?
3. 怎样布展台?
4. 对展出有什么特殊的要求?
5. 是否需要用鲜花和绿色植物来装饰?
6. 是否为参观者提供小吃和饮料?
7. 对服务工作还有什么建议或要求?

IV. Translate the following sentences into English.

1. 见到客人,要面带微笑,友好而得体地问候。
2. 与客人交谈要友好、热情、彬彬有礼。
3. 迅速、有效地回答客人的提问或对客人的要求做出反应,答复不了的话应亲自寻求答案。
4. 预测客人的需求并解决客人的难题。
5. 随时随地只要有必要、有可能,就应当追踪落实解决情况。

V. Translate the following sentences into English.

会展中心为国内外的一些组织机构提供会议或展览服务。他们提供综合性的会展服务,包括活动的策划、会议或展览设备的租赁、同声传译、文件翻译、宴会装饰、舞台表演等。一些会议型酒店还提供先进的会展设备如幻灯机、同传设备、视听设备和办公设备。

VI. Writing.

Write a composition for the service guidance of your Convention and Exhibition Center. The aim is to introduce the convention and exhibition facilities of your Convention and Exhibition Center.

Chapter Thirteen Shopping Service
商场部服务

Unit Thirty-one   Recommending the Article for the Guest
单元 31   为客人推荐商品

Unit Thirty-two   Displaying the Articles for the Customer to Choose
单元 32   展示商品供客人挑选

Service Position 服务岗位

With the rapid development of China's tourism, more and more foreign visitors have taken great interests in Chinese culture. In the shopping arcade of most large hotels, varied types of articles closely related to the Chinese culture have become more plentiful than ever before. Something typical Chinese such as jewelry, crafts, pure Chinese silk and Chinese arts, etc., is particularly in favor with foreigners. So the shopping arcade of the hotel, just like a "window", has displayed Chinese culture and civilization to the people all over the world.

Skills and Attainments 服务技能与素养

The shop assistants in the shopping arcade need to complete the following services in English: recommending articles for the guest, giving detailed explanations about the article that the guest prefers, including: characteristics of the article, how to use, introduction of its function and price, some special points for attention, as well as the cultural background related to the article, etc., and telling the guest where and how to pay. The above services require the shop assistants not only to have a good knowledge of shopping service but also to have an ability of high level of English. These are necessarily helpful to the sales of the products in the shopping arcade. Meanwhile, the shop assistants also make a channel for foreigners to have a better understanding of China.

Key Words and Expressions

shopping arcade	商场部
recommend (*v.*)	推荐
detailed (*adj.*)	具体的,细节的
article (*n.*)	商品
characteristics (*n.*)	特点
special points for attention	注意事项
cultural background	文化背景
related to	相关的
necessarily (*adv.*)	必然地,必定地
meanwhile (*adv.*)	同时,另一方面

Unit Thirty-one Recommending the Article for the Guest

单元 31 为客人推荐商品

Procedure of Service 服务流程

- Greet the guest.
- Ask what the guest wants.
- Ask what style, color and size the guest prefers.
- Recommend the article for the guest and ask the guest to try it on.
- Praise the article that fits the guest well.
- Tell the guest where and how to pay.

Points of Service Language 服务语言要点

1. **The polite expressions when greeting the customer** 礼貌用语

    Can I be of some assistance for you?

    Could I be of service to you?

    Are you being helped?

    有什么需要帮忙的吗?

2. **Asking what the customer wants and giving your recommendations** 询问顾客意愿并推荐商品

    What kind of ... would you like?

    您想要看看哪种……?

    How about this one?

    这件您觉得如何?

    What style do you prefer?

    您喜欢哪种款式?

    How do you like this design?

    您觉得这个款式怎么样?

    What color/size do you want?

您想要什么颜色/尺寸？
Would you like to have a sweater that's close-fitting or loose-fitting?
您想选的毛衣是紧身的还是宽松的？
Are they made of 100% cotton? Yes, sir. They're quite durable.
这些衬衣都是纯棉的吗？是的，它们很耐穿。

3. **Praising the article that fits the customer well** 夸赞商品很适合其本人可用以下方式

   I think it looks terrific on you.
   我觉得您穿上/戴上真是太漂亮了。
   This latest style is very popular nowadays.
   这是目前流行的最新款式。
   This dress looks good on you, Miss. I think it's a perfect fit.
   小姐，这件衣服您穿着很漂亮，我觉得非常合适。
   I think the color and style make you much younger.
   我觉得颜色和款式把您衬托得更年轻了。
   You've made a great/good choice.
   您算是选对了。（您的眼光真不错。）

4. **Introducing the articles to the customer** 向顾客介绍商品

   We have various selections. Let me show you some.
   我们有很多种可供选择。我可以拿给你看一看。
   We've got a wide selection for you to choose from.
   我们有非常多的样式可供您挑选。
   Everything sold here is real. And we have very good reputation in this business.
   这里出售的商品都是货真价实的。我们在这个行业享有盛名。
   Everything sold here comes with a guarantee of quality.
   在这里出售的商品都附带有质量保证书。
   It might be a little expensive, but the material is of the best quality. It's worth every penny of it.
   这件衣服虽然有点贵，但是用料质量上乘。非常值得买。
   As a matter of fact, all the dresses here are both colorfast and shrink-proof.
   事实上，我们这里出售的所有服装都不褪色也不缩水。
   We are the largest jade articles dealer in the city, and we have many patterns for you to choose from.
   我们是这个城市最大的玉器经销商。我们有多种样式供您选择。
   You've made a great choice. Many foreign friends come to buy porcelain ware of this kind.
   您算是选对了，很多到这里来的外国游客都会选这种瓷器。
   Among Chinese hand embroidery, Suzhou embroidery is considered the best one.
   人们普遍认为苏绣是中国手绣中最好的。

Chapter Thirteen   Shopping Service

商场部服务

Service Conversation 59

Shopping at the Jewelry and Crafts Shop

A: Shop Assistant
G: Guest

A: Good afternoon, sir. Could I be of service to you?
G: I'd like to buy something jade for my girlfriend.
A: OK. Here are all kinds of jades. How do you like this jade bracelet?
G: It looks very beautiful. But is it real jade? I want to send it to my girlfriend for her birthday.
A: Certainly, sir. Everything sold here is real. And we have a very good reputation in this business.
G: Can you show me some jade necklaces, please?
A: OK, how about this one? It is made of precious Chinese jade. Also, this style is very popular nowadays and your girlfriend will really like it.
G: Sure. It seems nice. How much does it cost?
A: It costs 300 RMB.
G: OK, I'll take it.
A: All right, I'll wrap it up for you. Would you please go to the cashier to pay for them?
G: That will be fine. Thank you.
A: You're welcome.

31-59 Shopping at the Jewelry and Crafts Shop.mp3

Practice Answer the questions according to the service conversation.

1. How do you greet your guest as a shop assistant?
2. For whom would the guest like to buy something of jade as a gift?
3. What kind of jade article does the guest prefer, a jade bracelet or a jade necklace?

Key Words and Expressions

jade bracelet	玉镯
genuine (*adj.*)	真正的
reputation (*n.*)	信誉
jade necklace	翡翠项链
precious (*adj.*)	珍贵的

latest style   最新款式

wrap up (v.)   包装起来

Service Conversation 60

Shopping at the Textile and Knitwear Shop

A: Shop Assistant

G: Guest

31–60 Shopping at the Textile and Knitwear Shop. mp3

A: Welcome to our shop. What can I do for you, ma'am?

G: I'd like to buy a silk dress. What style do you think would be most suitable for me?

A: Well, ma'am, your're so graceful and slim. Would you like a dress that's close-fitting or loose-fitting?

G: I'd like something close-fitting.

A: Sure. What do you think of this style? It is made of pure Chinese silk. It's velvety and the color is brilliant.

G: Ah, that's my favorite color. What are these red flowers on the dress?

A: They're peonies, the symbol of grace and nobility in Chinese culture.

G: That's wonderful. Can I try it on?

A: Yes, of course. The dressing room is over there.

G: I like the style very much and the size fits me nicely. What do you think?

A: I think it looks terrific on you.

G: OK, I'll take it. But I wonder if the color will wash out.

A: As a matter of fact, all the dresses here are colorfast. By the way, silk shouldn't be hung out in the sunshine.

G: Well, I see. How much do you charge for this?

A: 1,200 RMB.

G: All right. May I use my credit card here?

A: Sure.

Practice   Answer the questions according to the service conversation.

1. What does the guest want to buy?
2. How does the shop assistant recommend the silk dress to the guest?

3. What does the guest worry about at last?

Key Words and Expressions

silk (n.)	真丝,丝绸
suitable (adj.)	合适的
gracious (adj.)	优美的,优雅的
close-fitting (adj.)	紧身的
loose-fitting (adj.)	宽松的
velvety (adj.)	柔软的
brilliant (adj.)	鲜艳的,光亮的
pattern (n.)	图案,花样
nobility (n.)	高贵
go off (v.)	褪色
pure Chinese silk	真丝
colorfast (adj.)	不褪色的,不变色的

Notes

1. at the Jewelry and Crafts Shop　在珠宝工艺品部
2. at the Textile and Knitwear Shop　在丝绸纺织品部

Points of Service Performance 服务演练要点

- When serving the customers, the shop assistant should use the polite language.
  在为顾客服务时,注意使用礼貌服务用语。
- In many countries people don't carry a lot of cash with them when they go shopping. Paying by credit card and check is very convenient and much safer. So you'd better not forget to ask the customer how to make his payment after shopping.
  在许多国家,人们购物时很少随身携带大量现金。信用卡或支票结账非常方便且更加安全。所以,在客人购物结束时别忘了询问客人的付款方式。
- If the customer says: "I'm just looking." This means they want to choose the articles they prefer in no hurry without any interfering.
  如果客人说:"我只是看看。"说明他们不想被过分关注,希望自己慢慢挑选合意的商品。

Performance for Service 模拟演练

Task A

Performance in pairs according to the following two cards.

Guest Card	Guest name:	Anna Grace
	Nationality:	America
	Purpose:	to buy something typical Chinese as presents for her mother
	Ways of paying:	credit card

Shop Assistant Card	Goods: Suzhou embroidery(苏绣), jade bracelet, Cloisonne vase(景泰蓝花瓶), pearl earrings, etc.
	Suggestion: pearl earrings(珍珠耳环)
	How to pay

Task B

Mr. Smith, an English guest, wants to buy a shirt for himself. So Lisa, a shop assistant in the hotel, recommends a silk shirt to him and offers him many to choose. Mr. Smith knows little about Chinese silk. Lisa gives him so detailed explanations that Mr. Smith is quite pleased to take it. The size Mr. Smith wants is XL and the color he prefers is light grey.

Position Knowledge 岗位知识

- Our shop motto is to serve the guests heart and soul.
  我们商场的宗旨是全心全意为顾客服务。
- The departments of a hotel shop:
  酒店商场部的营销部门名称:
  Jewelry and Crafts Shop　珠宝工艺品部
  Shoes and Hats Department　鞋帽部
  Garments Shop　服装部
  Sports Goods Shop　体育用品部
  Domestic Appliances Shop　家用电器部
  Cosmetics Shop　化妆品部
  Chinaware Shop　瓷器部
  Chinese Arts and Stationery Shop　中国文化用品部
  Chinese Tea Counter　茶品部
  Pharmacy Counter　药品部
  Clock, Watch and Glasses Department　钟表、眼镜部
  Food and Beverage Department　食品饮料部
- Practical Sentences:
  实用句:
  ◆ It's said that the real jade will resist any scratching with metal.
  据说真正的玉是不怕金属刮擦的。

Chapter Thirteen　Shopping Service
商场部服务

◆ Cloisonne vases are well received the world over.
   景泰蓝的花瓶在世界各地都很受欢迎。
◆ Real emerald is always cool to the touch and will resist any scratching with metal.
   真翡翠摸起来有凉的感觉，而且不怕金属刮擦。
◆ The silk can be only washed in lukewarm water.
   真丝只能在温水中洗涤。

Exercises

Ⅰ. Topics for discussion.

1. If you are a shop assistant, in what way can you greet your customer?
2. As a shop assistant, how do you give your customer recommendations?
3. Please introduce the service procedure of shopping in English.

Ⅱ. Write out the questions according to the answers.

1. _____
   Yes. I'd like to get a silk dress.
2. _____
   This one? The style is really elegant. But I don't like that color.
3. _____
   Red in size L, please.
4. _____
   Thank you. That's wonderful! I'll take it.
5. Well, you may use the credit card or pay cash.
   _____

Ⅲ. Translate the following sentences into English.

1. 这是地道的中国式样。
2. 你觉得我适合穿旗袍吗？
3. 这副耳环是由天然珍珠做成的，光泽永远不会褪。
4. 先生，请告诉我您需要的尺寸？
5. 您想买点什么料子？
6. 丝绸不能在阳光下暴晒。
7. 如果您愿意，我可以让您看看其他的。
8. 您愿意我给您包在一起还是分开包装？

IV. Read the following passage and answer the questions.

Shopping in the US

Most stores in America are in the suburbs unlike ours which are downtown. The large number of people living in the suburbs is one of the reasons. But the most important reason is that there is no place for parking in the central city. People can find very large parking lots around the stores in the suburbs.

Shopping at a mall or a supermarket is quite simple. You walk in and pick up a shopping cart, which is free of charge, push the cart along the aisles and choose the articles on the shelves. When you get everything you need, push the cart to the check-out gate. After paying for the goods, you return the cart to its place by the door. That's it.

Stealing is almost impossible in a supermarket. For one thing, there are magnet bar codes on every article. When the goods are paid for, the computer will get rid of the magnet. If not, the magnet will make an alarm ring at the exit door and the police will appear. Besides, there are cameras which view and videotape every corner of the store.

To shop at a supermarket is very convenient. First, there is a wide range of items for you to choose. Second, the price there is reasonable. In addition, you can buy almost every daily necessity under one roof.

Unlike a mall or supermarket, a department store is salesperson served. Prices in department stores are often higher than in supermarkets. But they have many things that are not sold in supermarkets, and the quality of the merchandise is often better, too.

Most cities and states in the US collect a sales tax on almost everything you buy. The tax varies from place to place. The lower ones may be one or two percent and the higher ones may go up to eight or even ten percent.

Questions:

1. Why are most stores in America in the suburbs?
2. Why is stealing almost impossible in a supermarket?
3. Why is shopping at a supermarket very convenient?
4. What are the differences between a supermarket and a department store?
5. Do the consumers need to pay for using a shopping cart?

Unit Thirty-two Displaying the Articles for the Customer to Choose

单元 32 展示商品供客人挑选

Procedure of Service 服务流程

- Greet the customer.
- Find out what the customer wants.
- Recommend articles for the customer.
- Give the detailed explanations about the article that the customer prefers.
- Display many of the same kind of articles for the customer to choose from.
- Tell the customer where and how to pay.

Points of Service Language 服务语言要点

1. **Asking the customer how to make his payment**　询问客人的付款方式

   How will you be paying?
   How will you make your payment?
   How would you like to settle your bill?
   How would you like to make a payment, by credit card, in cash or with a traveler's check?
   您打算如何付款,是用信用卡、现金还是旅行支票?

2. **Bargaining with the customer for the articles**　讨价还价的表达方式

   It's too dear/expensive. I'm wondering if you can give us some discount.
   这个太贵了,能打点折吗?
   It's a real bargain.
   这是真正的便宜货。
   That's the best price.
   这是最好的价钱了。
   We have a one-price policy.
   我们的价格是固定的。

I can give you 10% off.

我可以给您打九折。

3. **Introducing the articles to the customer**　向顾客介绍商品

Chinese painting and calligraphy are the gems of Chinese culture.

国画和书法是中国文化的瑰宝。

Those ancient Chinese paintings are an important part of our national culture.

那些中国古画是我们民族文化的重要部分。

Tea should always be kept dry.

茶叶要保持干燥。

The black tea tastes strong and promotes digestion.

红茶味浓，而且有助于消化。

From the very beginning, tea was used as medicine.

茶最初被用作药材。

4. **Seeing a guest off**　送别客人

Please come again.

欢迎再次光临。

Please remember to take your bag.

请记得拿您的包。

Service Conversation 61

Shopping at the Chinese Arts and Stationery Shop

G：Guest

A：Shop Assistant

32 – 61　Shopping at the Chinese Arts and Stationery Shop. mp3

G：Excuse me.

A：Yes. What can I show you, sir?

G：I'm interested in those little stones. What are they used for?

A：For seal-cutting. It is a typical Chinese traditional art and has a history of 2,000 years. Look, we've got a wide selection of seals for you to choose from, such as Jixue stone, Shoushan stone, jade and crystal pieces.

G：Well, I would like to have a look at jade seals.

A：How do you like this one with a dragon on it? In China, the dragon seal is especially for gentlemen.

G: Oh, I guess it looks quite Chinese. I'll take it.

A: I'm glad you like it.

G: Also, I'd like to buy something for my wife. She's gotten interested in Chinese calligraphy these days. What do you recommend?

A: How about a set of the Four Treasures of the Study?

G: What are they?

A: They are composed of Xuan paper, a writing brush, an ink slab and an ink stick. She will like it.

G: I hope so. OK, how much are they altogether?

A: They come to 890 yuan. Please wait a moment. I'll wrap them up for you.

Practice	Answer the questions according to the service conversation.

1. What is the guest interested in?
2. How does the shop assistant make an introduction of the seals to the guest?
3. Finally, what has the guest bought for his wife?

Shopping at the Chinese Tea Counter

A: Shop Assistant

G: Guest

A: Good afternoon, sir. Are you being helped?

G: I'd like to have a look at Chinese tea.

A: We have Wulong Tea, Longjing Tea, Anxi Tie Guan Yin and so on. Which do you prefer?

32-62 Shopping at the Chinese Tea Counter. mp3

G: I was told there is a kind of Chinese tea called "Vigorous and Graceful Tea". Is that so?

A: Ah, that's Wulong Tea. It's a high quality green tea mixed with dried jasmine flowers. This kind of tea is fine both in appearance and in taste, and it also has a weight reducing effect.

G: Does it really have any special effect?

A: Yes, of course. That's why many foreign visitors, especially ladies, come to buy Wulong Tea in order to keep slim.

G: Wonderful. My wife is gaining weight these days. She's quite annoyed at her figure now.

A: She needs to exercise. But I suggest she also take some Chinese green tea as a must for her daily diet. It's quite effective.

G: Thank you. I'll take six boxes then.

A: All right, I'll wrap them up for you. Would you please go to the cashier to pay for them?

G: That will be fine. Thank you.

A: You are welcome.

Practice Answer the questions according to the service conversation.

1. What is Wulong Tea also called?
2. What special effect does Wulong Tea have?
3. What does the shop assistant suggest to the guest's wife?

Key Words and Expressions

seal-cutting (n.)	篆刻
typical (adj.)	典型的
traditional art	传统艺术
Jixue stone	鸡血石
Shoushan stone	寿山石
crystal (n.)	水晶石
jade seal	玉章
calligraphy (n.)	书法
the Four Treasures of the Study	文房四宝
ink slab	砚台
ink stick	墨
jasmine flowers	茉莉花

Notes

1. at the Chinese Arts and Stationery Shop　在中国文化用品部
2. at the Chinese Tea Counter　在茶品部

Points of Service Performance 服务演练要点

● The customers shopping in the hotel shop generally pay much attention to the brand, quality and design of the articles. The price is also considered, but the shop assistant shouldn't emphasize it too much.

在酒店购物的客人,一般会注重商品的品牌、质量、设计等因素。虽然价格也是他们考虑的要素之一,但不宜过分强调。

- If the articles which the customer has bought are antiques and valuables, the shop assistant still needs to remind him to keep the receipt or invoice well in case it is inspected by the customs.

  如果客人购买的是古玩或特别贵重的物品,还需要提醒客人保存好收据或发票,以备海关查验。

Performance for Service 模拟演练

Task A

Performance in pairs according to the following two cards.

Guest Card		
	Name:	John Smith
	Nationality:	America
	Purpose:	to buy something closely related to Chinese ancient culture
	Ways of paying:	cash

Shop Assistant Card		
	Goods:	Stone seals(石章), Chinese painting, the Four Treasures of the Study, Paper-cuts(剪纸)
	Suggestion:	Chinese painting
	How to pay	

Task B

A foreign customer wants to buy some Chinese tea, but he knows little about it. Having known what he wants, the shop assistant recommends Tie Guan Yin（铁观音）to him and gives him so detailed explanations about this tea. The customer is pleased to take it.

Position Knowledge 岗位知识

- Practical Terms and Expressions:

  茶的实用表达:

  green tea 绿茶   scented tea 花茶
  black tea 红茶   brick tea 砖茶
  pekoe 白毫   Tie Guan Yin 铁观音
  jasmine tea 茉莉花茶   chrysanthemum tea 菊花茶
  Pu'er tea 普洱茶   Wulong Tea (oolong tea) 乌龙茶

243

Longjing Tea (dragon well tea) 龙井茶

- Practical Sentences：

  实用句：

  - The Four Treasures of the Study are composed of Xuan paper, writing brush, ink slab and ink stick.

    宣纸、毛笔、砚台和墨被称为中国的文房四宝。

  - Seal-cutting is a typical traditional Chinese art and has a history of over 2,000 years.

    篆刻是典型的中国传统艺术，它已有2,000多年的历史。

  - Subject matters in Chinese painting are mainly landscape, portraiture, birds and flowers.

    国画的题材主要是山水、人物、鸟类和花木。

  - Tie Guan Yin is fine both in appearance and in taste, and it also has a weight reducing effect.

    铁观音无论外形还是口味均属上乘，而且它具有减肥效果。

  - The top grade Longjing Tea is manually baked. It is fresh green and has a sweetish and mellow taste.

    极品龙井茶是手工焙制的，它色泽碧绿，口味甘美醇和。

Exercises

Ⅰ. Topics for discussion.

1. As a shop assistant, how can you see a guest off after his shopping?
2. Suppose you are a shop assistant, what can you say if the guest asks you to give him some discount?
3. Please speak out some names of the Chinese tea in English.

Ⅱ. Translate the following sentences into English.

1. 请让我看一看那枚石/玉章。
2. 很多对中国文化感兴趣的外国游客都很喜欢国画。
3. 先生，您真有艺术眼光。
4. 我们有许多不同种类的传统国画。
5. 这可以算是典型的中国之旅的纪念品吧。
6. 您习惯喝什么茶？我习惯喝绿茶。
7. 中国的茶叶世界闻名。
8. 我们有红茶、绿茶和普洱茶。

Chapter Thirteen Shopping Service
商场部服务

III. Translate the following passage into Chinese.

Quality is always paid enough attention to by various consumers—whether the consumer is a housewife, an industrial corporation or a government agency. Then, what does the term "quality" mean? According to different people, quality may be understood in a variety of ways. It may be used to refer to grade of a product, as in the sentence "These are goods of first-rate quality", and it can also be used to refer to materials, workmanship or special features, such as "100% silk" "handcrafted" or "fireproof".

Chapter Fourteen　Other Service
其他服务

Unit Thirty-three　Lost and Found Service
单元 33　失物招领服务

Unit Thirty-four　Depositing Service
单元 34　寄存服务

Unit Thirty-five　Tourism Service
单元 35　旅游信息服务

Unit Thirty-six　Baby-sitting Service
单元 36　托婴服务

Service Position 服务岗位

The hotels offer miscellaneous services to cater to the guests' need, including lost and found service, depositing service, tourists assisting service, and baby-sitting service. Quality services in these fields could provide timely assistance to the guests when they are in need and impress them with warmhearted human care during their stay. The service motto of "creating a home far away from the guest's home" is embodied in these services. Some of the services are carried out at the Front Desk.

 Skills and Attainments 服务技能与素养

The clerks need to complete the following main services in English:
- Inform the Front Desk immediately after finding personal items that belong to the guest who is checking out or has already left the hotel. Keep the lost and found log. When the guest calls or comes in person to claim the items, assist him to fill in the property claiming form and sign. If a guest reports a loss, assist him to fill in the lost property report and start search immediately.
- Assist the guest to fill in the property depositing form while processing the depositing service. Give detailed explanation of the charge and procedure of the service. Remind the guest to keep the depositing tag and show it while withdrawing. As to valuables, provide the safety box.
- Provide the guest with tourism information including the introduction of famous travelling spots, transportation or expenses. Process the booking of guided tours or arrange transportation for the guest.
- Arrange the baby-sitting service for the guest in need. Assist the guest to fill in the baby-sitting service application form, check the information carefully. Pay attention to the guest's "special requirement" as that is closely related to the baby's personal condition. Arrange professional baby-sitters.

In providing miscellaneous services, the clerk needs to equip himself with career morals and the awareness of quality service. All the services above are frequently required by the guests in a star hotel and whether they can get satisfactory service is directly related to their recognition of the hotel image. A large amount of English conversation happens everyday in these sectors so that the clerks here are required to have higher language proficiency.

Key Words and Expressions

the lost and found log	失物拾物日志
property claiming form	失物认领登记表
lost property report	报失登记表
property depositing	物品寄存

Chapter Fourteen Other Service
其他服务

depositing tag	寄存条
safety box	保险箱
tourism information	旅游信息
introduction (*n.*)	介绍
transportation (*n.*)	交通
expense (*n.*)	花费
guided tours	全程导游陪同
baby-sitting (*n.*)	照看婴儿
special requirement	特殊要求
professional (*adj.*)	专业的
career moral	职业道德
quality service	优质服务
recognition (*n.*)	认识,认知
image (*n.*)	形象
sector (*n.*)	部门
language proficiency	语言能力

Unit Thirty-three Lost and Found Service

单元 33 失物招领服务

Procedure of Service 服务流程

To guest who reports a loss

- Greet the guest.
- Ask for the information of the lost items, including:
  Description of the item.
  Time when the item is last seen.
- Assist the guest to fill in the lost report.
- Ask for the name and contact number of the guest.
- Confirm the name and contact number of the guest.
- Arrange the search.

To guest who claims the item

- Greet the guest.
- Assist the guest to fill in the request slip.
- Ask the guest for his proof of identity.

Points of Service Language 服务语言要点

1. **Showing sympathy   表示同情用语**

   Don't worry, sir/madam, we'll see to it immediately.
   请您不要担心,我们会立刻为您查询。
   I am really sorry to hear this, but we'll try to help you with it.
   听到这件事很遗憾,我们会尽力帮助您的。
   I am sorry, it has not been found yet.
   很抱歉,还没有找到。

Chapter Fourteen Other Service
其他服务

2. Finding out the information about the lost items　了解失物信息

What is the make of your watch/phone/wallet?
您的手表/手机/钱包是什么牌子的？
What color is it?
是什么颜色的？
Is it brand new?
是崭新的吗？
Do you remember the last time you had it?
您记得最后看见它是什么时候吗？
Where had you been this morning/afternoon?
今天早晨您都去过哪里？

3. Finding out the reporter's information　了解报失人信息

May I have your name/room number/address?
能留下您的姓名/房号/地址吗？
Could you show me your ID card?
能否出示您的身份证？
Would you mind telling me your name/address?
可否留下您的姓名/住址？

4. Filling in the relevant forms　填写相关表格

Could you fill in the lost report?
您能填写报失单吗？
Would you mind finishing this request slip?
您能填写领物单吗？

Don't Worry, Sir

33 - 63 Don't Worry, Sir. mp3

C：Clerk

G：Guest

C：Good afternoon, sir. What can I do for you?

G：What a lousy day! I've just lost my mobile phone. All my contacts are in it. It's really important to me!

C：I can understand how you feel, sir. Don't worry. We'll try our best to help you. Do you remember the last time you used it or saw it, and where was it?

G: This morning. I got a call from my wife, and then I left the room with the phone on me.

C: Where did you go after that?

G: A lot of places. The souvenir shop, the café, and then I had my hair cut at the barber's. I think the mobile phone is still in the building.

C: Could you tell me your name and room number, please?

G: Sure. Paul Macleod, in Room 2017.

C: What is the make and model of your phone? And what's the color?

G: It is an old Ericsson phone, a straight one, and it's dark grey. It's so old that I don't think any one would want to steal it.

C: We'll arrange a search for it as soon as possible. If we find it, we will let you know immediately.

G: I hope you can. Thank you for your help.

C: You're welcome.

Practice Answer the questions according to the service conversation.

1. What does the guest lose?
2. Could you describe the item?
3. Where had the guest been before he found out the item was lost?

Claiming My Ring

33-64 Claiming My Ring. mp3

C: Clerk

G: Guest

C: Good morning. Sun Glory Hotel, lost and found office, can I help you?

G: Hello, this is Robert Brown.

C: Mr. Brown, what can I do for you?

G: I just checked out half an hour ago, but I am afraid I left my ring in a drawer in the bedroom.

C: May I have your room number please?

G: Room 1302.

C: What is the ring like?

G: It is a round gold one, with the name of a world famous football star.

Chapter Fourteen Other Service 其他服务

C: All right, we'll send the room attendant for it now. We'll see you at the lost and found office.

G: Thank you very much.

G: Hi, I am here to claim my ring. Sorry about that.

C: Don't mention it. Can I see your ID?

G: Sure, here you are.

C: Could you fill in this request slip?

G: OK.

C: Here is your ring, sir.

G: Thank you very much.

C: You're welcome. Have a nice day.

Practice Answer the questions according to the service conversation.

1. Why does Mr. Brown call the Lost and Found Desk?
2. Could you describe the item he lost?
3. What does Mr. Brown have to do in order to claim his item?

Key Words and Expressions

souvenir shop	纪念品店
barber (n.)	男性理发师
make (n.)	牌子
model (n.)	型号
immediately (adv.)	立即
signature (n.)	签字
request slip (n.)	取物单

Points of Service Performance 服务演练要点

On receiving a report of lost items, use the polite language and show your sympathy. Always be patient to the guest as he is usually in poor mood after losing items.

受理报失时要使用礼貌用语并对客人的遭遇表示同情。始终耐心对待客人,因为丢失物品的客人通常情绪不好。

Performance for Service 模拟演练

Task A

Performance in pairs according to the following two cards.

Guest Card	Guest name: Tom Smith Room number: Room 1039 Item: backpack Description: black, Puma make, with books, map and a kettle in it. Places he had been: the souvenir shop, the fitness center Telephone number: 139****7236

Clerk Card	Name of the guest Telephone number of the guest Room number of the guest Description of the lost item Lost report form

Task B

Mr. Bentley calls the Front Desk of Beijing Hotel from London to see if they found his book *Gone with the Wind*. He lived in the Room 1212 when he was here. The clerk checks the lost and found log and says yes. Mr. Bentley hopes the hotel can mail the book back to his home. His address is 3 Hope Street, Mount Lily, London, 3123. Please form the conversation according to above information.

Position Knowledge 岗位知识

- A clear and updated lost and found log must be kept on a daily basis. This will make the searching work more time-saving.
  要每天记好失物拾物日志,这样失物搜寻工作会更加节省时间。
- Patience and sympathy are key words for clerks at the Lost and Found Desk as the guests are apt to be upset after losing their personal items and may sometimes put the blame on our clerks. At this moment, the clerks must keep in mind that our guests and quality service are always the priority.
  耐心和同情心是失物招领部门人员工作的关键词,因为丢失物品的客人难免会情绪低落,甚至有时会把责任归于我们的工作人员。在这种情况下,服务员应把"服务至上,宾客至上"作为工作的纲领。

Chapter Fourteen　Other Service
其他服务

Ⅰ. Topics for discussion.

1. Introduce the service procedure of reporting the lost property in English.
2. Introduce the service procedure of claiming the property in English.

Ⅱ. Translate the following sentences into English.

1. 您在发现手表丢失之前都去过哪里？
2. 请问您的包裹是什么样子的？
3. 您能留下联系方式吗？
4. 请您不要着急，我们会马上安排人寻找。
5. 请您填写失物认领单。
6. 您能出示有效身份证件吗？

Ⅲ. Translate the following sentences into Chinese.

1. Patience and sympathy are key words for clerks at the Lost and Found Desk as the guests are apt to be upset after losing their personal items and may sometimes put the blame on our clerks. At this moment, the clerks must keep in mind that our guests and quality service are always the priority.
2. A lost and found is an office in a hotel where the guests can go to retrieve lost articles that may have been found by other guests or hotel staff. Some lost and found offices will try to contact the owners of any lost items if there are any personal identifiers available. Practically all will either give or throw away items after a certain period has passed to clear their storage.

Unit Thirty-four Depositing Service

单元 34 寄存服务

Main Service 主要服务

- Assist the guest to finish the Deposit Form or Valuables Deposit Form.
- Explain the terms of service.
- Give the guest a tag for withdrawing.
- Inform the guest of the cost of the service.

Points of Service Language 服务语言要点

1. **Polite expressions 礼貌用语**

    Good morning, would you like to deposit or withdraw something?
    早上好,您要存取什么吗?
    Can I be of any assistance to you, madam?
    夫人,能为您效劳吗?

2. **Informing the guest of the charge 告知收费标准**

    The service costs you ** yuan per bag per day.
    行李寄存需要支付每件每天**元。
    The safety box service is free.
    保险箱寄存服务是免费的。

3. **Explaining the terms of service 解释服务细则**

    If you need special care for your item, there is another form to fill out.
    如果您的物品需要特别照看,这里还有一张表需要填写。
    If you would like to use the items, please come here in person with the tag. After confirming your signature, we'll open the box.
    如果您想使用物品,请携带标签亲自过来。在核对您的签名后,我们会打开保险箱。

Chapter Fourteen   Other Service
其他服务

Luggage Depositing

34 – 65   Luggage Depositing. mp3

G: Guest

C: Clerk

G: Excuse me. I'll be checking out at noon. I wonder whether I could leave my luggage here after I check out.

C: Yes, sure. We do provide luggage storage service. When will you collect them?

G: A week later.

C: I see. When will you be checking out?

G: About 11:30.

C: Then shall we arrange the bellman to pick up your luggage at 11:00?

G: Sure.

C: May I have your room number please?

G: Room 1210.

C: Room 1210. We will collect your luggage at 11:00 in the morning. Would you come to the service desk after that to get your storage receipt?

G: Sure. By the way, may I ask the daily rate for storing my luggage?

C: It's 5 yuan per bag per day.

G: I see. Thanks a lot.

C: You're welcome.

Practice Answer the questions according to the service conversation.

1. How many days does the guest want to deposit his luggage for?
2. What is the charge for the service?

Safe-Deposit Box

34 – 66   Safe-Deposit Box. mp3

C: Clerk

G: Guest

C: Good evening, sir. May I help you?

G: Yes. I'd like to use a safe-deposit box. Will a laptop fit into it?

C: Let me see. I think it's all right.

C: Could you tell me your name and room number?

G: Bob Green. My room number is 1012.

C: Please put your items in this bag, and we'll seal it. Do you need special handling for your item? If so, there is another form to fill out.

G: Well, it's actually not very expensive. I don't think I need any special handling.

C: Could you sign your name here?

G: Sure.

C: Thank you. Here's your tag. If you would like to use the items, please come here in person with the tag. After confirming your signature, we'll open the box.

G: I see. Thank you.

C: You're welcome.

> **Practice** Answer the questions according to the service conversation.

1. What does the guest want to put in the safety box?
2. Why does the clerk ask the guest whether he needs special care or not?
3. How can the guest withdraw his thing?

Key Words and Expressions

luggage (*n.*)	行李
storage (*n.*)	储存
collect (*v.*)	提取
arrange (*v.*)	安排
receipt (*n.*)	收据、收条
deposit (*v.*)	存
safety box (*n.*)	保险箱
laptop (*n.*)	笔记本电脑
seal (*v.*)	密封
confirm (*v.*)	确认

Points of Service Performance 服务演练要点

If the guest needs a safety deposit box to store valuables, remind the guest to keep the tag carefully.

如果客人需要保险箱寄存贵重物品,提醒客人仔细保存标签。

Chapter Fourteen Other Service
其他服务

Performance for Service 模拟演练

Task A

Performance in pairs according to the following two cards.

Guest Card		
	Guest name:	Jane Young
	Room number:	Room 1020
	Item:	jewelry
	Special care:	required

Clerk Card
- Name of the guest
- Room number of the guest
- Safety box application form
- Issue the tag
- Explain the terms of claiming the item

Task B

Mr. Huber just arrives at the Jianguo Hotel and wants to have his luggage checked for half an hour. Li Bin, the clerk at the Front Desk helps him go through the formalities. Please form a dialogue according to above information.

Position Knowledge 岗位知识

The depositing service and safety box service involve the guests' personal belongings and wealth. Therefore, the strong sense of responsibility of the hotel party is highly essential in these services. Ordinarily, such services are free of charge in spite of the involved duty. For the guests' interests, the clerk must remind them to require special care for the valuables, which will ensure high level of care and proper compensation in case the items are lost or damaged.

保管箱和寄存的问题涉及客人财产或贵重物品，酒店的相关责任也因此特别重大。一般酒店都提供免费保管箱服务，虽然是免费服务，但其中涉及的责任可能会很大。当客人寄存贵重物品时，工作人员一定要提醒寄存人对贵重物品申请特别看管，这样酒店会采取特别保护措施，一旦丢失或损失，也能得到相应赔偿。

Exercises

I. Topics for discussion.

Why is it important to ask the guest whether he needs special care for the valuables?

II. Complete the following dialogue.

C: Clerk

G: Guest

C: Good evening, sir. May I help you?

G: Yes. I would like to use a ___1___ to store my digital products.

C: Could you tell me your ___2___ and ___3___?

G: Bob Green. My room number is 1012.

C: Do you need ___4___ for your item?

G: Well, I think so. They are important to me.

C: Could you ___5___ your name here?

G: Sure.

C: Thank you. Here is your ___6___. If you would like to use the items during the period of storage, please come here in person with the tag. After ___7___ your signature, we will open the box.

G: I see. Thank you.

C: You are welcome.

III. Translate the following sentences into English.

1. 我们有寄存服务。
2. 你需要行李员在11点为您提行李吗?
3. 请问寄存行李每天的收费是多少?
4. 如果在寄存期间您要领取物品,请您亲自过来,出示取物牌。我们核对签字后会为您打开保险箱。
5. 如有贵重物品,请申请特别看管。

Unit Thirty-five Tourism Service   单元 35 旅游信息服务

Main Service 主要服务

- Give the guest directions about the location of certain place.
- Provide the guest with tourism information such as:
  the name of the traveling sites;
  the transportation;
  the entrance fee.
- Arrange transportation for the guest.
- Book guided tours on request.

Points of Service Language 服务语言要点

1. **Showing the directions   指示方位**

   The Lama Temple is located on ...road.
   雍和宫位于……路。
   You can take bus No. 1, and then change to bus No. 2 at...
   您先坐 1 路,然后在……站换乘 2 路。
   Cross the road, go down three blocks and you will see the gallery.
   穿过这条路,向前走三个街区就能看到美术馆了。
   Please go straight and then turn right at the traffic lights.
   直走,在红绿灯处向右拐。

2. **Giving traveling advice   提供旅游建议**

   I suggest you go to the Summer Palace.
   我建议您去颐和园。
   Are you looking for a package deal or just transportation and hotels?
   您想要全程随团还是只订交通和酒店?

Showing the Way

35-67 Showing the Way. mp3

R: Receptionist

G: Guest

R: Good morning. May I help you?

G: Yes. I want to go to Jingshan Park. See? This is the name. Could you tell me where it is?

R: Certainly yes, sir. It is not far from here. You could either go by public transportation or taxi. I'd be pleased to arrange a taxi for you if you like.

G: I prefer to go by bus. Could you show me the way?

R: Well, it's just opposite to the Forbidden City. Just take the subway to Dongsi Station and then take bus No. 112 to the Forbidden City Stop.

G: Thank you very much. By the way, do you know the entrance fee?

R: It's very cheap. Just 2 yuan.

G: OK, I see. Thank you!

R: Enjoy your trip!

Practice Answer the questions according to the service conversation.

1. How can the guest get to Jingshan Park?
2. What's the entrance fee of Jingshan Park?

Booking a Tour

35-68 Booking a Tour. mp3

G: Guest

R: Receptionist

G: Good morning.

R: Good morning. What can I do for you?

G: I'm looking for someplace to spend the weekend. What do you have that's good and not too expensive?

R: Do you want to go alone, or with a group? Are you looking for a package deal or just transportation and hotels?

G: With a group. Do you have any special offers?

R: For a group tour, we have the Emperor Tomb package. It includes transportation, tour guides, hotels, meals, and the entrance fee for Dong Ling. It is an all-expenses-paid tour: the price includes all meals and insurance.

G: How much is that?

R: 1,000 RMB.

G: How about their service?

R: They're very good. We haven't received any complaints about them so far. They take care of their guests very well.

G: We'll think it over and let you know.

R: That's fine.

(Next day)

G: Hello.

R: Great to see you again.

G: We've decided to go with the Emperor Tomb Tour.

R: That's fine. I can book that for you. Could you tell me your name, room number, and cell phone number, please?

G: Sure. Grace Smith, in Room 2016. My cell phone number is 139 **** 9963.

R: Here are the details of the trip and the contract. Could you read and sign your name at the bottom?

G: OK.

R: Thank you. The travel agency will pick you up at the hotel at 7 o'clock this Saturday morning. And the fee is 1,000 RMB. We accept both cash and credit cards.

G: I will pay by credit card.

R: This way, please.

R: Is there anything else I can do for you?

G: I guess that's it. Thank you.

R: You're welcome. Have a nice trip.

Practice Answer the questions according to the service conversation.

1. What kind of trip does the guest need? A long journey or just two-day tour?
2. What kind of tour package does the guest prefer?
3. What's the name of the package he chooses?

public transportation　　　　　公共交通
package deal　　　　　　　　　全包括的选择
emperor tomb　　　　　　　　帝王陵墓

Points of Service Performance 服务演练要点

If the guest would like to book a tour with the receptionist at the front desk, remind him to read the trip contract carefully.

如果客人愿意在前台订下随团旅游,一定要提醒客人仔细阅读合同。

Performance for Service 模拟演练

Task A

Performance in pairs according to the following two cards.

Guest Card	Guest name:	Jane Young
	Room number:	Room 1020
	Query:	places of interests in Beijing

Clerk Card	Introduce:
	the Forbidden City, the Summer Palace and the Temple of Heaven, Central Business Districts, the International Trade Center zone, the Financial Street, Zhongguan Village
	Recommend:
	guided day tour
	a free traveling brochure

Task B

The Silvers are going to Chaoyang Park for a pop music festival held in the evening, but they don't know the way very well. The event is a joint effort of both Chinese pop singers and some foreign bands. Please form a conversation to show them the way to Chaoyang Park and briefly exchange some ideas about the pop music festival.

Position Knowledge 岗位知识

The staff providing traveling assistance must have sound knowledge of the tourism attractions and the transportation in the city, and more importantly, they must be able to use English at higher level. Therefore, staff in this position should be motivated to update their knowledge and perspectives towards the tourism facilities in the city so as to provide the guests with accurate information.

旅游信息咨询指导岗位需要前台工作人员具备相关的城市交通及景点知识和较好的英语表达水平,因此,员工要积极更新自己的知识结构,增加对旅游设施服务的了解,以提供给客人准确、有效的信息。

Ⅰ. Topics for discussion.

What kinds of skills are required as a receptionist at the Front Desk?

Ⅱ. Read the passage and answer the questions.

Modern Beijing

Beijing thrives today as the political and cultural capital of China as well as a center of international activities. Great changes have taken place since the founding of the People's Republic of China in 1949. The city walls were demolished(拆除)to facilitate transportation and allow for general expansion. By 2004, the population exceeded 14.9 million, and the total municipal area was increased to over 16,800 square kilometers. The city is presently divided into 16 districts: Dongcheng, Xicheng, Chongwen, Xuanwu, Chaoyang, Haidian, Shijingshan, Fengtai, Shunyi, Changping, Mentougou, Tongzhou, Fangshan, Daxing, Huairou and Pinggu. In addition to these urban districts, the municipality(自治区) is comprised of two counties: Miyun and Yanqing.

Plans for future development retain the symmetrical(对称的) layout of the old city on its north-south axis(轴线), extending out into the suburban districts.

With Tian'anmen at the center, offices along 38-kilometer-long Chang'an Boulevard will concentrate on state, political and economic affairs. The areas around the Palace Museum(Forbidden City) and city gates as well as the lakes—Zhongnanhai, Beihai and Houhai—have been designated landmark districts. And with a look to the future, an increasing number of historical, cultural and revolutionary sites are being renovated and opened to the public.

Questions:

1. What's the population in Beijing by the year of 2004?
2. How many districts are there in Beijing?
3. What are the sights to see in the central area of Beijing?
4. What is the plan for future development of the city?

Unit  Baby-sitting Service

单元 36 托婴服务

Main Service 主要服务

- Assist the guest to finish the Service Application Form.
- Explain the cost of the service.
- Arrange professional baby-sitters on request.

Points of Service Language 服务语言要点

Ask about the detailed information of the baby 询问婴儿信息

How old is your baby?
请问您的孩子几岁了?

What's the gender?
男孩还是女孩?

Is he/she in good health?
他/她的健康状况怎么样?

Do you have any special requirement in the service?
您有什么特别要求吗?

Service Conversation 69

Baby-sitting Service

36-69 Baby-sitting Service. mp3

G: Guest
C: Clerk

G: Excuse me. I wonder whether you could do me a favor.

Chapter Fourteen   Other Service
其他服务

C: I'm willing to try my best, ma'am. What's the matter?

G: My husband and I want to go out this evening. We need someone to look after our baby. Is such service available here?

C: Yes. We have qualified baby sitters.

G: Are they experienced?

C: Yes, ma'am. They are all well-educated and reliable.

G: That's good. Could you tell me what you charge for this service?

C: It's 90 yuan an hour, for a minimum of 2 hours.

G: That's all right.

C: Please keep in mind that a 100 yuan cancellation fee applies if the reservation is cancelled within 12 hours of the starting time of the service.

G: I see.

C: If you need the service, here is a confirmation form for you to sign. It includes the time of the service, basic information about your baby and your signature.

G: OK, I'll finish it right away. Thank you. Here you are.

C: Thank you, ma'am. We'll arrange the service soon. Just bring your sweetheart here at the time designated on the form. Have a good night.

Practice   Answer the questions according to the service conversation.

1. What's the charge of the baby-sitting service in the hotel?
2. In what occasion is there a cancellation fee?

Key Words and Expressions

available (*adj.*)	有的;可用的
qualified (*adj.*)	有资质的
reliable (*adj.*)	可靠的
cancellation fee	取消费
apply (*v.*)	被收取;适用
designate (*v.*)	指定

Please double check the baby-sitting service application form to ensure all the important information about the baby is included.

在客人填写完托婴服务申请表后一定要仔细检查以保证所有关于婴儿的重要信息都包括在内了。

Performance for Service 模拟演练

Task A

Performance in pairs according to the following two cards.

Guest Card

Guest name: Michelle Kin
Room number: Room 1312
Contact No.: 135 * * 83
Two children:
John Kin   age 4
Ben Kin   age 2
Special requirement:
Ben is having flu. He needs to take medicine.
Time: Thursday, 13th of August, from 9 a.m to 6 p.m.

Clerk Card

Name of the guest
Room number of the guest
Name of the baby
Age of the baby
Baby's health condition
Explain the charge:
90 yuan per hour for a minimum of 2 hours

Task B

Mrs. Roger is inquiring about the baby-sitting service at the Front Desk of Sun Glory Hotel. Zhang Ling gives her a detailed explanation of the service charge and terms. Please form a dialogue based on your knowledge of the baby-sitting service.

Chapter Fourteen　　Other Service
其他服务

Ⅰ. **Fill in the blanks in the following baby-sitting service application form according to the cards in task A.**

```
                        Application Form
    Full name/s of parent/s    _____
    ( title i. e. Mr. /Mrs. )

    Contact numbers    Home    _____
                       Mobile  _____
                       Other   _____

    E-mail address            _____
    Room Number               _____
    Date Babysitter Needed    _____
    Start Time _____  Finish Time _____
    Details of Children
    Name  _____  Age  _____  M/F
    Name  _____  Age  _____  M/F
    Special Requirements (e. g. medical needs) _____

    I/We agree to abide by the information in the terms and conditions.


    (attached to this form)
    Signed: _____
    Dated: _____
```

Ⅱ. **Translate the following sentences into Chinese.**

1. Baby-sitting is the practice of temporarily caring for a baby on behalf of the child's parents. The sitter is normally contracted one night at a time. The term probably originated from the action of the caretaker "sitting on" the baby in one room, while the parents were entertaining or busy in another.

2. In providing the baby-sitting service, the clerk needs to equip himself with career morals and the awareness of quality service. Keep a clear record of the baby's situation, the parents' requirement and the accurate starting time of the service so as to coordinate the qualified babysitters to carry out the service.

Key to the Exercises
练习答案

Chapter One　Front Desk Service

Unit One

Ⅱ. **Answer the following questions.**

1. By credit card/In cash/With(By) a traveler's check.
2. What's your occupation, please?/Please tell me your occupation.
3. I'm afraid that your room is not ready yet. Would you mind waiting, please? We are very sorry for the inconvenience.
4. Here is the receipt. Please keep it.

Ⅲ. **Translate the following sentences into English.**

1. You're always welcome. We are glad to serve you at any time. Have a pleasant stay here.
2. Just a minute, please. A bellman will show you to your room. I hope you will enjoy your stay here.
3. Please fill in the registration forms—your nationality, age, occupation, passport number, and your signature.
4. Would you please sign your name here?
5. Your key cards and breakfast vouchers are all in the envelopes with your names on them.
6. Miss White, a moment, please. Let me check the registration list. Thanks for waiting so long. You have a reservation of 11 standard rooms and a suite room for four nights, correct?

Ⅳ. **Translate the following sentences into Chinese.**

1. 在餐厅和酒吧用餐后签单时您得出示这张房卡。
2. 有您要的房间。您住几个晚上?
3. 没有听懂或没有听清客人的英文,切忌猜测,更不要假装明白。当然也不用怕。礼貌地请客人再说一遍,如"对不起,打扰了,请再说一遍。"或"对不起,我没有听懂,能否再重复一遍?"。
4. 真不凑巧,您上次住的那个套间今天上午被预订了。不过我们还有一个面湖的套间,价格和您上次住的套间一样。

5. 我们提倡传统的良好仪态和彬彬有礼,要在实践中使这些成为你的第二天性——使这习惯成自然。

Unit Two

Ⅱ. Read the following passage and answer the questions.

1. The hotel staff should always be polite and helpful.
2. It means "write down in a hurry".
3. He should then make a short apology and express his understanding of the guest's situation or sympathy with the guest.
4. Only when he puts himself in the guest's shoe, can he look at the problem from the other person's perspective.

Ⅲ. Translate the following sentences into English.

1. We do apologize for the inconvenience.
2. I assure you that it won't happen again.
3. I'm very sorry. We might have overlooked some details. Thank you for bringing the matter to our attention. Wait a minute, please. I'll send a housemaid immediately.
4. Mr. Smith asks Wang Ping whether he has an extra pillow and a hair-dryer.
5. A pleased guest leaves the hotel with a warm memory of the hospitality he has enjoyed and an inclination to repeat his visit to our hotel.

Chapter Two   Reservation Desk Service

Unit Three

Ⅱ. Write out the questions in room reservation according to the answers.

1. What kind of room would you like/prefer?
2. For how many nights?/How long will you be staying?
3. How many guests will there be in your party?
4. How much do you charge?/Could you tell me the room rate?
5. Could I have your name, please?

Ⅲ. Translate the following sentences into English.

1. We don't have a single room available. Would you mind a standard room?
2. I want to reserve a family suite facing the lake.
3. We'll extend the reservation for you.
4. It's my pleasure. We look forward to your arrival.
5. Sorry, we won't have any vacancy today. But we can recommend another hotel if you like.
6. There is a 15 percent deduction for a group reservation.

Unit Four

II. Write out the questions in room reservation according to the answers.

1. In whose name was the reservation made?
2. In what way was the reservation made?
3. What was the date of the reservation?
4. How many nights would you like to extend?
5. How much do you charge?
6. How would you like to change?

III. Translate the following sentences into English.

1. It's my pleasure. Mr. Davis, we look forward to your visit.
2. I'd like to extend my reservation for three more nights.
3. Do you think it's possible for us to change the reservation?
4. How and in whose name has the reservation been made?
5. Mr. Ramsay, you need 20 standard rooms and a business suite altogether from 7th to 9th of May. Is that right?
6. Miss Rose Berry, I'll cancel your reservation from May 6th for 3 nights altogether. My name is Li Hai. We look forward to another chance to serve you.

IV. Translate the following sentences into Chinese.

1. 大多数宾馆、饭店将无保证预订房保留到当天下午6点钟,无保证预订房延长保留24小时。
2. 我们会尽快传真给您以确定您的预订。
3. 真对不起,我们现在没有空房。
4. 我是Marcus Ramsay,从纽约给你们打电话,我得改变预订日期。

Chapter Three Concierge Desk Service

Unit Five

II. Write out the questions according to the answers.

1. How many pieces of luggage are there in your team?
2. What can I do for you?
3. What is your room number?/May I know your room number?

III. Translate the following sentences into English.

1. Would you like to check luggage?
2. You can/may claim your luggage with the luggage tag.
3. You may/can leave your luggage in the Concierge.
4. Wait a moment, please. I'll bring a trolley.
5. Is there anything valuable or breakable in your bag?

Unit Six

II. Write out the questions according to the answers.

1. What kind of vehicle would you like/prefer?
2. May I know your returning time, please?
3. Where would you like to go?

III. Translate the following sentences into Chinese.

1. 包车来回划算。
2. 请稍等。出租车15分钟就到。
3. 接您到机场的车已停在酒店的停车场。

Chapter Four   Cash Desk Service

Unit Seven

II. Write out the Chinese names of the following currencies and then fill in their codes.

1. 澳大利亚元   A $
2. 加拿大元   Can $
3. 港元   HK $
4. 新西兰元   ZN $
5. 新加坡元   S $
6. 美元   US $
7. 英镑   £
8. 人民币元   RMB ¥
9. 日元   JAN ¥
10. 欧元   EUR

III. Answer the questions.

1. Any kind will be OK.
2. I'm afraid that you'd better to change it at the Bank of China or the Airport Exchange Office (a specialized foreign exchange bank).
3. Please fill in your passport number, the total amount, your room number or permanent address, and sign your name here as well.
4. Because the guest is required to show it at the Customs when he goes back to his country. (If the guest wants to change the RMB left back into his native currency at a specialized foreign exchange bank /at the Bank of China or the Airport Exchange Office, he is required to show the memo.)
5. According to today's rate of exchange, 2,600 US dollars is equal to 17,420 yuan RMB.

IV. Decide whether the following sentences are true or false.

1. False   2. True   3. False   4. False   5. True   6. False

Ⅴ. **Translate the following sentences into English.**

1. How much would you like to change, sir?
2. We change foreign currencies according to today's exchange rate.
3. The exchange rate of US dollar to RMB is 1∶6.70.
4. 600 US dollars. The exchange is 4,080 yuan RMB.
5. We hope you have enjoyed your stay in the hotel.
6. According to today's rate of exchange, every 100 US dollars in cash comes to RMB 680.
7. By the way, how can I change my RMB left back into Canadian dollar when I go back to my country?
8. Here's your memo. Please keep it well. You are required to show it at the Customs when you go back to your country.
9. Seeing the passport of the guest, you need to get the information as to the name, nationality, the passport number and the date of expiry.
10. When filling in the exchange memo, ask the guest to fill in his passport number, the total sum, room number or permanent address and sign his name.

Unit Eight

Ⅱ. **Speak English fluently according to the Chinese situations. Some situations can be expressed in many ways.**

1. The check-out time is 12:00 at noon.
2. Are you going to pay in cash or by traveler's check?/How will you settle your account, in cash or by traveler's check?/How would you like to make your payment, in cash or by traveler's check?/How do you wish to settle your account, sir? In cash, or by traveler's check?
3. It totals 4,567 yuan./Your bill comes/amounts to 4,567 yuan./Your bill makes a total of 4,567 yuan.
4. We hope you'll be staying with us again. Have a good trip!/We hope you have enjoyed your stay in the hotel./We hope we will have another opportunity of serving you./It's my pleasure. Hope you will enjoy your journey./Glad to have severed you. Have a good trip!

Ⅲ. **Translate the following sentences into English.**

1. Please wait a moment, Miss White. I'll draw up your bill. Your bill totals 6,500 US dollars. Would you like to check it?
2. You have paid a deposit of 1,000 US dollars. Give me your receipt, please.
3. What kind of credit cards do you honor?
4. Traveler's check is welcome.
5. There's a 5% merchant commission you must pay if you use a credit card.

Ⅳ. Fill in the blankets and then translate the passage into Chinese.

1. checking out
2. should
3. in cash
4. receipt of deposit
5. by credit card
6. whether
7. credit limit
8. with traveler's check
9. asking
10. correct

Unit Nine

Ⅱ. Translate the following sentences into English.

1. I must apologize for the inconvenient.
2. Here is the money you've overpaid.
3. When a guest makes a complaint against the bill to you, be sure to repeat the points of what the guest says to you in order to confirm.
4. I think there is something wrong with the bill. You have overcharged.

Ⅲ. Fill in the blanks.

1. I'd like to check out.
2. Please give me the keycard. /Would you give me the keycard?
3. Have you had any bill in the restaurant?
4. I'll draw up your bill for you.
5. How would you like to pay?
6. My personal check.
7. I'm sorry/I'm sorry, according to the policy
8. Could I take a print of your card?
9. Take your card and the receipt.
10. It's my pleasure.
11. We hope you have enjoyed your stay in the hotel.
12. We hope we will have another opportunity of serving you.

Chapter Five   Telephone Desk Service

Unit Ten

Ⅱ. Write out the questions according to the answers.

1. Good morning. This is Overseas Operator. May I help you?
2. Certainly, sir. I'd be glad to help you. What number are you calling, please?
3. Would you please tell me to whom you would like to speak?
4. Do you want to make a pay call or a collect call?
5. May I have your name and room number, please?
6. Could you hang up, please? I'll call you back as soon as I can.

Ⅲ. **Translate the following sentences into English.**

1. Would you like me to place the call for you?
2. You may call directly from your room. It is cheaper than going through the operator.
3. I'm sorry. The line is busy. Shall I ask him to call you back later when the line is free?
4. —Could you put me through to Room 103, please?
   —Certainly, sir. Whom would you like to speak with?
5. Thank you for waiting, sir. Please go ahead, you're through.

Ⅳ. **Read the following passage and answer the questions.**

1. The list of "White Pages" includes the names, addresses, and telephone numbers of people in the area.
2. The list of "Yellow Pages" includes all the businesses, hotels, restaurants, shops, theaters, and services in the area.
3. You can find the emergency number you want inside the front cover of the phone book.
4. Operators. And this kind of call is more expensive.

Unit Eleven

Ⅱ. **Write out the questions according to the answers.**

1. Good evening. This is the Hotel Operator. May I help you?
2. Certainly, sir. At what time?
3. What kind of wake-up call would you like, by phone or by knocking at the door?
4. Sure. Let me confirm your name and room number.
5. Mr. Calwell in Room 1025, tomorrow morning at 7:15. OK, we'll give you a call in the morning. Anything else I can do for you?

Ⅲ. **Translate the following passage into Chinese.**

接电话时,你应该立即表明身份,即使你很忙,也要礼貌、友好地向对方致意。不要让打电话的人等的时间太长。如果要询问信息或接听另一个电话,你有必要给对方再打回去。当你的办公室里有客人到访时,长时间打电话是很不礼貌的。如果这个电话不能很快结束,你应该告诉对方一会儿再打过去,不过事后千万别忘了。

Chapter Six Housekeeping Service

Unit Twelve

Ⅱ. **Write out the English equivalents to the following.**

1. pillow   2. quilt   3. blanket   4. extra blanket   5. sheet
6. bed cover/bed spread   7. curtain   8. carpet   9. electric pot
10. ashtray   11. sewing   12. table lamp/reading lamp   13. laundry bag
14. coat hanger   15. laundry list   16. clothes brush

Ⅲ. Translate the following sentences into English.

1. Good morning, Mr. White. May I do your room now?
2. When would you like me to clean your room, Mr. Smith?
3. I'm always at your service.
4. The sale of the rooms constitutes approximately 50 percent or more of the total revenue.
5. What time would/will be convenient for you?
6. Good evening, sir. May I do the turn-down service now?
7. If you need any help, you may call the Room Center by dialing 9.
8. The room is no longer available.

Ⅳ. Translate the following sentences into Chinese.

1. 做晚床就是将床罩拿走,将靠电话那一边的被子角掀起,折成三角形,放好枕头。接着放下窗帘,打开一些灯。最后收拾好浴室,放上一些干净的毛巾并准备好热水。
2. 在客房部,客人常常会向客房部工作人员提出加床要求,但是客房部工作人员没有权力直接给客人加床。这时,要求客人打电话到前台以获得许可,或者要求客人直接到前台办理加床手续。只有在获得前台许可之后,服务员才能给客人加床。

Unit Thirteen

Ⅱ. Translate the following sentences into English.

1. Which breakfast would you prefer, American or continental?
2. Which kind of juice would you like/prefer, grapefruit or orange?
3. Would you like ham or bacon with your eggs?
4. There is an extra service charge of 10% for the room service.
5. Your order will arrive in 15 minutes, see you.
6. We offer three types of breakfast: American, continental and Chinese. Which one would you prefer?
7. We'll add the cost to your room bill. Please sign your name and room number here on the bill.
8. Thank you for using room service. Enjoy yourself. Goodbye.

Ⅲ. Read the following passage and answer the questions and then translate it into Chinese.

1. To create a home away from home for all the traveling guests who need rest, food and drink is the operation aim of the hotel.
2. Firstly, we should regard our guests as our family members and try our best to meet with the demands that the guests have put to us. Secondly, we should be good at finding out or predicting the demands that the guest don't put to us and satisfy them.
3. Only we can provide our guests with the most sincere service to make their stay here convenient, comfortable and enjoyable, will they have the feeling of staying at their homes.

Unit Fourteen

II. Translate the following sentences into English.

1. Thank you for bringing the problems to our attention. And I apologize to you for the inconvenience as well. The repairman will come to your room in five minutes.
2. I've come to repair the facilities in the bathroom. Can you please tell me what the trouble is in detail?
3. Generally speaking, there is no potable water in Chinese hotels. So we can warn the foreign guests to drink boiled water or bottled water.
4. Thank you for what you've said.
5. If the guest doesn't know how to use the electric facilities in the room, show him how to use it carefully or give some explanations.
6. You're welcome. I'm always at your service.
7. I want to keep some documents and valuables in the safe in my room, but I don't know how to use it.

Chapter Seven Restaurant Service

Unit Fifteen

II. Read the following passage and answer the questions.

Part 1

1. Lenovo Company wants to reserve suites as well as a big conference hall.
2. "Perks" includes breakfast and coffee hours, which is offered complimentarily by the hotel when the guest reserves a suite.
3. The conference hall is 10,000 yuan RMB per night.

Part 2

1. The company chooses the routine entree and chef's choice for the banquet.
2. The company wants the French service, including the free pour during the banquet.
3. The minimum charge for each attendee is 400 yuan RMB per person, premium brands excluded.
4. No. Because tastes of the guests are different.

Unit Sixteen

答案略。

Unit Seventeen

I. Fill in the blanks.

1. Good evening. May I take your order now

2. What for the main course
3. How would you like your steak done
4. What soup would you like
5. Anything else

Ⅱ. Translate the following sentences into Chinese.

1. 你喜欢哪一种口味,是甜的还是辣的?
2. 一般来说,粤菜比较清淡,川菜浓烈而辛辣,沪菜比较油,而京菜香而且有点咸。
3. 这道菜色、香、味俱全。

Unit Eighteen

Translate the following sentences into English.

1. May I serve it to you now?
2. May I move this plate to the side?
3. May I take your plate?
4. I'm terribly sorry, sir. I seem to have brought the wrong dish.

Unit Nineteen

Ⅰ. Fill in the blanks.

1. there is something wrong with my order
2. I seem to have brought a wrong dish
3. I'm afraid we can't serve you the cheesecake/I have to say sorry to you again
4. Can you tell me the reason/But why
5. Is there anything else you want/Is there anything else I can do for you, sir

Ⅱ. Translate the following sentences into English.

1. Can I pay here?
2. Thank you for your coming.
3. I think there is a mistake in the bill.
4. Can I pay with this credit card?
5. May I have the receipt, please?

Ⅲ. Translate the following sentences into Chinese.

1. 能否安排一张靠近花园的桌子?
2. ——您的香槟酒是先上还是和主菜一起上?
   ——请先上。
3. 我上错菜了,很抱歉。
4. 总共220元,含10%的服务费。
5. 是合单还是分开付账呢?

Chapter Eight Bar Service

Unit Twenty

I. Please speak out the English counterparts of the following words.

1. on the rocks   syrup   ice water   soft drink
   dessert wine   alcohol   tonic water   base
   aperitifs   dessert wines   liqueurs   gin
   vodka   tequila   rum   whiskey
   brandy   beer   bitter   cocktail
   soda water   ginger ale

2. bottle opener   champagne bucket   corkscrew   straw
   ice shaver   mixing glasses   icemaker   beer mug
   champagne glass   tumbler   wine glass   goblet
   brandy glass   tapering glass

3. cherry   strawberry   lemon   olive
   clove   mint   pineapple   grapefruit
   grape

II. Translate the following sentences into English.

1. Would you like to sit by the window or by the bar counter?
2. Would you like bottle beer or draught beer?
3. I am glad to do that. The most popular one in China is Yan Jing. Would you like to have a try?
4. We have orange, pineapple, grapefruit, mango, peach and tomato juice.
5. Give me one ice-cold beer, please.
6. We have all the ranges from aperitifs to brandy.

III. Read the following passage and answer the questions.

1. The percentage of revenue earned from selling liquor.
2. They are passed down from the western United States.
3. The bar is only open to guests with a particular membership.
4. Loud music, subdued lighting, dress code and admission policy.

Unit Twenty-one

II. Fill in the blanks.

1. medium-rare one
2. far away from the band
3. do apologize
4. have the chips changed right away
5. would you mind

Ⅲ. Translate the following sentences into English.

1. Thank you for telling us about it, sir. I'll look into the matter at once.
2. I'll speak to the person in charge and ask him to take care of the problem.
3. Please relax, madam. I will take care of it according to your request.
4. Sorry, sir, I will solve the problem for you as soon as possible.
5. I'm awfully sorry for my carelessness.

Ⅳ. Translate the following sentences into Chinese.

1. 您想要开胃酒还是白葡萄酒？
2. 您要不要尝一尝我们的特别鸡尾酒？
3. 您的苏格兰威士忌要加冰吗？
4. 这是45元，找的钱作为小费吧。
5. 非常感谢您。但是我们这里不允许收客人小费。

Chapter Nine Business Center Service（Ⅰ）

Unit Twenty-two

Exercises

Ⅱ. Translate the following sentences into Chinese.

在会议设施入口处的便利位置可满足您所要的专业需求。我们的商务中心配备了互联网、办公服务和用品、通信租赁、运输和接收及私人迷你套房的租赁。

Ⅲ. Read the following service conversation and answer the questions.

1. He wants to print some documents in his thumb drive.
2. The employee resizes the chart and inserts the page number
3. The charge is 120 yuan.
4. He would like to pay in cash.

Unit Twenty-three

Exercises

Ⅱ. Translate the following sentences into Chinese.

在这个时代，互联网的使用量增加了，互联网通过我们的移动设备进入我们的家庭和任何地方，访问信息变得更加容易。因此，使用互联网已成为提供抽象产品的酒店的一项义务。

Ⅲ. Translate the following sentences into English.

1. Whether you're traveling for business or pleasure, you need reliable internet service.
2. One thing to keep in mind when traveling is that not all places have great Wi-Fi access.
3. Hotels can replace their front desk computers with more efficient mobile computers, and staff members can be given a personal tablet to assist them with their jobs.

Chapter Ten Business Center Service(Ⅱ)

Unit Twenty-four

Ⅱ. **Write out the questions according to the answers.**

1. I'd like to book an air ticket from Beijing to Singapore on February the 10th.

2. What time would you like to take the train?

3. What is the train number?

4. How would you like to pay, by credit card, with WeChat or Alipay?

Ⅲ. **Translate the following sentences into English.**

1. Bullet trains run very frequently between Shanghai and Hangzhou.

2. Which seat would you like, second-class seat, first-class seat or business-class seat?

3. Sorry, the direct fight is fully booked. Do you mind transferring at Hong Kong International Airport?

4. Which one do you prefer, a window seat or an aisle seat?

Ⅳ. **Translate the following paragraph into Chinese.**

如果你想让我为你安排行程,我建议你乘坐中国国际航空公司从北京直飞悉尼的航班,然后再在澳大利亚维珍航空公司订悉尼飞布里斯班的航班。你可以在悉尼停留一到两天,休息调整一下,看看悉尼的风土人情。爬上悉尼海港大桥看一看;到悉尼歌剧院欣赏一场表演;去悉尼塔瑞噶野生动物园邂逅考拉,并抱一抱它;到达令港的水族馆观赏世界上唯一一对在展出的儒艮。在飞往布里斯班之前,别忘了在沃森湾吃一顿海鲜大餐。

Unit Twenty-five

Ⅱ. **Write out the questions according to the answers.**

1. What is inside your parcel?

2. We offer DHL, FEDEX, EMS and SF Express. Which one do you prefer?

3. What payment would do like? Cash on shipment or Cash on delivery?

4. When would you like the courier to pick up the parcel?

Ⅲ. **Translate the following sentences into English.**

1. Does your parcel have any fragile items?

2. We can offer traditional Chinese cuisine and folk music performance at the luncheon.

3. To deliver this parcel, SF Express provides speedy express and standard express.

4. Free high speed WiFi covers all meeting areas.

5. The professional Business Centrepersonnels with dedicated event services can help to arrange anything including transportation, accommodations, technological and communications support.

Ⅳ. **Translate the following sentences into Chinese.**

1. 根据包裹的重量和体积,为客人提供快递估价。

2. 问询快递类型、包裹重量、尺寸和快递里程。
3. 快递费用确认之后,立刻通知快递员取件。
4. 高天花板的1,220平方米的凯悦宴会厅非常适合举办大型会议和活动。

Chapter Eleven   Health & Recreation Center Service

Unit Twenty-six

Ⅱ. **Write out the questions according to the answers.**

1. How many lanes do you like to have, one or two?
2. Would you like to take on the marking board?
3. What facilities do hou have here?
4. Do you have any special rules while playing?

Ⅲ. **Translate the following sentences into English.**

1. Please wipe off the machines after you finish using them.
2. There are such classes as martial arts, yoga, and Pilates.
3. This exercise is good for your arms.
4. Please put on sneakers before entering the court. If you didn't bring shoes by yourself, you can rent at the service counter.
5. The charge is one basket for 30 minutes (include less than it) for one unit.
6. You'd better warm up before the exercises in order to avoid ankle sprain, muscle injury or knee hurt.

Ⅳ. **Answer the questions according to the passage.**

1. Bowling began in Germany and Holland.
2. Before A.D. 4th century, bowling was only a religion ceremony.
3. In 16th century, the Holland immigrants brought this game to America.
4. In mid-19th century, this game was first named "bowling".
5. 答案略。

Unit Twenty-seven

Ⅱ. **Translate the following sentences into Chinese.**

洗浴服务是酒店为满足客人排毒、放松需求而提供的一系列服务的总称,主要包括洗浴、桑拿、水疗、香熏泡浴、游泳、搓澡、按摩等项目。不同酒店根据自身情况设置不同的项目。

Ⅲ. **Read the following passage and answer the questions.**

1. There are four. They are Dry Sauna Bath, Damp Sauna Bath, Salt Sauna Bath, and Ice Sauna Bath.
2. Dry Sauna Bath, also called Turkish bath, started in Eastern Europe. It has an effect of sweating weight off, accelerating blood circulation and metabolism.
3. Damp Sauna Bath, also named as Finland Bath, is that people stay in a very hot

room to let the human body absorb steam. It has an effect on helping to dilate blood capillary and smooth the skin.

4. Salt Sauna Bath, is that people stay in a room whose four sides are coated with salt to let the body absorb the molecule which gives out from the salt by high temperature.

5. Ice Sauna Bath, is a comparative cold place where people can stay for a while between the dry or wet sauna.

6. Rubdown popular among the people in China is a simple health care treatment. The technician gives the guest a rubdown with a damp towel to massage his back and other places of the body after they take a shower.

Unit Twenty-eight

Ⅱ. Write out the questions according to the answers.

1. And how about the contents of the songs?
2. Are you our hotel guest?
3. Would you please tell me how to use the machine when we sing?
4. How is your KTV parlor like?

Ⅲ. Translate the following sentences into English.

1. If you have any problems, please let the technician know.
2. Our hotel is well equipped with first-class stereo and lighting systems.
3. The environment and equipment in our hotel are first class, and of the computers are very fast.
4. You can first select the codes of the songs you prefer and then press the key "input".
5. Please use our network according to the rules and regulations of the Guests' Notice issued by the hotel.
6. The sound levels have already been adjusted well. Please do not twiddle with the equipment.

Chapter Twelve Convention & Exhibition Center Service

Unit Twenty-nine

Ⅱ. Translate the following sentences into English.

1. Good morning. We want to hold a meeting in your hotel. May I speak to the person in charge?
2. Our conference center has just been equipped with full simultaneous interpretation facilities.
3. Can you give us the information in detail about your services and the price list of your services? Only in this way, can we make a good plan for the conference.
4. Glad to see you, too. I'd like to have a discussion about some details of the confer-

ence services with you.

5. The suppers on the first day and the last day of the conference are banquets.

Ⅲ. **Translate the following sentences into Chinese.**

1. 他们还需要电传、复印、秘书办公服务和20台笔记本电脑。
2. 请把贵宾的名单交给我,以便为他们安排合适的房间。
3. 从"会议服务指南"里,我知道你们能提供非常先进的会议设施。请问能否提供电传、复印、秘书办公服务?
4. 先生,上午好。请问您是开会报到吗?
5. Robinson 先生,您预订的房号是3678,这是一个豪华套间。给您房卡,这是您的会议证章和会议塑料袋。
6. 来自 Colombia 大学的 Peter Moran 博士前来开会报到,他预先登记过。

Unit Thirty

Ⅲ. **How to ask the guest about the service demands in exhibition?**

1. What kind of exhibition will you hold?
2. How can we arrange the exhibition halls?
3. How about setting up the stands?
4. Do you have any special demands for the exhibitions?
5. Would you like some flowers and plants to decorate the booths and the halls?
6. Will you provide some snake and refreshment for the visitors?
7. Are there any other suggestions and demands for our service work?

Ⅳ. **Translate the following sentences into English.**

1. Smile and offer an appropriate hospitality comment when seeing a guest.
2. Speak to the guest in a friendly, enthusiastic and courteous tone and manner.
3. Answer the question and request of the guest quickly and efficiently, or take personal responsibility to get the answer.
4. Anticipate guest needs and resolve quest problems.
5. Follow up wherever and whenever necessary and possible.

Ⅴ. **Translate the following sentences into English.**

The Convention and Exhibition Center is responsible for offering convention service or exhibition service to some organizations both from home and aboard. It provides comprehensive convention and exhibition services including the activities planning, convention and exhibition equipments leasing, simultaneous interpretation, documents translation, ballroom decoration, stage performance and so on. Some of the conventional hotels have a remarkable reserve of advanced convention and exhibition equipments, ranging from the slide projector, the full simultaneous interpretation facilities to the audio and video equipments and the office equipments.

Chapter Thirteen Shopping Service

Unit Thirty-one

II. Write out the questions according to the answers.

1. Good afternoon, Miss. What can I do for you?
2. What do you think of this style? It is very popular among young ladies nowadays.
3. What color do you prefer? And what's your size?
4. This dress looks good on you, Miss. I think it's a perfect fit.
5. One more thing, how shall we pay for what we buy?

III. Translate the following sentences into English.

1. It's perfect Chinese traditional design.
2. Do you think a Chipao will suit me?
3. It's made of natural pearls and the luster will never fade out.
4. Will you please tell me what size you need, sir?
5. What material do you prefer?
6. The silk shouldn't be hung out in the sunshine.
7. If you would like, I can show you some other pieces.
8. Would you please wrap them together or separately?

IV. Read the following passage and answer the questions.

1. The most important reason is that there is no place for parking in the central city.
2. Because there are magnet bar codes on every article. If you take away articles without paying, the magnet will make an alarm ring at the exit door and the police will appear. Besides, there are cameras which view and videotape every corner of the store.
3. Firstly, there is a wide range of items. Secondly, the price is reasonable. Thirdly, consumers can buy almost every daily necessity under one roof.
4. (1) A department store is salesperson served. But in a supermarket people can choose the articles on the shelves without the help of salesmen.

    (2) Prices in department stores are often higher than in supermarkets.

    (3) In department stores, you can buy many articles that are not sold in supermarkets, and the quality of the merchandise is often better, too.
5. No, they don't.

Unit Thirty-two

II. Translate the following sentences into English.

1. Please let me have a look at the cutting/jade seal.
2. Many foreign visitors who are interested in Chinese culture are fond of Chinese painting.
3. Well, sir. I should say you've got artistic eyes.
4. We have many different kinds of Chinese traditional paintings.
5. This can be taken as typical souvenirs of a journey to China.

6. What kind of tea are you used to? I'm used to green tea.

7. Chinese tea is world-famous.

8. We serve black tea, green tea and Pu'er tea.

Ⅲ. **Translate the following passage into Chinese.**

质量总是被各种不同的消费者给予足够的重视——不管是家庭主妇、实业公司还是政府机构。那么,质量这个术语的含义到底是什么呢? 不同的人从不同的角度来理解质量。在"这些产品是一流的"这个句子中,质量指的是产品的等级。而在"100%丝绸""手工工艺制作""耐火、防火"等语句中,它又被用来表示产品的原材料、工艺和特性。

Chapter Fourteen　　Other Service

Unit Thirty-three

Ⅱ. **Translate the following sentences into English.**

1. Where had you been before you found you lost the watch?
2. Could you describe your package?
3. Could you leave your telephone number?
4. Take it easy, sir. We will arrange the search immediately.
5. Please fill out the request slip.
6. Could you show your valid ID?

Ⅲ. **Translate the following sentences into Chinese.**

1. 耐心和同情心是失物招领部门人员工作的关键词,因为丢失物品的客人难免会情绪低落,甚至有时会把责任归于我们的工作人员。在这种情况下,服务员应把"服务至上,宾客至上"作为工作的纲领。
2. 在失物招领部门,客人可以前去领取他们丢失的东西,这些东西可能是其他客人或者酒店工作人员捡到的。如果在失物上有失主的联系方式,失物招领部门会主动联系失主前来领取。在实际操作上,当一段时间过去之后,失物招领部门会将无人认领物品处理以清仓。

Unit Thirty-four

Ⅱ. **Complete the following dialogue.**

1. safety box　　2. name　　3. room number
4. special care　　5. sign　　6. tag
7. confirming

Ⅲ. **Translate the following sentences into English.**

1. We do provide the luggage storage service.
2. Shall we arrange the bellman to pick up your luggage at 11:00?
3. May I ask the rate for depositing my luggage per day?
4. If you would like to use the items during the period of storage, please come here in

287

person with the tag. After confirming your signature, we will open the box.
5. Please require special care for valuables.

Unit Thirty-five

Ⅱ. Read the passage and answer the questions.

1. more than 14.9 million
2. 18
3. Tian'anmen, Chang'an Boulevard, the Palace Museum (Forbidden City), Zhongnanhai, Beihai and Houhai.
4. Extend out to the suburban area based on the city center north-south layout.

Unit Thirty-six

Ⅱ. Translate the following sentences into Chinese.

1. 托婴服务是指为婴儿的父母暂时照看婴儿。照看者通常一次签订一晚的合同。这个词语可能来源于照看者在房间中坐在婴儿旁边这个动作，而婴儿的父母则在娱乐或忙其他事情。
2. 工作人员在提供托婴服务时要具备职业道德和优质服务意识。对婴儿情况、父母要求及服务开始时间都要做详细记录，以便于安排合格的照看者履行服务。

参考文献

[1] 肖璇. 现代酒店英语实务教程[M]. 北京:世界图书公司,2006.
[2] 郭兆康. 饭店英语[M]. 北京:旅游教育出版社,2003.
[3] 李红. 敢说饭店服务英语[M]. 北京:机械工业出版社,2005.
[4] 陈昕. 酒吧服务训练手册[M]. 北京:旅游教育出版社,2006.
[5] 刘友道. 饭店管理实用英语[M]. 北京:外文出版社,2006.
[6] 程中锐. 饭店工作英语[M]. 北京:中国旅游出版社,2002.
[7] 张伟. 饭店英语[M]. 天津:南开大学出版社,2008.
[8] 唐莉. 饭店情景英语[M]. 北京:中国人民大学出版社,2011.
[9] 魏新民. 酒店情景英语[M]. 北京:北京大学出版社,2011.
[10] 李晓红. 旅游英语综合教程[M]. 北京:中国人民大学出版社,2011.
[11] 胡扬政. 酒店英语服务实训[M]. 2版. 北京:清华大学出版社,2016.
[12] 夏伟华. 酒店英语[M]. 上海:复旦大学出版社,2015.
[13] 胡扬政. 高职酒店英语课程改革探索与研究[J]. 中国科教创新导刊,2008(29):189-190.
[14] https://www.sf-express.com.
[15] https://www.airchina.com.cn.